Fountas & Pinnell

Leveled Literacy Intervention

System Guide

GOLD SYSTEM

Irene C. Fountas
Gay Su Pinnell

Heinemann, Portsmouth, NH

Heinemann
361 Hanover Street
Portsmouth, NH 03801–3912
www.heinemann.com

Offices and agents throughout the world

The Cataloging-in-Publication data is on file with the Library of Congress.

ISBN 978-0-325-04825-3

Editor: Betsy Sawyer-Melodia and Jill Harden
Production: Lynne Costa
Cover and interior designs: Lisa Anne Fowler
Typesetter: Gina Poirier Design
Manufacturing: Deanna Richardson

Printed in China
0713/13000122
18   17   16   15   14   13   RRD   1   2   3   4   5

CONTENTS

Section 2	Implementing the *LLI Gold System*	21

Section 3	*LLI Gold System* Lesson Overview	31

Section 6	Assessment and Record Keeping in the *LLI System*	95

Leveled Literacy Intervention Gold System

▶ *LLI:* Fifteen Key Characteristics of Effective Literacy Intervention

When readers struggle, there is a critical need for highly effective, small-group interventions that will get them back on track as soon as possible. There are some basic implementation principles that are essential if the intervention is expected to work effectively (see Figure 1.1).

We want interventions to be short term and intensive, with flexible entry and exit points so that individual needs may be accommodated in a small-group situation. If the intervention is early and effective, then the length will be shorter; however, students who are very far behind may need a year or even more of effective supplementary instruction. The layers of intervention should be flexible enough that the teacher can group and regroup students.

Lessons must be supplemental to good classroom instruction; it is the *combination* of high-quality classroom teaching and intensive small-group intervention lessons that enables learners to make accelerated progress, catch up with their peers, and continue to perform at expected levels for the grade.

Lessons must be frequent—five days a week is preferred—*every* week so that readers can gain and sustain momentum and acceleration is possible. And, the teacher-to-student ratio must be as low as possible. For the greatest impact in a short-term intervention, we recommend a ratio of 1:3 for children performing at earlier levels (kindergarten, grades 1 and 2) and 1:4 for students performing at higher levels (grades 3 through 12).

Providing excellent intervention lessons depends on the expertise of teachers. The teachers of struggling readers and writers should be exceptionally skilled in systematic observation, in the assessment of reading behaviors, and in teaching for the range of strategic actions that proficient readers use. *All* teachers of struggling readers

Basic Implementation Characteristics

- Intensive
- Short term
- Supplementary
- Daily lessons
- Low teacher-student ratio
- Taught by expert teacher
- Communication with classroom and home

FIGURE 1.1 Basic Implementation Characteristics

(classroom and intervention teachers) need opportunities to continually increase their understanding of the reading and writing processes and the behavioral evidence that reveals competencies. The expert intervention teacher is able to make effective decisions that meet the diversity of student needs.

Finally, excellent communication and teamwork among all who have a role in supporting the students' progress are required for an intervention to help individual students. Students' families need to know the goals of the intervention as well as what students will be expected to do for homework. Good communication between classroom and intervention teachers is essential so that they are working toward the same goals. It is critical to have a shared set of curriculum goals such as those detailed in *The Continuum of Literacy Learning, PreK–8* (Pinnell & Fountas 2011). *Leveled Literacy Intervention* is built on the foundation of the description of text characteristics and strategic actions described for each level, A to Z in this comprehensive tool.

When all of the basic implementation requirements are in place, we need to dig deeper into research on literacy learning and reading difficulties to inform the design of teaching. What *happens* in the intervention must affect change. Many struggling students sit daily in 30- to 45-minute intervention lessons, yet little improvement is evident in what they are able to do independently. Remember that *progress* is not enough; these struggling readers need to make *faster progress* than their peers, and that is the whole purpose of intervention. They may be disengaged or bored. They may work diligently at mechanical tasks that they do not connect in a lively way to real reading and writing. To be effective, the intervention lessons must incorporate everything we know about what students need to learn, especially those who are experiencing difficulty.

A review of the research reveals fifteen key characteristics of effective literacy intervention that are essential for intermediate and middle grade students as well as secondary school students who need to improve reading abilities. These characteristics address the kind of teaching that struggling readers and writers need. The extent to which the intervention program can meet *all* of these goals will indicate its potential for effectively helping struggling readers and writers.

1. ***Provide books that engage the intellect and build knowledge.*** Struggling readers and writers are the students who are most in need of high-quality, engaging books that represent a variety of genres. Ongoing access to new books is a major factor in motivation. Students want material that is relevant, fresh, interesting, and appropriate to their age group—they need the chance to engage with new information, interesting current topics, and fascinating plots and characters. Too often, texts for struggling readers are shockingly inferior and not very interesting. The success of any intervention ultimately depends on students being fully captivated by the books they read and write about.

2. ***Increase reading volume by engaging students in a large amount of successful reading every day.*** Quantity matters. A key factor in the success of an intervention is the amount of real reading that students do—and that is especially true for English language learners. Struggling readers need a great deal of authentic, high-success reading. The experiences make it possible, ultimately, for them to *teach themselves* by using strategic actions effectively. The amount of time students spend reading is a significant predictor of vocabulary size and success.

3. ***Provide students with choice in reading material to increase motivation.*** Choice is a highly motivating factor in reading comprehension; choice increases engagement. Students are more likely to read purposefully if they can choose texts that reflect their individual interests. Interventions may need to have students read high-interest texts that are selected and sequenced so that the teaching can be efficient and effective, but they should also provide students with many opportunities for choice reading so they can build their reading lives.

4. ***Assure proficient grade-level reading by matching texts to readers' current abilities, and then provide teaching to expand quickly to new levels.*** Readers who struggle need a careful, effective match to a text, one that enables them to read more challenging material through which they can increase proficiency. Texts should be matched to students' instructional level, and students must be supported by teaching that will ensure that readers use strategic actions effectively. In this way, they can progress up a "ladder of difficulty" (a gradient of texts) and build their reading

power. Matching texts to readers allows for *highly accurate reading,* which is essential (although not sufficient) for good reading comprehension.

5. ***Support the development of independent, self-initiating, self-regulatory behaviors, and transfer to performance in multiple contexts.*** Students who have difficulty with reading and writing sometimes become dependent and passive in instructional contexts. They need to develop independent, self-initiating, self-regulating behaviors that will transfer to classroom work. Independence can be developed through teaching that focuses on principles and through helping students build strategic actions they can apply to many texts. They need to be able to take what they learn to do as readers and apply their reading competencies in all content areas.

6. ***Increase reading of nonfiction texts and teach students how to read a variety of nonfiction genres including expository, narrative, procedural, and persuasive.*** Knowledge and understanding of a variety of genres, including nonfiction genres, is a powerful factor in comprehension. Nonfiction texts allow students to become engaged with real information that is relevant to their lives and worlds. Expository texts employ language, features, and structures that are different from those found in fiction texts. Students need exposure to these texts and explicit teaching in how to read them. Extensive reading of nonfiction supports new vocabulary learning, particularly of content words, and builds background knowledge.

7. ***Demonstrate and teach for comprehension—strategic actions for thinking within, beyond, and about the text.*** Comprehension is an active process that engages readers' thinking before, during, and after reading. It involves the smooth orchestration of many systems of strategic actions. Readers must derive not only the literal meaning of texts but the big ideas and messages of both fiction and nonfiction texts. They need to be able to understand the relevance of texts to themselves, others, and the world. Students who have found the reading process difficult often become mechanical; they struggle so much to decode words that they have little attention left to think deeply about the meaning. The construction of meaning is critical to proficient reading. Readers need to think critically and analytically about texts.

8. ***Help students monitor their reading through brief, temporary metacognitive attention that supports deeper understanding of fiction and informational texts.*** Readers in the intermediate, middle school grades, and secondary level need to build awareness of the kind of thinking that the text requires of them through brief metacognitive attention that supports their understanding of texts. For example, they need to monitor their understanding of a text and search for and use more information as needed. They need to check understanding by comparing one kind of information with another. They need to know how to analyze how a text is organized and use the structure to gain a deeper (or faster) understanding of the content or the narrative. They consciously (and later unconsciously) form expectations of a genre so that even before reading they can make predictions and also evaluate the text for quality. They need to learn to articulate their own thinking, giving evidence from personal experience or from the text. By teaching readers how to articulate their thinking for a short time, they can internalize an awareness of the demands of various texts.

9. ***Provide systematic study of how words work (phonics and word structure) to increase students' ability to rapidly take words apart while reading and construct words effectively while writing.*** Many students who have literacy difficulties struggle to learn words as isolated units. They need to understand powerful principles of phonics and word study so they can see connections in words and apply their understandings in reading and writing. Students' knowledge of meaningful word parts, root words, base words, and affixes, for example, helps them take words apart while reading and contributes both to decoding proficiency, the expansion of vocabulary, and spelling in the process of writing.

10. ***Focus on intentional vocabulary development that helps students develop strategies for connecting words and using morphology and word parts.*** Vocabulary knowledge is one of the most important factors in reading with understanding. All students, especially those who are struggling in reading, need both explicit instruction *and* rich engagement in texts, supported by oral language. This teaching is especially important for those students who are taking on vocabulary in a language different from the language

spoken in their homes and communities. There is no more powerful way to expand word knowledge than through reading and talking about texts; but students also need intentional, systematic teaching of strategies for acquiring new vocabulary so they can expand their academic vocabulary as well as their content vocabulary. Struggling students also need to *learn how to learn vocabulary from reading and talking*, so they can continue to add to their vocabularies independently.

11. *Teach for fluency in reading (pausing, phrasing, word stress, intonation, rate, and integration).* Struggling readers and writers need the experience of reading written text as language—smooth, with pauses and intonation that reflect the communication of meaning. Readers need to move along at a good rate—not too fast and not too slow—while avoiding very fast, robotic reading. Laborious reading of texts that are too hard interferes with the building of a processing system of reading. Students need appropriate texts at independent and instructional levels to support learning to read fluently; and they need explicit instruction in many dimensions of fluency—pausing, phrasing, intonation, word stress, and rate. The end goal is orchestrated processing across all types of text.

12. *Engage students in talk about texts that expands thinking and supports their development of complex, academic language.* Students not only need a chance to read; they need opportunities to engage in meaningful dialogue with their peers about books. Collaboration fosters interest and aids comprehension, and successful reading is also enhanced by "accountable talk" about texts. This kind of talk is more complex and is likely to support both comprehension and vocabulary development. There is a need for real talk, the kind of thoughtful discussion of ideas that moves beyond question and answer to genuine conversation that inquires into the multiple interpretations and bigger, important ideas in texts.

13. *Engage students in writing about reading to deepen comprehension and expand writing skills.* There is a strong relationship between reading and writing. When students write about reading in a way that is meaningful to them, they select, organize, and integrate information. Writing enhances reading comprehension, and it also helps students to see text structure and to

think about aspects of the writer's craft. Conversely, reading contributes to writing through expanded knowledge of craft, language (grammar), and new vocabulary and content.

14. *Support the specific needs of English language learners, adapting lessons in ways that assure their access and give them opportunities to understand English.* English language learners sometimes become categorized as struggling readers because of their limited knowledge of both English syntax and vocabulary as well as the language to talk about content and concepts. Engaging them in reading and talking about a variety of meaningful texts enables them to rapidly expand their knowledge. As they engage with texts, they need more intensive teaching of syntax and vocabulary, as well as clarification of content and the use of figurative language. They can also benefit from word study that helps them connect words and notice their structures.

15. *Provide fast-paced, intensive, and highly structured lessons that help students develop all areas of proficient reading.* Intervention lessons for intermediate, middle grade, and secondary students should be 45 minutes long and include a variety of encounters with written text and attention to the essential elements of proficient reading at those levels. True efficiency depends on carefully designed lessons with a dynamic combination of research-based instructional approaches. In addition, struggling readers need predictability to help them build confidence. Lessons must be designed carefully, using a sequence of texts that build on each other in many ways. The intervention lesson structure should include extensive reading of texts at the independent and instructional level, close reading for deep comprehension, vocabulary instruction, fluency instruction, phonics/word study, and writing about reading.

► What Is *Leveled Literacy Intervention*?

Leveled Literacy Intervention (LLI) is a small-group, supplementary intervention designed for students who find reading and writing difficult. These students are the lowest achievers in literacy at their grade level and are not receiving another literacy intervention. The goal of *LLI* is to bring students to grade-level achievement in reading. The *LLI* systems (a total of seven) have been designed to bring students from the earliest level A (kindergarten level) to level Z, which represents competencies needed at the middle and secondary school level.

Leveled Literacy Intervention is based on the F&P Text Level Gradient™. Each level of text makes increasing demands on the reader, but the demands and resulting changes are gradual. By actively participating in intensive lessons on each level, readers have the opportunity to expand their reading and writing abilities. With the support of instruction, they stretch themselves to read more complex texts with accuracy, fluency, and comprehension—and to write with more complexity. With these goals in mind, students effectively engage in the reading and writing process every day.

We use the term *leveled* because leveled books are a key component in helping students become competent readers and accessing texts of increasing complexity. Each book is carefully designed, analyzed, and sequenced to provide enough support and the right amount of challenge so the reader can learn on the text and make small steps toward grade-level goals.

The Critical Role of a Gradient of Text

The F&P Text Level Gradient™, created and refined as a teaching and assessment tool over the past twenty years, consists of twenty-six points on a gradient of reading difficulty (see Figure 1.2). Each point on that gradient, from the easiest at level A to the most challenging at level Z (Z+ in special cases), represents a small but significant increase in difficulty over the previous level. The Z+ category creates a twenty-seventh point that indicates adult-level reading. In the *LLI Gold System*, the books begin at level O and continue through level T, with a total of 192 related lessons.

LLI is a *literacy* intervention system. Through systematically designed lessons, you support learning in both reading and writing. Also, you help students expand their knowledge of language and of words and how they work. At every level in the *LLI Gold System*, there are 24 standard lessons, followed by 4 novel study lessons, and 4 optional test preparation lessons. Over a span of two days of standard lessons, students read books, write about reading, and receive explicit teaching

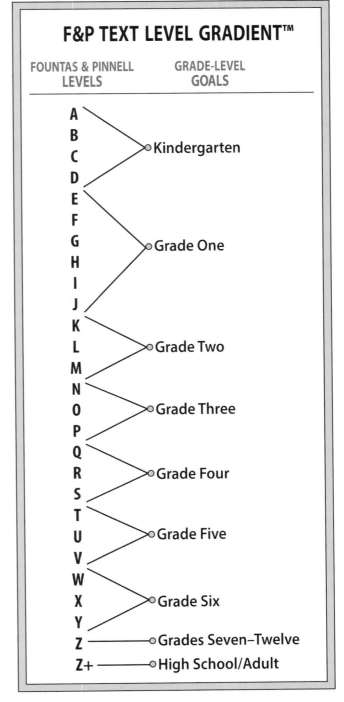

FIGURE 1.2 F&P Text Level Gradient™

in phonics and word study. In the Writing About Reading section, students develop critical strategies that deepen their understanding of texts and can be applied in classroom contexts across subject areas.

When the learners are reading with proficiency, you can provide scaffolds that allow them to progress to higher levels. In *LLI*, students have many opportunities to process texts that are not too difficult and not too easy, allowing them to learn on the text.

While readers are progressing along the gradient, they receive specific instruction in phonics and word study; but it is the daily opportunity to *apply* what they know to reading and writing continuous text that enables students to make accelerated progress. Additionally, you provide explicit instruction in comprehension as the students discuss the texts, and you intentionally draw their attention to aspects of a text that they need to understand.

Key understandings for each text are indicated in the lessons and on the Recording Forms used for conducting reading records in standard even-numbered lessons. Monitor students' comprehension closely as they respond to texts. Reading records make it possible to monitor progress over time systematically, and assessment of phonics and word analysis, reading behaviors, fluency, and comprehending are built into each lesson.

The F&P Text Level Gradient™ is the foundation of *The Continuum of Literacy Learning, PreK–8* (2011), which provides a level-by-level description of the demands of the texts on readers at each level as well as the corresponding competencies to teach for, assess, and reinforce. You will find the specific competencies on a continuum of behaviors and understandings to notice, teach, and support at the end of each level in the *LLI Gold System Lesson Guide*.

▶ *Leveled Literacy Intervention* Within a Comprehensive Educational System

LLI is available to schools that want to make it a part of a comprehensive literacy system. It is a streamlined, easy-to-implement, small-group intervention that is proven effective. The *LLI* system includes original leveled books created especially for the intervention. Districts and schools can incorporate *LLI* into their present system, with these goals in mind:

- ❏ Help a large number of students enter the world of literacy.
- ❏ Help teachers learn the value of a well-selected sequence of texts.

- ❏ Help teachers learn to plan and implement small-group lessons that are very efficient and effective.
- ❏ Suggest language that will help teachers learn precise ways of teaching that they can internalize and apply in many instructional settings.
- ❏ Create a system within which multiple needs, at many levels, can be met.

Ultimately we expect coherent, many-layered systems that embrace highly effective classroom teaching alongside multiple interventions—some highly individualized and others supportive in systematic ways—to help all students who are having difficulty learning to read and write (see Figure 1.3). We strongly recommend *Leveled Literacy Intervention* as a component of that system.

Who Is *LLI* For?

The *LLI* system is designed to be used with small groups of students who need intensive support to achieve grade-level competencies. It is designed to serve the lowest-achieving students in the grade who are not receiving another supplementary literacy intervention. It also provides strong support for students who are acquiring English as an additional language and are receiving classroom reading instruction in English. You may also decide to include students who are identified as having special needs if the content of the *LLI* intervention meets the educational program specifications for the student. We recommend early intervention, such as Reading Recovery® in grade 1 and the implementation of *LLI* in the early grades (K–3), to prevent large numbers of students from entering grade 4 below grade level.

LLI in Grade 4

LLI Gold is particularly important for the lowest-achieving students in grade 4 and for students in higher grades who are reading below level T. It serves to catch students up and prevent literacy difficulties in subsequent years of schooling. We suggest that classroom teachers engage fourth-grade students in rich literacy opportunities—including interactive read-aloud, book clubs, shared writing, guided reading, and independent reading and writing in readers' and writers' workshop—as part of the classroom instructional program.

A Many-Layered System of Literacy Intervention

Grade Level	All Students	Students Who Need Extra Literacy Support	
K	Good classroom teaching	*LLI* through level E	For lowest-achieving
1	Good classroom teaching	Reading Recovery®, if available	For lowest-achieving
		LLI through level K	For lowest achieving not in Reading Recovery, including Special Education and ELL
2	Good classroom teaching	*LLI* through level N	For lowest-achieving, including Special Education and ELL
3	Good classroom teaching	*LLI* through level Q	For lowest-achieving, including Special Education and ELL
4	Good classroom teaching	*LLI* through level T	For lowest-achieving, including Special Education and ELL
5	Good classroom teaching	*LLI* through level W	For lowest-achieving, including Special Education and ELL
6–12	Good classroom teaching	*LLI* through level Z	For lowest-achieving, including Special Education and ELL

FIGURE 1.3 A Many-Layered System of Literacy Intervention

Even with many high-quality literacy opportunities, some students struggle with literacy learning. An intervention system gets them back on track so they can benefit fully from classroom instruction. *LLI* can give these students the boost they need to begin grade 5 at the same level as their peers.

LLI for English Language Learners

Each lesson in the *LLI System* provides specific suggestions for supporting English language learners who are selected for the program (also see *When Readers Struggle, L–Z: Teaching That Works*, in press). Use your school or district criteria for language proficiency to determine eligibility for reading instruction in English. English language learners benefit greatly from conversation with an adult and interaction with a very small group of students. They also benefit from reading the large amount of continuous text in *LLI*. Through reading, talking,

and writing about reading, they extend their knowledge of the structure of English and expand their vocabularies. The *LLI* lesson is ideal for these students because of the opportunities for increased language modeling—oral language surrounds every element of the lesson. In addition, the group size and instructional approaches allow for decision making based on the specific strengths and needs of the students.

If students cannot follow your instructions or participate fully in the activities of the group, you may want to give them whatever language support your district offers before placing them in an *LLI* group. The *LLI System* provides lesson-specific, text-specific suggestions for supporting English language learners who are selected for the program. In addition, you can keep some general suggestions in mind as you work across lessons. We list suggestions in four categories: oral language, reading, writing, and phonics and word study (see Figure 1.4). These ideas will be helpful as you work with English language learners as well as with other students who can benefit from extra support. You will also find specific suggestions in every lesson and a comprehensive chapter in *When Readers Struggle, L–Z: Teaching That Works* (in press).

▶ The *LLI* Systems

Five systems are currently available for *LLI*:

- *Orange System:* levels A through E*
- *Green System:* levels A through K*
- *Blue System:* levels C through N
- *Red System:* levels L through Q
- *Gold System:* levels O through T

Two additional systems are in production, and dates for release are available at www.fountasandpinnell.com:

- *Purple System:* levels R through W
- *Teal System:* levels U through Z

Lessons across the seven systems progress from level A (beginning reading in kindergarten) through level Z, which represents competencies at the middle and secondary school level. Each level within the systems provides:

- ❏ A combination of reading, writing, and phonics/word study.
- ❏ Emphasis on teaching for comprehending strategies.
- ❏ Explicit attention to genre and to the features of nonfiction and fiction texts.
- ❏ Special attention to disciplinary reading, literature inquiry, and writing about reading.
- ❏ Specific work on sounds, letters, and words in activities designed to help students notice the details of written language and learn how words "work."
- ❏ Close reading to deepen and expand comprehension.
- ❏ Explicit teaching of effective and efficient strategies for expanding vocabulary.
- ❏ Explicit teaching for fluent and phrased reading.
- ❏ Use of writing about reading for the purpose of communicating and learning how to express ideas for a particular purpose and audience using a variety of writing strategies.

There are specific *Lesson Guides* for each *LLI System*, and the systems are coordinated with the grade levels at which they will most likely be used; however, educators may make other decisions as they work to match the program to the needs of particular readers. *The systems overlap in levels, but books and lessons for each system are unique, with no overlap of titles or lessons.* You may choose to extend the number of lessons at a level on the F&P Text Level Gradient™ by using a set of lessons and titles from another system. For example, after teaching at level P in the *LLI Gold System*, you may decide that students need a few additional lessons at that level. You can use level P books and lessons from the *LLI Red System* to meet your students' needs. If after teaching at level T in the *Gold System*, students need *additional* lessons, you can use level T books and lessons from the *LLI Purple System* for that purpose. You may also decide to spend *fewer* days at a level when you have observable evidence that the students control almost all the competencies specified at the level. These competencies are listed in the pages at the end of each level of the *Lesson Guide*, in the excerpt from *The Continuum of Literacy Learning*.

The *LLI* books have been written specifically for the intervention system. Written by children's authors and illustrated by high-quality artists, they are designed to provide engaging, age-appropriate material while at the same time offering increasingly sophisticated learning opportunities so that students can build a reading process over time.

Orange System (Levels A–E*)

The books and lessons in the *Orange System* begin with level A and continue through level E. They provide a significant amount of easy reading for students who are having difficulty becoming oriented to print and learning the function of letters and sounds. The books were written with the interest levels of five-year-olds in mind. The *Orange System* is designed to *prevent* further confusions by establishing a strong foundation at easy levels.

The *LLI Orange System* is specifically designed to address the interests and needs of kindergarten students

---

*The levels in the *LLI Orange* and *Green* systems are being extended to accommodate increased instructional level expectations. A "booster" package will be available for those who have already purchased the *Orange* and *Green* systems.

Suggestions for Working with English Language Learners

Supporting Oral Language

- Make instructions highly interactive, with oral language surrounding everything students are learning.

- Use short, simple (but natural sounding) sentences instead of long, complex ones that students will have difficulty following.

- Have the students repeat unfamiliar vocabulary and language structures, if needed.

- When introducing books, use some of the language of the text in a conversational way, and have students repeat the language several times to help them remember the English syntax.

- Show students what you mean when you give directions. You may need to act out certain sequences of actions and have students repeat those actions while you coach them. Have them repeat directions to each other or say them aloud as they engage in the activity. Support them during their first attempts rather than expecting independence immediately.

- Give English language learners more "wait and think" time. You could say, "Let's think about that for a minute" before calling for an answer. Demonstrate to students how to think about what you are going to say. Set expectations that students will share their thinking.

- Before they share with the group, give students opportunities to talk briefly with a partner so that they can try out the language they want to use to express their thinking.

- Paraphrase and summarize for students. Repeat the directions or instructions several different ways, watching for feedback that they understand you.

- Remember that typical English language learners usually understand more than they are able to express verbally. Ask students if they understand, and repeat, if needed.

- Expand students' sentences in a conversational way during discussion (rather than correcting them) to encourage active participation.

- If possible, learn some important words and expressions in the students' language. Encourage them to share with you.

Supporting Reading

- Involve students in some shared reading. They can benefit from repeated reading, especially if the language is different or more complex than the language they can currently use in speech. This experience gives students a chance to practice language, learn the meaning of the words, and use the sentence structures of English. Several repetitions of a new language structure, within a meaningful and enjoyable activity, will enable a student to add the new literacy structure to her repertoire. This may take place during the book introduction, or after reading, but is also reinforced during fluency practice—in Readers' Theater, echo reading, and assisted reading.

- Check understanding to see if you need to explain a concept or vocabulary word that would be familiar to most English speakers but might not be for ELLs.

- Direct attention to illustrations and graphic text features, and use understandable oral language when you introduce texts to students. Repeat as needed.

- Help learners relate new words to words they already know. Before, during, and after reading, check with students to be sure they understand the vocabulary and concepts. Allow time within the lessons, and encourage students to bring up any words they do not understand.

- Be sure students understand the prompts you are using before you ask them to demonstrate what they have learned. English language learners might need support for their understanding of the concepts.

- Encourage students to read aloud to a parent or sibling at home, even if that parent or sibling is not yet fluent in English. If her parents are not fluent in English, encourage the student to talk about the books and stories she is reading in her first language.

FIGURE 1.4 Suggestions for Working with English Language Learners

continues

Suggestions for Working with English Language Learners

Supporting Writing

- Value and allow students to draw as a way to represent their thinking.

- Help them connect their ideas represented in drawing to the language they want to write.

- Demonstrate how to say words slowly and segment multisyllable words, providing individual help and demonstration, as needed.

- Surround students' independent writing with a great deal of oral language. Talk with students, and help them express their ideas and expand oral language before they write.

- Learn something about the sound system of students' first languages. That knowledge will give you valuable insights into the way they attempt their first spellings. For example, notice whether they are using letter/sound associations from the first language or whether they are actually thinking of a word in the first language and trying to spell it.

- Help students use standard pronunciation and spelling of words. They need to develop a sense of the visual features of words—how a word *looks*.

- Notice how English pronunciation improves as students experience reading and talking.

Supporting Phonics and Word Study

- The "hands-on" activities in *LLI* lessons will be very helpful to your English language learners. Students will have a chance to manipulate word magnets and word cards and play games with words. Repeat activities that you find most beneficial for your students.

- Be sure that your handwriting (printing) on all charts is clear and consistent so that students who are working in another language are not confused by a variety of unfamiliar letter forms.

- Make sure that your English language learners are sitting where it is easy for them to see the charts.

- When possible, use a concrete object to help students learn a concept.

- Enunciate your own words clearly and accept students' approximations. If they are feeling their own mouths as they say (or approximate) the sounds, they will be able to make the connections. Sounds and letters are abstract concepts, and the relationships are arbitrary. Building understanding of letter-sound correspondence will be especially complex for students whose sound systems do not exactly match that of English. They may have trouble saying the sounds that are related to letters and letter clusters.

- Accept alternative pronunciations of words with the hard-to-say sounds, and present the written forms to help learners distinguish between them. Sounds that are like each other, have similar tongue positions, and are easily confused—such as *s* and *z*, *r* and *l*, *sh* and *ch*, *f* and *v*—can be difficult for English language learners to differentiate. They often have trouble with inflected endings (*s, ed*) because they have not yet achieved control of the language structure.

- Speak clearly and slowly when working with students on distinguishing phonemes and hearing sounds in words, but do not distort the word so much that it is unrecognizable. Distortion may confuse English language learners in that it may make one word sound like another that they do not know.

- When discussing concepts such as *beginning, ending, first,* and *last,* be sure students understand these concepts.

FIGURE 1.4 Suggestions for Working with English Language Learners (*cont.*)

who are identified as having difficulties after the first few months of kindergarten and is also helpful for students who are learning English as it provides easy reading and plenty of opportunities to talk about texts.

Green System (Levels A–K*)

The books and lessons in the *Green System* begin with level A and continue through level K. The books in the *Green System* were written with the interest levels of six-year-olds in mind. The *Green System* is specifically designed to address the interests and needs of first grade students who are identified as reading below expected grade level. In schools that use Reading Recovery it is recommended that the lowest achieving students receive Reading Recovery instruction, and the next tier of students receive *LLI* instruction. The *Green System* can also be used for ELL students and special education students for whom the lessons meet the educational program specifications.

Blue System (Levels C–N)

The books and lessons in the *Blue System* begin with level C and continue through level N. The books were written with the interest level of seven- to eight-year-old students in mind. The *Blue System* is designed to address the interests and needs of second graders who are reading below grade level, or older students who are reading below level N. It has also been effectively used with ELL students and special education students for whom the lessons meet the educational program specifications.

Red System (Levels L–Q)

The books and lessons in the *Red System* begin with level L and continue through level Q. Each level in the *Red System* consists of 28 lessons plus 4 optional test preparation lessons. The lessons provide students with opportunities to read a variety of genres. Students engage in intensive work in comprehension, vocabulary fluency, phonics, word study, and writing about reading. The *Red System* is specifically

designed to address the interests and needs of third graders (approximately 8–9 years old), but may be used with older students who are reading below level Q. It can also be used with ELL students and special education students for whom the lessons meet the educational program specifications.

Gold System (Levels O–T)

The books and lessons in the *Gold System* begin with level O and continue through level T. The *Gold System* is specifically designed to address the interests and needs of fourth graders who are reading below grade level, older students reading below level T, and for ELL students and special education students for whom the lessons meet the educational program specifications. The *Gold System* includes the same number of books and lessons as the *Red System*. Books are written and illustrated to be appealing to readers about nine or ten years old.

Purple System (Levels R–W, in press)

The books and lessons in the *Purple System* begin with level R and continue through level W. The *Purple System* is specifically designed to address the interests and needs of fifth graders who are reading below grade level, older students reading below level W, and for ELL students and special education students for whom the lessons meet the educational program specifications. The *Purple System* includes the same number of books as the *Red* and *Gold Systems*. Books are written and illustrated to be appealing to preadolescents (ages 10–12).

Teal System (Levels U–Z, in press)

The books and lessons in the *Teal System* begin with level U and continue through level Z. The *Teal System* is designed specifically to address the needs of middle and secondary school students who are reading below grade level and for ELL students and special education students for whom the lessons meet the educational program specifications. The *Teal System* includes the same number of books as the *Red*, *Gold*, and *Purple Systems*. Books are written to be appealing to adolescents (ages 12 and up) and engage them in disciplinary reading.

*The levels in the *LLI Orange* and *Green Systems* are being extended to accommodate increased instructional level expectations. A "booster" package will be available for those who have already purchased the *Orange* and *Green Systems*.

▶ *LLI Gold System* Components

In Figure 1.5 you see the key components provided for implementing the *Leveled Literacy Intervention Gold System*.

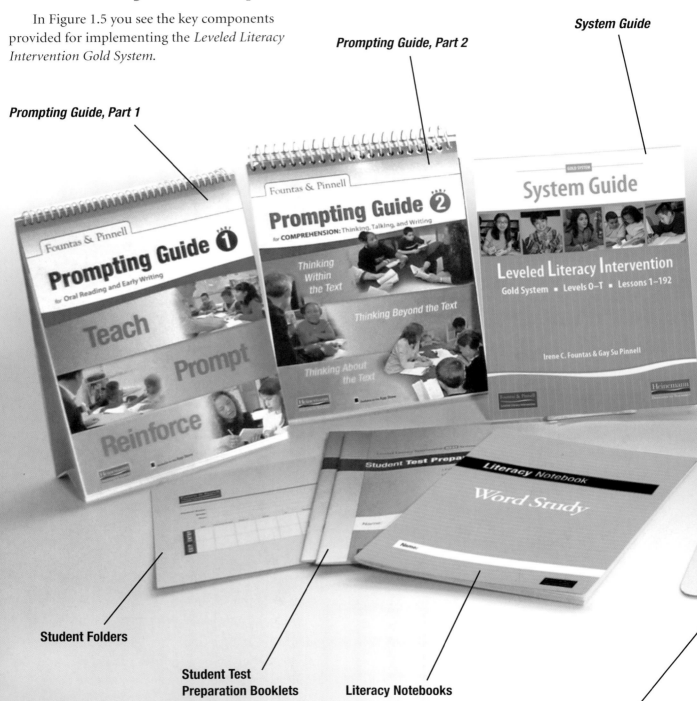

Prompting Guide, Part 1

Prompting Guide, Part 2

System Guide

Student Folders

Student Test Preparation Booklets

Literacy Notebooks

F&P Calculator/Stopwatch

FIGURE 1.5 *LLI* Components

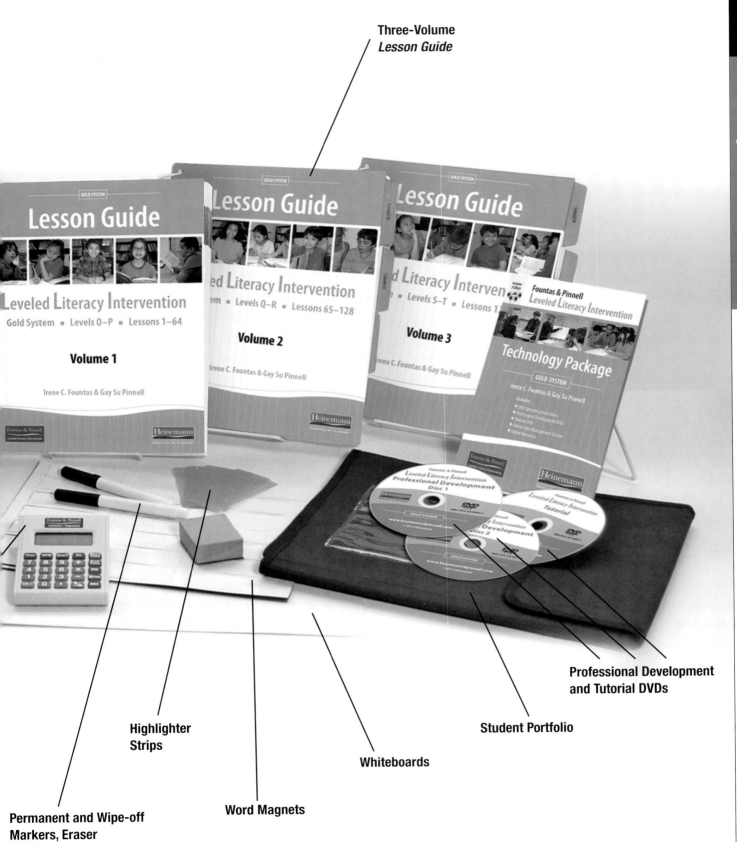

Three-Volume
Lesson Guide

Professional Development
and Tutorial DVDs

Student Portfolio

Whiteboards

Highlighter
Strips

Word Magnets

Permanent and Wipe-off
Markers, Eraser

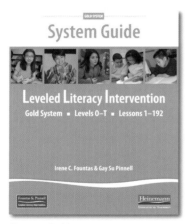

System Guide

SYSTEM GUIDE

The *System Guide* provides a comprehensive overview of the components and implementation of the *LLI Gold System*.

Lesson Guide

LESSON GUIDE

The three-volume *Lesson Guide* for the *Gold System* includes 192 lessons for teaching students in small groups. The guides help you provide high-quality, fast-paced lessons that support reading, writing, and language development.

At the end of each of the levels O–T, you will find the specific continuum that specifies the important behaviors and understandings to notice, teach, and support for the level.

Leveled Books

BOOKS

In the *Gold System*, learning takes place with the foundational support of 24 leveled texts and one full-length novel at each level O through T, for a total of 150 different titles in the system. The *Gold System* includes six copies each of the 150 titles (900 student books in total): a teacher copy, four student copies to be used within a group, and one extra copy for replacement as needed. (Additional copies or replacement copies can be ordered from Heinemann.) The back cover of each book shows the genre, level, book/lesson number, and total number of running words. For each book, there is a description that students can read to help them preview the book and an author's note on the inside back cover. This material is designed for the *teacher to read to the students*. You have the option to use this material. Within the collection there is a strong emphasis on disciplinary reading and thinking across texts. The complete list of titles in the *Gold System* can be found in Appendix A, beginning on page 128. They include a wide variety of genres, including biography, memoir, narrative nonfiction, expository nonfiction, realistic fiction, historical fiction, and fantasy. They also include a variety of series books and two-way books, which are single volumes containing two related books that present a topic from two different perspectives in two different forms.

Series Books

A *series* is a set of texts that are connected in some way—characters, setting, or ideas. In the *LLI Gold System*, there are two kinds of series books—fiction and nonfiction.

❑ Fiction series books feature the same characters in the same settings (or a couple of related settings) by the same author. The characters are identifiable and, in general, remain unchanged except for sometimes learning by solving problems.

❑ Nonfiction series books are connected by a larger theme or idea. They have different content, but each elaborates on a concept or overarching theme.

The series books in the *Gold System* may be read in any order, and it is not necessary to have read a previous book to understand a current one. (This feature is different from books with sequels in which characters grow older and change, as in the Harry Potter books.) Also, the series books in *LLI* are short (24 to 32 pages) so that they can be read in a day; however, reading several or all of the books in a series will give readers a sustained experience in getting to know characters or thinking about a big idea.

There are several advantages to using series books. In general, series books promote thinking across texts and increase engagement. See Appendix E for a detailed description of the series books and the rationale for including them in *LLI*.

Novels

Six full-length novels (6 copies each) are provided at the end of each level O–T, to help students build stamina by reading longer texts.

Gold System Novels

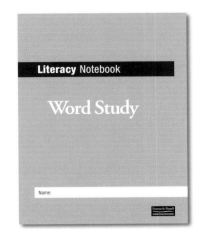

LITERACY NOTEBOOKS (PACK OF 96)*

Consumable 72-page notebooks are provided to extend word study and writing about reading portions of the lessons. There are packs of 16 per level with lined pages, glossary of terms, and other reference material to use for students' writing and word study. The Literacy Notebook is in a two-way format, allowing students to use the Word Study section or flip the notebook over to use the Writing About Reading section.

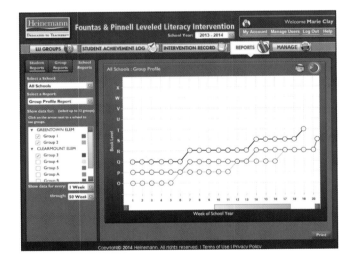

LLI ONLINE DATA MANAGEMENT SYSTEM (ODMS)

The *LLI* Online Data Management System is a secure and efficient way for teachers and school and district administrators to collect, analyze, and report student assessment data according to district

---

*Replacement copies can be ordered from Heinemann at www.fountasandpinnell.com.

requirements. A one-year individual teacher subscription to this secure, Web-based data management system is included with the initial purchase of the *LLI Gold System*. After year one, subscriptions are per teacher per year (for an unlimited number of students) and include unlimited access for school and district administrators. The product code for accessing ODMS is included in the Technology Package and User Guide. For a product tour and downloadable user manuals, go to www.heinemann.com/fountasandpinnell/student-progress-monitoring.aspx.

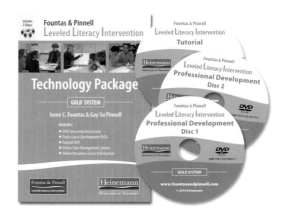

TECHNOLOGY PACKAGE: PROFESSIONAL DEVELOPMENT AND TUTORIAL DVDS, AND USER GUIDE

This three-DVD set is composed of two Professional Development DVDs and a Tutorial DVD. The first features model lessons, instructional procedures, and an overview of the system. The Tutorial DVD provides instruction and practice coding, scoring, analyzing, and interpreting reading records to inform instruction. The User Guide supports all the technological components of *LLI*.

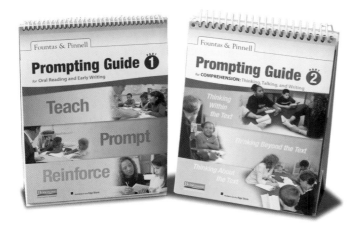

PROMPTING GUIDE PART 1 FOR ORAL READING AND EARLY WRITING

This professional resource contains reference flip charts that contain precise language that can be used to teach for, prompt for, and reinforce effective strategic actions during reading and early writing.

PROMPTING GUIDE PART 2 FOR COMPREHENSION: THINKING, TALKING, AND WRITING

This guide is a tool that provides specific language for supporting students' thinking, talking, and writing about reading. Prompts for book discussions and reading conferences are included. The guide is organized in categories and color coded so that you can turn quickly to the area needed and refer to it as you teach.

ONLINE RESOURCES

Some of the resources listed in the You Will Need section of each lesson can be printed from the Online Resources site at www.fountasandpinnell.com/resources.

The inclusion of these materials will save you valuable preparation time. The product code for accessing this site is included in the Technology Package and User Guide.

The contents of the Online Resources for *LLI* are organized by two main sections: General Resources and Lesson Resources.

General Resources includes items that you will need on multiple occasions throughout *LLI* so we recommend you print multiple copies in advance and keep them on file. Some of the General Resources include:

❑ Intervention Record

❑ Lesson Records for Standard, Novel Study, and Test Preparation Lessons

❑ Guide for Observing and Noting Reading Behaviors

❑ Coding and Scoring Errors at-a-Glance

❑ Reflection Guide

❑ Communication Sheets for Group and Individuals

❑ Reading Graph

❑ Student Achievement Log

❑ Phonics/Word Study Game Directions and Game Boards

❑ Word Cards

❑ Translations of Parent Letters (French, Spanish, Hmong, Haitian-Creole)

Lesson Resources are specific to lessons and can be accessed by lesson number. Some of the Lesson Resources include:

❑ Recording Forms for taking reading records

❑ Readers' Theater activities

❑ Phrased Reading activities

❑ Practice Sorts

❑ Word Cards

❑ Graphic Organizers

❑ Word Lists

❑ Phonics/Word Study Games

❑ Parent Letters (English)

---

*Replacement copies can be ordered from Heinemann at www.fountasandpinnell.com

F&P CALCULATOR/STOPWATCH

This valuable tool automates the calculation of an accuracy rate and doubles as a stopwatch to calculate reading rate (WPM).

STUDENT FOLDERS (PACK OF 16)*

The *LLI Gold System* includes a set of folders to organize and store reading records and other data for each student. These folders can be passed on each year as part of students' records. The inside of the folder includes a graph for tracking a student's entry level, progress throughout *LLI*, and exit-level information.

LESSON FOLDERS

The system also includes 192 sturdy plastic lesson folders to store books, lessons, and other ancillary material needed for each lesson.

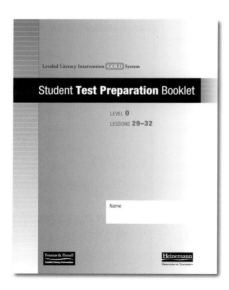

STUDENT TEST PREPARATION BOOKLETS (12 PACKS OF 6)*

The consumable booklets, one for each of the six levels, include selections and test items for the optional Test Preparation Lessons.

STUDENT PORTFOLIOS (PACK OF 16)

Sturdy student portfolios are for students to organize and transport *LLI* books, Literacy Notebooks, class work, and homework between school and home.

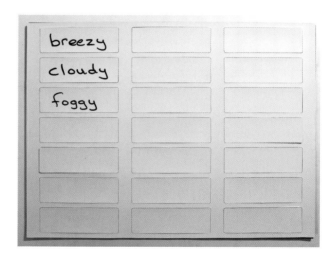

WORD MAGNETS (PACK OF 900)*

Blank sheets of word magnet cards are used to create the cards for phonics/word study lessons, using permanent or wipe-off markers.

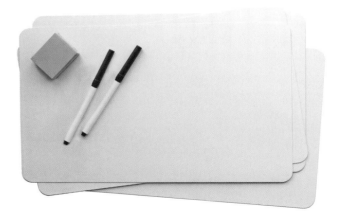

MAGNETIC WHITEBOARDS (PACK OF 6)*

Student whiteboards, pens, and word magnets are used during phonics/word study lessons.

PERMANENT AND WIPE-OFF MARKERS AND ERASER

For use with word magnets and whiteboards. The permanent marker is for creating word magnets to be reused again and again. The wipe-off marker is for practicing words on the whiteboard.

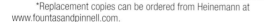

*Replacement copies can be ordered from Heinemann at www.fountasandpinnell.com.

HIGHLIGHTER STRIPS

For highlighting words or parts of words in phonics/word study activities. They can also be used for helping students' eyes to move more quickly along the print.

Optional Purchases Outside the System

WHEN READERS STRUGGLE, L–Z: TEACHING THAT WORKS (IN PRESS)

This volume is a comprehensive professional book to support effective teaching in the lessons. Each lesson will refer you to chapters that will be helpful in developing your professional expertise in working with students who find literacy learning difficult.

FOUNTAS & PINNELL LLI GOLD SYSTEM CHOICE LIBRARY

The *Fountas & Pinnell LLI Gold System Choice Library* includes 150 carefully selected high-quality books in a range of genres and topics written by authors your students will enjoy. The library offers a wide range of longer books for your students to build reading stamina. A significant factor in the progress of intermediate and middle school students is the opportunity to read a variety of genres and topics related to their own interests. An increase in the volume of reading will support your students' accelerated progress. The library is an important investment in the independent reading opportunities of your readers.

After *LLI* lessons, you can give students a few minutes to check books in and out of the collection to read during independent reading in class or at home. Accompanying teacher material provides a summary, prompts, and the level of each book for your reference in guiding students in making good choices. We are not suggesting that students choose the books by level but that you assure students find a book that they will be able to read successfully.

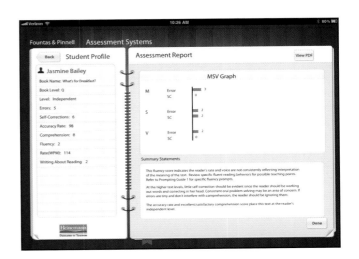

FOUNTAS & PINNELL *LLI* READING RECORD APP FOR IPADS*

Reading record software that performs the following functions:

- ❏ Saves individual reading record assesments and summary assessments as PDFs.
- ❏ Times the conference and calculates oral reading and accuracy rate, self-correction ratio, fluency, and comprehension scores.
- ❏ Records the assessment conference.
- ❏ Syncs data to the Online Data Management System (ODMS).

*Available through Apple iTunes App Store.

Implementing the *LLI Gold System*

▶ Initial Assessment of Students

When implementing the *LLI Gold System*, your goal is to identify the lowest-achieving students in grade 4 and find the instructional reading level for each of them. A valuable source of information is the classroom teacher who has worked with the students for the last year or for the first weeks of school and who has had the opportunity to notice both the strengths and the needs of the students. The classroom teacher may be able to recommend several students for systematic assessment of reading levels and other competencies. If the students are reading below level O, you will need to begin with the *Red System*.

▶ Finding the Instructional Reading Levels of the Lowest-Achieving Students

For entry into *LLI*, it will be necessary to assess the students' instructional and independent reading levels. Systematic assessment is very helpful because the more precise you and the classroom teacher are in your initial assessment, the more effective you will be in your teaching. If the classroom teacher can give you the recent reading records from the *Fountas & Pinnell Benchmark Assessment System 2*, you will not need to readminister it.

Using the *Fountas & Pinnell Benchmark Assessment System 2*

If possible, we recommend that you or the classroom teacher use the *Fountas & Pinnell Benchmark Assessment System 2* to determine the instructional reading level for each of your students because the levels will correlate precisely to *LLI* levels. You will be able to identify each student's specific reading level according to the levels used in this intervention. The *Fountas & Pinnell Benchmark Assessment System 2* will also provide critical information on the student's reading strengths and processing needs, comprehension, and fluency. Using *The Continuum of Literacy Learning,* you can link learning needs directly to instruction. In addition, you will be able to select specific assessments from the section called "Optional Assessments" in the *Benchmark Assessment System 2* for diagnostic purposes. For example, at the grade 4 level, you may want to use any of the following:

❑ Reading High-Frequency Words—Students read 500 high-frequency words.

❑ Phonograms—Students read words with phonogram patterns.

❑ Consonant Blends—Students say words and identify consonant clusters.

❑ Vowel Clusters—Students read words with vowels that appear together and represent one sound.

❑ One- and Two-syllable Words—Students say a word, clap for each syllable, and identify the number of syllables in the word.

❑ Vocabulary in Context—Students define words in context by using information in a sentence, paragraph, or whole text.

Some of the assessments are quick and may be administered in a small group. All of the assessments will provide a wealth of information to inform your instruction.

Using Other Benchmark Assessment Systems

If you do not have access to the *Fountas & Pinnell Benchmark Assessment System,* you can use other benchmark assessments you have in your school or district. Many publishers provide correlation charts to connect their assessment systems with the Fountas and Pinnell levels. You may find the following correlation chart (see Figure 2.1) helpful, although the Fountas & Pinnell Assessment Levels and the Reading Recovery levels are the most reliable and the most closely matched to this intervention.

Alternative Assessments

If you do not have access to a benchmark assessment, you can use the information from any assessments used in the district and select the lowest performers. Once you have identified these students, you may want to use a quick informal assessment of reading level using leveled books. If you are using a basal system, the correlation chart in Figure 2.1 may be helpful in selecting students who are reading below level.

Assessment Using Leveled Books

A quick and informal way to assess students is to have an individual student read aloud one or two books at a particular text level. If you have leveled books in your school, select one or two from that collection. Assess the percentage of words read accurately, and note specific errors (substitutions, omissions, insertions). The level at which the student reads with 90–94% accuracy (levels A–K) and satisfactory comprehension or 95–97% accuracy (levels L–Z) and satisfactory comprehension is the student's instructional level. You may want to use the F&P Calculator/Stopwatch to quickly determine an accuracy rate.

You will have an assessment of accuracy and also insights into the kind of actions and the information the student is using when errors are made (for example, words that look like other words or words that are inaccurate but make sense). Errors can sometimes illustrate a student's strengths and give you insights in how to help him. The Tutorial DVD included in the system will help you to analyze your students' reading behavior.

Following the reading, involve the student in a conversation that will help you know what he understood from the text. You can encourage the student's thinking with prompts and questions, but the assessment should not feel like an interrogation.

If the level is too difficult, move down the levels until you find something the student can read at an instructional level with good understanding. If the level seems easy, move up the levels until you find the book that is too hard. Start your instruction with the level a student can read with 90–94% accuracy (levels A–K) and satisfactory comprehension or 95–97% accuracy (levels L–Z) and satisfactory comprehension.

Instructional Grade-Level Equivalence Chart

Grade	Fountas & Pinnell Level	Basal Level	Reading Recovery® Level	Rigby Level	DRA Level
Kindergarten	A	Readiness	1	1–2	A, 1, 2
Kindergarten	B		2	3–4	
Kindergarten	C	PP1	3, 4		
Kindergarten	D	PP2	5, 6	6	4
Grade 1	E	PP3	7, 8	7	6, 7, 8
Grade 1	F	Primer	9, 10	8	10
Grade 1	G	Grade 1	11, 12	9	12
Grade 1	H	Grade 1	13, 14	10	14
Grade 1	I	Grade 1	15, 16	11	16
Grade 1	J	Grade 1	17, 18	12	18
Grade 2	K	Grade 2	19, 20	13–14	20
Grade 2	L	Grade 2		15	24–28
Grade 2	M	Grade 2		16–17	
Grade 3	N	Grade 3		18	30
Grade 3	O	Grade 3		19	
Grade 3	P	Grade 3		20	34–38
Grade 4	Q	Grade 4			40
Grade 4	R	Grade 4			
Grade 4	S	Grade 4			44
Grade 5	T	Grade 5			
Grade 5	U	Grade 5			
Grade 5	V	Grade 5			
Grade 6	W	Grade 6			
Grade 6	X	Grade 6			
Grade 6	Y	Grade 6			
Grade 7, 8 and Above	Z	Grade 7, 8			

FIGURE 2.1 Instructional Grade-Level Equivalence Chart

▶ Selecting Students for the Intervention

If students are reading below the level indicated for grade 4 at a specific time of the school year, you may want to select them for *LLI*. Remember, these are approximations and are not to be used in rigid ways.

We have designed a general Instructional Level Expectations chart (Figure 2.2). Use this chart to keep goals in mind for each grade level, but be flexible based on the goals of your school/district.

In your school, you may have many students who do not meet expectations for grade-level reading—many more than can be served in the intervention. In this case, begin with the students who need the most help and serve all you can. On the other hand, your school or district may have higher-level expectations than are indicated in the chart so some students may need intervention to meet your school/district-specific goals. If students cannot fully participate and learn from the level of instruction in the classroom, they can benefit from *LLI*. Adjust the levels accordingly.

Forming *LLI* Groups

Any form of grouping requires some compromise. Ideally, you try to meet individual needs and provide the very specific instruction that each reader needs to move forward, but sometimes logistics require forming groups that have students who vary by one level. You can keep many factors in mind as you thoughtfully create groups. It helps that in *LLI*, you work with a small group and you have the advantage of many interactions to support language development and understanding. Within the group

Fountas & Pinnell

INSTRUCTIONAL LEVEL EXPECTATIONS FOR READING

	Beginning of Year (Aug.–Sept.)	1st Interval of Year (Nov.–Dec.)	2nd Interval of Year (Feb.–Mar.)	End of Year (May–June)
Grade K		C+	D+	E+
		B	C	D
		A	B	C
				Below C
Grade 1	E+	G+	I+	K+
	D / E	F	H	J
	C	E	G	I
	Below C	Below E	Below G	Below I
Grade 2	K+	L+	M+	N+
	J / K	K	L	M
	I	J	K	L
	Below I	Below J	Below K	Below L
Grade 3	N+	O+	P+	Q+
	M / N	N	O	P
	L	M	N	O
	Below L	Below M	Below N	Below O
Grade 4	Q+	R+	S+	T+
	P / Q	Q	R	S
	O	P	Q	R
	Below O	Below P	Below Q	Below R
Grade 5	T+	U+	V+	W+
	S / T	T	U	V
	R	S	T	U
	Below R	Below S	Below T	Below U
Grade 6	W+	X+	Y+	Z
	V / W	W	X	Y
	U	V	W	X
	Below U	Below V	Below W	Below X
Grade 7	Z	Z	Z+	Z+
	Y	Y	Z	Z
	X	X	Y	Y
	Below X	Below X	Below Y	Below Y
Grade 8+	Z+	Z+	Z+	Z+
	Z	Z	Z	Z
	Y	Y	Y	Y
	Below Y	Below Y	Below Y	Below Y

KEY

- Exceeds Expectations
- Meets Expectations
- Approaches Expectations: Needs Short-Term Intervention
- Does Not Meet Expectations: Needs Intensive Intervention

The Instructional Level Expectations for Reading chart is intended to provide general guidelines for grade-level goals, which should be adjusted based on school/district requirements and professional teacher judgement.

06/26/2013

DEDICATED TO TEACHERS

FIGURE 2.2 Instructional Level Expectations Chart

you will interact with individuals to support their development.

Once you determine the instructional levels of the students, create small groups of readers who are similar enough that you can begin lessons at a particular level. In the *Gold System*, we strongly recommend that you work with four students at a time, and then (later in the year), work with another group of four in the 45-minute teaching slot. You will serve four students in each teaching slot across the year. In this way you will ultimately serve at least eight students in one teaching slot, but only four at a time to achieve better results. From time to time you may make other decisions; however, we recommend a group of four so that you can:

❑ Observe closely and provide strong individual support.

❑ Keep all students in the group highly engaged throughout the lesson.

❑ Use precise language to prompt for effective reading strategies while listening to individual readers.

❑ Observe closely and interact with students as they write to support the development of writing strategies.

❑ Promote interaction among students.

❑ Maintain efficiency in time management.

Students do not always fall neatly into just the right number of groups! After all, they are individuals who cannot be defined by "reading level." You will probably have to do some problem solving when you begin to group students. Your goal is to group the students so that the level of instruction is appropriate for them all. Start the group at a text level that allows every student to begin with success. Here are some suggestions:

❑ Make some "one level" compromises. Four students whose instructional levels are O, O, P, and P, for example, may be able to read together and benefit from the intervention lessons starting at level O. Remember that if they move quickly, you can skip lessons. Just be sure you use *The Continuum of Literacy Learning* in your decision making. Review the behaviors and understandings needed at the level, and be sure you have gained strong evidence. You can challenge individuals through the writing opportunities and through the use of choice libraries.

❑ If you are working alongside a teacher in a classroom, make arrangements for students from the "next door" classroom to join the group you are teaching.

❑ Take students at the same level from different classrooms (but be sure that it doesn't take too much time to assemble them in the space where you are teaching).

Your priority should be to group students efficiently and effectively so that you can teach them at the appropriate level. (See Section 7 for Frequently Asked Questions.)

You may move a student from one group to another at any time. Sometimes, after a few weeks, teachers look at their data on all the students and re-form their groups. Depending on the students' strengths and needs, it is not usually a problem if a student experiences a few lessons for the second time or skips a few books and lessons.

▶ Management of *LLI* Groups
Scheduling *LLI* Groups

The *LLI System* is designed to provide intensive short-term support. Students need five lessons per week (four as a minimum) so that what they learned the previous day can be reinforced and built upon the following day. Five lessons is ideal if it is possible to accommodate in the schedule. It is important that the lessons are a supplement *to*, not a substitute *for*, classroom small-group reading instruction at the elementary level. Good, consistent small-group teaching in the classroom is a key factor in supporting ongoing learning. The supplementary teaching will allow the students to make faster-than-average progress and catch up with their peers.

Supplemental, intensive small-group instruction is the key to intervention that will bring students to grade level performance. Readers who struggle need to participate in both classroom reading instruction and intensive instruction through *LLI* to close the achievement gap.

For each 45-minute teaching slot in your schedule, you will be able to work with one group. As students reach grade-level performance, you can start another group in the teaching slot. If you have five teaching slots per day, you will be able to work with at least ten

LLI groups in the school year. If you have six teaching slots, you will be able to teach at least twelve groups per year. This means that you can serve from 30 to 48 of the lowest-achieving students in a school year!

The length of time spent in *LLI* lessons will vary depending on how far below grade level the students are when they enter the system (see Figure 2.3). If you complete all 28 lessons at a level (24 standard lessons and 4 novel study lessons), it should take 5.5 weeks (or 5 weeks, 3 days) per level. Note that this plan does not include the optional Test Preparation Lessons. You may not need to have students complete all lessons at a level. If you find the students demonstrate almost all of the

behaviors listed in *The Continuum of Literacy Learning* page found at the end of the level in your *Lesson Guide*, you could give students the extra books at the level for home reading and move to the next level.

We have created Figure 2.4 to show the work of one intervention teacher across a school year. Notice how the teacher began the year with five groups, in five teaching slots per day. As each group reached the level performance goal and exited the intervention, the teacher started with another group. By the end of the year, the teacher brought 40 students to grade-level expectations and helped another 12 students make progress toward grade level.

Estimated Time in *LLI Gold System*

Entry Level	0 →	P →	Q →	R →	S →	T →
# of Lessons	28	28	28	28	28	28
Approximate # of Weeks	5.5	5.5	5.5	5.5	5.5	5.5

1. Students may not need all 28 lessons at a level.
2. Test Preparation Lessons are not included in this plan.

FIGURE 2.3 Estimated Time in *LLI Gold System*

One Intervention Teacher with Five Teaching Slots Per Day

This chart demonstrates how one intervention teacher with five teaching slots works with fifty-two students over the course of one school y

Week	1	2	3	4	5	6	7	8	9	10	11	12	13	14	15	16
	Assessment & Grouping			Red (Group of 4)												
	Assessment & Grouping			Red (Group of 4)												
	Assessment & Grouping			Gold (Group of 4)												
	Assessment & Grouping			Gold (Group of 4)												
	Assessment & Grouping			Purple (Group of 4)												

FIGURE 2.4 One Intervention Teacher with Five Teaching Slots Per Day

If you have only the *Gold System*, concentrate your efforts on grade 4 students reading below grade level. If they are reading below level O, you will need the *Red System* to begin at lower levels.

Entering the System

Use your assessments to determine a specific starting point for the system. This means that you may start with the intervention at the beginning of any level. It is important to start at a level where you are confident the students will find success. If you are uncertain about where to start, begin at a lower level. You can always decide not to spend all 28 days at a level if students find the material very easy. You can move to the beginning of the next level, or you can just skip to the Novel Study and optional Test Preparation Lessons (if used), then proceed to the next level.

Coordinating *LLI* Lessons with Classroom Instruction

Once the students have entered the *LLI System*, your partnership with the classroom teacher will be critical in helping students make fast progress to catch up with their peers. The following suggestions may be helpful, but you may have many more ideas:

❏ Talk with the classroom teacher about the importance and benefits of daily *LLI* lessons and frequent small-group instruction in the classroom.

❏ Invite the classroom teacher to observe an *LLI* lesson. Talk about what behaviors and strategies you observed and how you could provide cohesion in instruction for these students.

❏ Share the Lesson Record or other record-keeping charts, such as the Reading Graph, on a regular basis so you both have the same information on student progress. You may also want to use the communication forms that can be downloaded from the Online Resources site.

❏ Ask for any information the classroom teacher may have that will inform your teaching (e.g., Writing Folder, Reading List).

❏ Share the student's Literacy Notebook frequently, and discuss with the classroom teacher the writing that shows evidence of learning.

❏ Show the classroom teacher the Parent Letter (in English and other languages) and other materials so they are aware of what is expected at home. Though you cannot count on home practice for the student's success in the intervention, any extra practice will be a bonus. The time might be provided in the classroom for some students, as needed.

Amount of Time in the System

The approximate amount of time students need in the system will be related to the entry level and the distance to grade-level performance. Depending upon

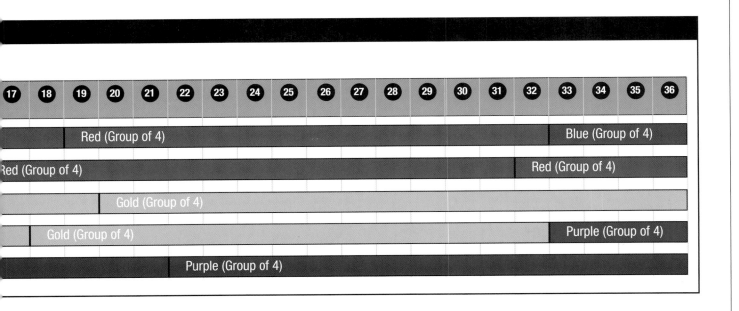

how far below grade level they are when they enter the system, most students in grade 4 should reach grade level in 18–24 weeks with daily lessons (five per week) and strong teaching, If students enter a full year or more below grade level, they should experience significant progress, but they may not reach grade level as quickly.

You may decide to keep the students a few weeks longer if they are approaching grade-level performance, but keep in mind that this will delay the entrance of other students needing the intervention, or shorten the amount of time they are able to spend in the system.

Exiting the System

When you and the classroom teacher observe evidence that the students are reading well at the end of a series of lessons and are performing at least on grade level, you can use your final reading record as an indicator of the student's competencies. Ideally, you will have the *Fountas & Pinnell Benchmark Assessment System* so you or the classroom teacher can re-administer the leveled assessments to confirm your observational notes, the classroom performance, and your final reading record. Figure 2.5 can be used to identify grade-level goals or competencies. Adjust it to fit your school or district expectations.

We have created Figure 2.6 to show the progress of *LLI* students who have made accelerated progress with daily, intensive, supplemental instruction. The top line shows the progress of an average-achieving student, making a years' progress in a year. The bottom line shows a student who enters grade 4 about a year behind and continues to learn slowly. Comparing the top and bottom lines, you see how the gap between achieving

Grade-Level Goals			
Grade	Beginning	Mid-year	End
3	M/N	0	P
4	P/Q	R	S

FIGURE 2.5 Grade-Level Goals

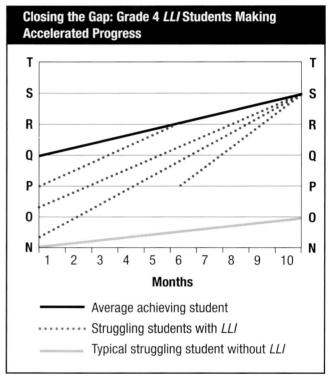

FIGURE 2.6 Closing the Gap: Grade 4 *LLI* Students Making Accelerated Progress

and low-achieving students widens. The four dotted middle lines show *LLI* students who entered below grade level and made accelerated progress to close the gap and work at the level of their grade-level peers.

▶ Getting Organized for Teaching

A Space for Teaching

LLI lessons can be taught just about anywhere that you can accommodate yourself and the group of four students. You can use a section of the classroom, a space outside the classroom, or a small room. The materials are not bulky, and at any one time, it takes only a folder of materials to teach a group of students. You will need a small space in which you can place students so that they are facing you and will not be distracted.

Selecting a Table

Use a table that allows your students to face you directly and also allows them to see clearly when you write on a chart or hold up the whiteboard. A horseshoe table, a round table, or a rectangular table will work well so that you can look directly at your students all the time. Notice the height of the table and have the legs adjusted if needed. The table should come to just above the students' waists so they can hold books and look down at them.

Planning and Organizing for *LLI* Lessons

The intervention lessons are designed to require a minimum of teacher planning time, but you will need to read the books, review and think about the week's lessons, and print out the corresponding materials from the Online Resources site. If you choose not to use some materials, you can decide not to print them.

The first section of your *Lesson Guide*, called Getting Organized for Teaching, will be helpful in the process because it shows what you will print from the Online Resources site and what other supplies you will need prior to starting the teaching.

Some suggestions for planning are listed below:

❑ Review the *Lesson Guide* for the appropriate lessons. Notice the You Will Need list at the top of the first lesson page. The first materials listed are supplied in the program. These are followed by the supplies you should have at your school. To the right is a list of items that you can print out from the Online Resources site. Those items that you may want to print out once at the beginning of the intervention have a check mark.

❑ Print the Lesson Record Form and other materials specific to the lesson.

❑ Consult word lists at the back of the *Lesson Guide* to make word magnets and put in sealable bags or plastic containers for re-use.

❑ Be sure to have supplies such as magnet letters, highlighter strips, markers, whiteboards, and stick-on notes, organized and in proximity for quick access during lessons.

❑ Have all materials for a group in a plastic tub or basket (e.g., Literacy Notebooks, new books for the lesson, magnetic letters, word magnets).

❑ Read the books and the lessons and note any lesson variations needed with stick-on notes.

❑ Have your *Prompting Guide, Part 1* and *Prompting Guide, Part 2* ready to use. You may want to quickly review the suggested pages of the guides that you know you will need to use. Place a stick-on note on those pages.

❑ Take note of transitions and think about how to save time.

❑ Have record-keeping forms, such as the Recording Form and the Lesson Record form, ready with the students' names on them.

❑ Have your F&P Calculator/Stopwatch ready to use.

❑ Consider placing a small rolling cart next to your table for markers, whiteboards, and other materials or supplies.

❑ If you move from classroom to classroom, consider a special container to organize your materials or a small rolling cart. For customized *LLI* teaching carts, visit www.copernicused.com.

MATERIALS AND SUPPLIES FROM YOUR SCHOOL

You will need to gather some basic supplies for your lessons:

❑ A whiteboard and dry-erase markers for teacher demonstrations during phonics and writing.

❑ Chart paper for phonics/word study and writing.

- Two sets of small, multicolored lowercase magnetic letters for teacher demonstrations during word work.
- Magnetic letters arranged alphabetically for use with students. You can use them to demonstrate or have students work with word parts.
- Paper or card stock for printing games and some charts.
- One-inch-wide correction tape to cover errors in students' Literacy Notebooks.
- Stick-on notes for marking places in books.

GROUP MATERIALS

Some basic materials for teaching a group are listed below:

- Plastic folders for the particular lessons, in which you can place the new books.
- Plastic folder for the previous day's lesson, in which you have placed the books that students will reread.
- *Lesson Guide* for today's lesson.
- Word magnets, whiteboards, markers, and games you have prepared (in clear, sealable bags).
- Highlighter strips.
- A folder for the group with Lesson Records and completed Recording Forms for students as well as Recording Forms for the week.
- Literacy Notebook for each student.

LLI Gold System Lesson Overview

▶ *Lesson Guide* Organization

There are a total of 192 lessons in the *LLI Gold System.* The lessons are divided among the three volumes of the *Lesson Guide.* Three kinds of lessons are included:

- ❏ 144 Standard Lessons
- ❏ 24 Novel Study Lessons
- ❏ 24 Optional Test Preparation Lessons

The *Lesson Guide* includes tabbed dividers for levels O–T. Each level contains 24 standard lessons, followed by 4 Novel Study sequences and 4 optional Test Preparation Lessons (Figure 3.1). The last item in each tabbed section is *The Continuum of Literacy Learning* for that level.

In this section, we provide a brief overview of the lesson frameworks, all of which provide structure to support smooth, well-paced lessons that will become very comfortable for you. The students also benefit from the predictability of the lesson structures as they learn familiar lesson procedures.

LLI Gold System Lesson Guide Organization

Volume	Lesson #s	Level	Lesson Type
1	Getting Organized for Teaching		
	1–24	O	Standard
	25–28		Novel Study Sequence
	29–32		Test Preparation (Optional)
	33–56	P	Standard
	57–60		Novel Study Sequence
	61–64		Test Preparation (Optional)
2	65–88	Q	Standard
	89–92		Novel Study Sequence
	93–96		Test Preparation (Optional)
	97–120	R	Standard
	121–124		Novel Study Sequence
	125–128		Test Preparation (Optional)
3	129–152	S	Standard
	153–156		Novel Study Sequence
	157–160		Test Preparation (Optional)
	161–184	T	Standard
	185–188		Novel Study Sequence
	189–192		Test Preparation (Optional)

FIGURE 3.1 *LLI Gold System Lesson Guide* Organization

▶ Pacing the Lessons

The *LLI Gold System* lessons are designed to be taught in a 45-minute time slot, five days per week for optimal results and intensity. In contrast to the *Orange, Green,* and *Blue* systems, the *Red System* and the *Gold System* lessons require more time.

- ❏ Books are longer and more complex.
- ❏ More time is required for comprehension, vocabulary, or fluency instruction.
- ❏ Student writing is more complex.

If a 45-minute time slot is prohibitive, see Appendix D, pp. 152–154, for a 30-minute variation of each lesson type, but work toward a 45-minute period when possible to get the full impact of the intervention.

Following the overview of each lesson framework in this section we have provided Lesson Framework charts to guide you toward this goal (see Figures 3.4, 3.6, 3.8).

▶ The Lesson Frameworks

Within the standard lessons, there are two types of lesson frameworks: one for the odd-numbered lessons and one for the even-numbered lessons. The majority of the *LLI* lessons follow the frameworks.

The framework of the novel study sequence is similar in many ways to the standard lessons but has been adjusted to accommodate the reading of a chapter book over four days, along with book club discussions.

The optional test preparation lessons have their own framework, designed to support students as they learn and practice test-taking strategies to help them meet the demands of standardized testing.

Overview of Odd-Numbered Standard Lesson Framework

Figure 3.2, which follows, shows an overview of an odd-numbered standard lesson.

Lesson Information The lesson number and level, the system, new book title, and genre.

Materials

A list of materials for the lesson. Most are included in the *LLI System* package, but some are more generic items that should be available from your school. Items in the right column are available for printing from the Online Resources site. Also included here are covers of the new book and the one to be reread.

Goals

The specific teaching goals for the lesson are organized in three categories: comprehension, word study/ vocabulary, and fluency. Choose the goals that apply to comprehension, vocabulary, or fluency, depending on the needs of your students.

How the Book Works

A statement to help you think about the overall structure of the text—the way the writer has organized and presented the information. Consider it as you introduce the text, and invite students to notice features of the text.

Text Analysis

An analysis of the new book separated into the ten characteristics that are used to analyze books.

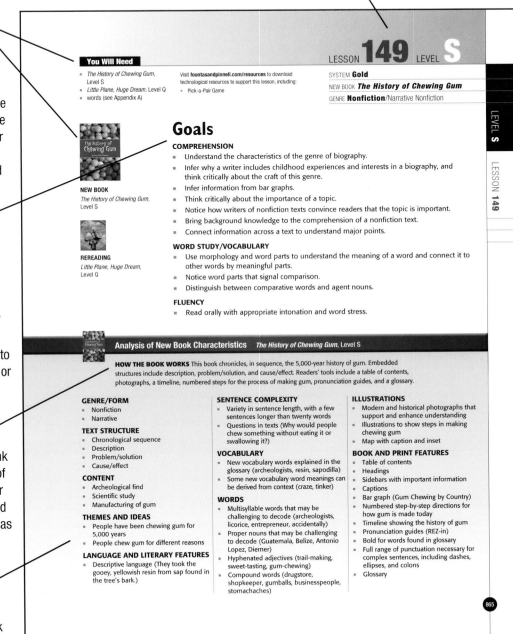

FIGURE 3.2A An Example of an Odd-Numbered Standard Lesson (Page 1 of 6)

Part 1: Discussing Yesterday's New Book

Cover of yesterday's new book and suggestions for discussion.

Key Understandings

Statements of key understandings from the text. Use these to help you guide the discussion and to observe for evidence of comprehension.

Messages

A statement conveying the main or "big" ideas of the text.

Part 2: Revisiting Yesterday's New Book

Suggestions for three choices: comprehension, vocabulary, or fluency, depending upon the needs of your students.

Discussing Yesterday's New Book

REREADING
Little Plane, Huge Dream,
Level Q

PROMPTING GUIDE, PART 2
Refer to pages 22 and 52 as needed

Revisiting Yesterday's New Book

Options and Suggested Language

✓ *Choose one:*
- ○ Comprehension
- ○ Vocabulary
- ○ Fluency

REREADING
Little Plane, Huge Dream,
Level Q

■ Invite students to share their thinking about *Little Plane, Huge Dream.* Some key understandings they may express:

Thinking **Within** the Text	Thinking **Beyond** the Text	Thinking **About** the Text
■ From boyhood, Maynard Hill loved making model airplanes. ■ In college, he learned how to build and fly model planes with radio controls. ■ He built model planes that set 23 world records. ■ When he was 77, he flew a model plane from Canada to Ireland, setting a record.	■ Maynard Hill was motivated to be successful by his love of model airplanes. ■ His persistence, despite many disappointments, was rewarded. ■ A person is never too old to pursue a dream.	■ The table "Fifth Time's the Charm!" summarizes the information of the five TAM flights. ■ Questions in the text represent Hill's thinking and give insights into his character. ■ The photograph of the magazine cover provides authenticity to the story.

MESSAGE It may take longer than you ever imagined, but with persistence and the right skills, you can make your dreams come true.

Comprehension Infer and Critique

Let's look back at your reading from yesterday to talk about your thinking.

■ **Close Reading** *The writer of a biography often begins by telling about the subject's childhood. Read page 3, and then let's talk about the experiences in Maynard Hill's childhood that influenced his entire life.* [Students read and respond.]

■ **Confirm Thinking** *You noticed that even as a young boy, Maynard loved airplanes and made many model airplanes. He loved watching them soar even a short distance, and that is probably why he worked all his life to achieve his dream at age 77. Do you think this information is important in helping readers understand the subject of the biography? Why or why not?* [Students respond.]

Vocabulary Use Morphology and Word Parts: *previous*

Let's look back at your reading from yesterday to think together about word meaning.

■ *Take a look at the bar graph on page 7 that shows how Maynard broke the previous record.* Have students find the word *previous* on the graph. Write *previous* on the whiteboard and then divide it into syllables (*pre/vi/ous*). *Read the label on the graph and talk with your partner about what* previous *means.* [Students read and respond.] Have partners share their definitions with the group.

■ Previous *means "coming before." Take a look at the beginning word part,* pre-. Write *preschool, preheat,* and *preview* on the whiteboard. *When* pre- *is used as a prefix, it usually means "before."* Invite students to talk about the meanings of all four words and the connections they see among them.

FIGURE 3.2B An Example of an Odd-Numbered Standard Lesson (Page 2 of 6)

Part 3: Phonics/Word Study

The major concept for the teaching.

Principle

A concise statement of the phonics/word study principle students need to understand and learn to use.

Example

An example of a chart you will create for students, or the work they do related to the principle.

PROMPTING GUIDE, PART 1
Refer to pages 18 and 19 as needed

Fluency Echo Reading: Intonation and Word Stress

Let's look back at your reading from yesterday to think about how your reading sounds.

- Turn to page 14, and listen while I read the last two paragraphs. *I'll try to make my voice show how important this last chance was to Maynard and how exciting the call from Ireland was.*
- Read the paragraphs with good intonation and word stress. *What did you notice?* [Students respond.]
- *You noticed that my voice went up and down, and I stressed, or emphasized, some words more than others. In the last paragraph, I stressed* finally *and* ground *and that made it sound like an exciting moment.*
- Have the students read the paragraphs the same way.

Phonics/ Word Study

Agent Nouns

Principle Some words name people who do things (*farmer, driver, swimmer*). The *-er* ending is also used for comparison (*smaller*).

beggar	cheaper
dreamer	quicker
sailor	smaller
shopper	
skater	

Say and Sort

- Show the following words: *actor, bigger, darker, farmer*. Use any word that the students might not understand in a sentence. *What do you notice about these words? Which ones are alike?* [Students respond.]
- Help students see that two of these words name people who do things and the others are words that compare.
- Show *builder, jogger,* and *writer*. *What are the base words?* [Students respond.] Underline *build, jog,* and *write*. *How was each word changed to make a word that names a person?* [Students respond.] Help students see that the verbs became nouns when *-er* was added.
- Give partners the following words: *beggar, cheaper, dreamer, quicker, sailor, smaller, shopper, skater*. Have them sort the words into two columns.
- *What did you notice when you sorted the words?* [Students respond.]
- Help the students notice that agent nouns can have spelling changes and can end in *-er, -or,* or *-ar*.
- Summarize the lesson by restating the principle.
- Give the students the Pick-a-Pair Game to play in class or at home.

867

FIGURE 3.2C An Example of an Odd-Numbered Standard Lesson (Page 3 of 6)

Part 4: Reading a New Book

Suggestions for supporting students' proficient reading of a new instructional level text.

Genre Focus

A statement indicating the key genre characteristics of the new book.

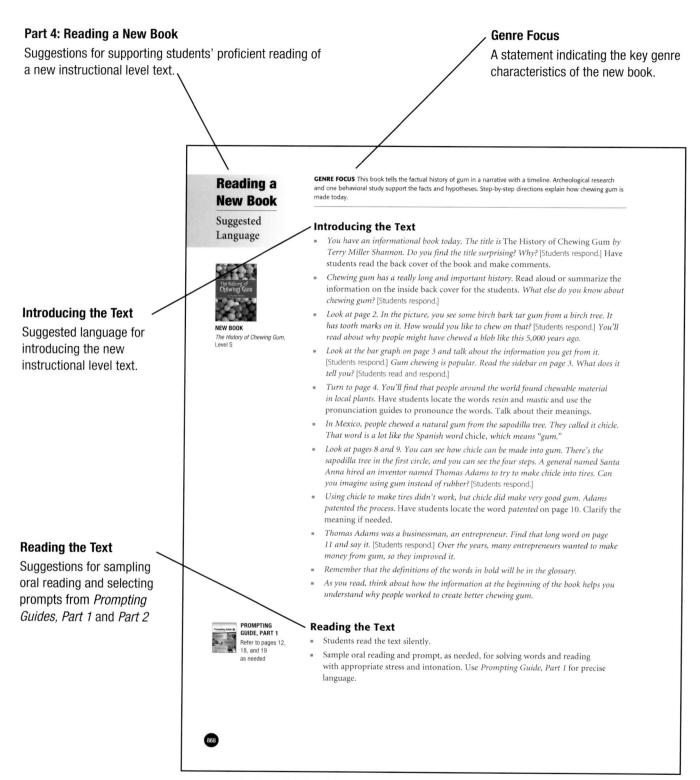

Reading a New Book

Suggested Language

NEW BOOK
The History of Chewing Gum,
Level S

Introducing the Text

Suggested language for introducing the new instructional level text.

Reading the Text

Suggestions for sampling oral reading and selecting prompts from *Prompting Guides, Part 1* and *Part 2*

PROMPTING GUIDE, PART 1
Refer to pages 12, 18, and 19 as needed

GENRE FOCUS This book tells the factual history of gum in a narrative with a timeline. Archeological research and one behavioral study support the facts and hypotheses. Step-by-step directions explain how chewing gum is made today.

Introducing the Text

- *You have an informational book today. The title is* The History of Chewing Gum *by Terry Miller Shannon. Do you find the title surprising? Why?* [Students respond.] Have students read the back cover of the book and make comments.

- *Chewing gum has a really long and important history.* Read aloud or summarize the information on the inside back cover for the students. *What else do you know about chewing gum?* [Students respond.]

- *Look at page 2. In the picture, you see some birch bark tar gum from a birch tree. It has tooth marks on it. How would you like to chew on that?* [Students respond.] *You'll read about why people might have chewed a blob like this 5,000 years ago.*

- *Look at the bar graph on page 3 and talk about the information you get from it.* [Students respond.] *Gum chewing is popular. Read the sidebar on page 3. What does it tell you?* [Students read and respond.]

- *Turn to page 4. You'll find that people around the world found chewable material in local plants.* Have students locate the words *resin* and *mastic* and use the pronunciation guides to pronounce the words. Talk about their meanings.

- *In Mexico, people chewed a natural gum from the sapodilla tree. They called it chicle. That word is a lot like the Spanish word* chicle, *which means "gum."*

- *Look at pages 8 and 9. You can see how chicle can be made into gum. There's the sapodilla tree in the first circle, and you can see the four steps. A general named Santa Anna hired an inventor named Thomas Adams to try to make chicle into tires. Can you imagine using gum instead of rubber?* [Students respond.]

- *Using chicle to make tires didn't work, but chicle did make very good gum. Adams patented the process.* Have students locate the word *patented* on page 10. Clarify the meaning if needed.

- *Thomas Adams was a businessman, an entrepreneur. Find that long word on page 11 and say it.* [Students respond.] *Over the years, many entrepreneurs wanted to make money from gum, so they improved it.*

- *Remember that the definitions of the words in bold will be in the glossary.*

- *As you read, think about how the information at the beginning of the book helps you understand why people worked to create better chewing gum.*

Reading the Text

- Students read the text silently.

- Sample oral reading and prompt, as needed, for solving words and reading with appropriate stress and intonation. Use *Prompting Guide, Part 1* for precise language.

868

FIGURE 3.2D An Example of an Odd-Numbered Standard Lesson (Page 4 of 6)

Discussing and Revisiting the Text

Suggestions for inviting students to share their thinking about the text they read.

Messages

A statement conveying the main or "big" ideas of the text.

Teaching Points

A suggested teaching point plus a reminder to select other points from the *Prompting Guides, Part 1* and *Part 2.*

Key Understandings

Statements of key understandings from the text. Use these to help you guide the discussion and to observe for evidence of comprehension.

PROMPTING GUIDE, PART 2
Refer to page 35 as needed

Discussing and Revisiting the Text

- Invite students to talk about what they learned from reading *The History of Chewing Gum.*
- *Why do you think Terry Shannon wanted to tell this story? What is her message?* [Students respond.]
- *Sometimes something we take for granted, like gum, may have a really long, interesting history. It makes life more interesting when you know more about everyday items like gum. Also, the story of gum tells you a lot about how entrepreneurs work to make money.*
- Continue the discussion, guiding students toward the key understandings and the main message of the text. Some key understandings students may express:

Thinking *Within* the Text	Thinking *Beyond* the Text	Thinking *About* the Text
• An archeologist discovered a 5,000-year-old blob of tar with tooth marks. • Native Americans chewed the resin from spruce trees. • Businesspeople changed the gum recipe to make money. • People chew gum for many reasons—it tastes good, freshens breath, keeps teeth healthy, and improves alertness and memory.	• People in the United States chew more gum than people in other countries. • The most common ingredient in gum over the years has come from trees. • Although people have been chewing gum for centuries, it is only recently that flavors and colors have been added.	• The timeline serves as a summary of the history of gum described in the narrative. • An archeological finding and a scientific study support the authenticity of the text. • The topic is interesting for young readers because gum is a popular treat and forbidden in most schools.

MESSAGE We can often make things better through hard work and experimentation.

PROMPTING GUIDE, PART 2
Refer to page 52 as needed

Teaching Points

- Based on your observations, use *Prompting Guide, Part 2* to select a teaching point that will be most helpful to the readers. You may also use the suggestion below.
- *Talk about the information on pages 2 and 3 and then share your thinking about why the writer might have included it.* [Students respond.]
- *The writers of nonfiction texts sometimes start by convincing readers that the topic is important. Did you find this information convincing? Did it make you feel that this topic is important?* [Students respond.] *Also, chewing gum is very popular around the world. That means a lot of chewing gum is sold. So when you read the rest of the book, you knew that if people could make better chewing gum, they could make a lot of money.*
- *If you write an informational text like this one, you may want to start by providing some information to show how the topic is important.*

869

FIGURE 3.2E An Example of an Odd-Numbered Standard Lesson (Page 5 of 6)

Classroom and Homework

An optional game, sort, or activity to complete for homework or classwork.

Assessing Reading and Writing Behaviors

A list of reading and writing behaviors to notice as you observe student behaviors. Some may not be applicable, depending upon which option you chose for revisiting the text.

Supporting English Language Learners

Important considerations for supporting English language learners in this particular lesson.

Professional Development Links

Suggestions for accessing other professional resources, connected to the concepts and teaching in this lesson.

Classroom and Homework

- Play the Pick-a-Pair Game for practice with noun agents.

Assessing Reading and Writing Behaviors

Observe to find evidence that readers can:

- understand and describe characteristics of the genre of biography.
- infer and state why a writer includes childhood experiences and interests in a biography; think critically about the craft of this genre.
- infer and discuss information from bar graphs.
- think critically about and discuss the importance of a topic.
- notice and discuss how writers of nonfiction texts convince readers that the topic is important.
- share background knowledge related to a nonfiction text.
- connect and discuss information across a text to understand major points.
- use morphology and word parts to understand the meaning of a word, and connect it to other words by meaningful parts.
- notice word parts that signal comparison.
- distinguish between comparative words and agent nouns.
- read orally with appropriate intonation and word stress.

Supporting English Language Learners

To support English Language Learners, you can:

- **be sure** students understand the phrase *influenced his entire life* during Comprehension work.
- **ensure** understanding of prompting language.
- **check** how students use nonfiction text features to extend their understanding.
- **demonstrate** pronunciation of multisyllable words (e.g., *archeologists, licorice, entrepreneur, accidentally*).
- **check for** understanding of *wads of gum, inventor, experiments, substance,* and *in style today.*
- **be sure** students understand how to derive meanings of new words from context; model as necessary.
- **observe** students reading longer, complex sentences with appropriate stress and intonation.
- **demonstrate** using bar graphs to get new information.

Professional Development Links

Professional Development and *Tutorial* DVDs, *LLI Gold System*
View "Instructional Procedures for Phonics/Word Study: Say and Sort" on the *Professional Development DVD.*

Genre Study: Teaching with Fiction and Nonfiction Books
Read Chapter 9, "Understanding Biography: Learning from the Lives of Others."

Teaching for Comprehending and Fluency: Thinking, Talking, and Writing About Reading, K–8
Read pages 178–182 of Chapter 13, "Understanding the Demands of Nonfiction Texts."

Leveled Literacy Intervention System Guide, LLI Gold System
Read "Teaching Standard Lessons (Odd-Numbered)" in Section 4.

 870

FIGURE 3.2F An Example of an Odd-Numbered Standard Lesson (Page 6 of 6)

Overview of Even-Numbered Standard Lesson Framework

Figure 3.3, which follows, shows an overview of an even-numbered standard lesson.

Lesson Information

The lesson number and level, the system, new book title, and genre.

Materials

A list of materials for the lesson. Most are included in the *LLI System* package, but some are more generic items that should be available from your school. Items in the right column are available for printing from the Online Resources site. Also shown are covers of the new book and one to be reread.

Goals

The specific teaching goals for the lesson are organized in four categories: comprehension, word study/vocabulary, fluency, and writing about reading. Choose the goals that apply to comprehension, vocabulary, fluency, or writing about reading, depending on the needs of your students.

How the Book Works

A statement to help you think about the overall structure of the text—the way the writer has organized and presented the information. Consider it as you introduce the text, and invite students to notice features of the text.

Text Analysis

An analysis of the new book separated into the ten characteristics that are used to analyze books.

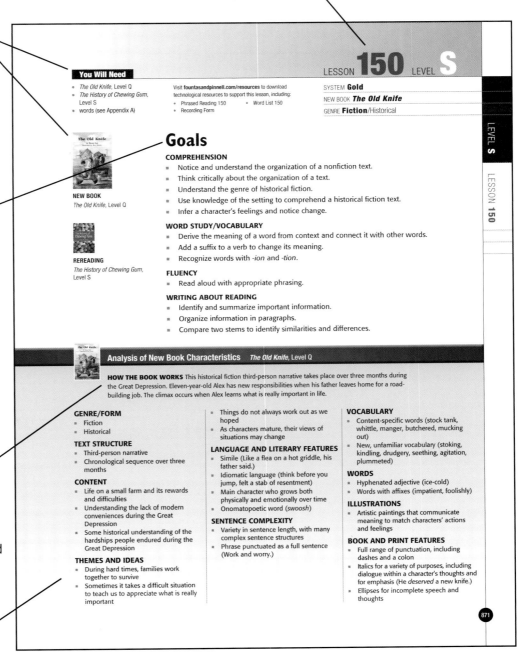

FIGURE 3.3A An Example of an Even-Numbered Standard Lesson (Page 1 of 6)

Part 1: Revisiting Yesterday's New Book

Cover of yesterday's new book and suggestions for three choices: comprehension, vocabulary, or fluency, depending upon the needs of your students.

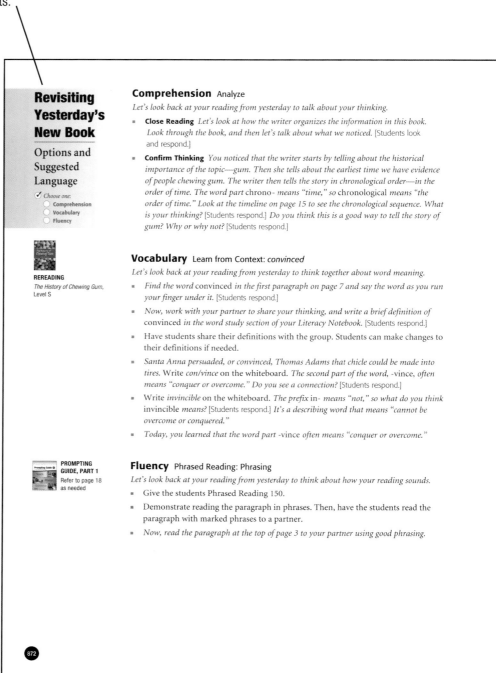

Revisiting Yesterday's New Book

Options and Suggested Language

☑ *Choose one:*
○ Comprehension
○ Vocabulary
○ Fluency

REREADING
The History of Chewing Gum,
Level S

PROMPTING GUIDE, PART 1
Refer to page 18 as needed

Comprehension Analyze

Let's look back at your reading from yesterday to talk about your thinking.

- **Close Reading** *Let's look at how the writer organizes the information in this book. Look through the book, and then let's talk about what we noticed.* [Students look and respond.]
- **Confirm Thinking** *You noticed that the writer starts by telling about the historical importance of the topic—gum. Then she tells about the earliest time we have evidence of people chewing gum. The writer then tells the story in chronological order—in the order of time. The word part* chrono- *means "time," so* chronological *means "the order of time." Look at the timeline on page 15 to see the chronological sequence. What is your thinking?* [Students respond.] *Do you think this is a good way to tell the story of gum? Why or why not?* [Students respond.]

Vocabulary Learn from Context: *convinced*

Let's look back at your reading from yesterday to think together about word meaning.

- *Find the word* convinced *in the first paragraph on page 7 and say the word as you run your finger under it.* [Students respond.]
- *Now, work with your partner to share your thinking, and write a brief definition of* convinced *in the word study section of your Literacy Notebook.* [Students respond.]
- Have students share their definitions with the group. Students can make changes to their definitions if needed.
- *Santa Anna persuaded, or convinced, Thomas Adams that chicle could be made into tires.* Write *con/vince* on the whiteboard. *The second part of the word,* -vince, *often means "conquer or overcome." Do you see a connection?* [Students respond.]
- Write *invincible* on the whiteboard. *The prefix* in- *means "not," so what do you think* invincible *means?* [Students respond.] *It's a describing word that means "cannot be overcome or conquered."*
- *Today, you learned that the word part* -vince *often means "conquer or overcome."*

Fluency Phrased Reading: Phrasing

Let's look back at your reading from yesterday to think about how your reading sounds.

- Give the students Phrased Reading 150.
- Demonstrate reading the paragraph in phrases. Then, have the students read the paragraph with marked phrases to a partner.
- *Now, read the paragraph at the top of page 3 to your partner using good phrasing.*

872

FIGURE 3.3B An Example of an Even-Numbered Standard Lesson (Page 2 of 6)

Part 2: Rereading and Assessment

Suggestions for guiding students to reread part of yesterday's new book for a specific purpose and for assessing one reader's processing.

Part 3: Writing About Reading

Suggestions for using one of three forms of writing (shared, independent, or dictated) as well as the type of writing used to write about yesterday's new book.

Rereading and Assessment

Suggested Language

PROMPTING GUIDE, PART 1
Refer to pages as needed to reinforce reading behaviors or

PROMPTING GUIDE, PART 2
Refer to pages 13 and 35 as needed

- **Rereading for a Purpose** *Starting on page 7 in* The History of Chewing Gum, *reread as far as you can in the time we have. Be sure to pay attention to and think about the headings. As you read, think about what you learned about the work of inventors and entrepreneurs—what they do and what they have in common.*

- **Assessment** While other students read for a purpose, listen to one student read the section identified in *The History of Chewing Gum*. Code the reading behavior on the Recording Form. Engage the student in a brief comprehension conversation, give scores for fluency and comprehension, and select a brief teaching point that will be most helpful to the reader. Analyze the record later.

Writing About Reading

Suggested Language

Independent Writing Short Write

- Talk with the students about what inventors and entrepreneurs do and what they have in common. *Because they are always thinking and noticing, sometimes inventors make new discoveries when looking for something else. Entrepreneurs are always trying to improve their products so they can sell more.*

- *In the writing section of your Literacy Notebook, write three paragraphs telling what you have learned about the ways inventors and entrepreneurs work. Write the first paragraph about inventors and the second paragraph about entrepreneurs. In the third paragraph, write what is true about both inventors and entrepreneurs.*

- You may want to list on the board what should be included in the assignment.

Student Sample

Sample of the writing students complete.

> Inventors are scientists. They do experiments and are always observing and getting new ideas. What they notice gives them ideas to help them make new discoveries.
>
> Entrepeneurs are business people. They are always looking for ways to improve some things so they can sell more.
>
> Both inventors and entepeneurs keep on investigating and getting new ideas. They are always looking for ways to make their inventions and products better.

873

FIGURE 3.3C An Example of an Even-Numbered Standard Lesson (Page 3 of 6)

Part 4: Phonics/Word Study
The major concept for teaching.

Principle
A concise statement of the phonics/word study principle students need to understand and learn to use.

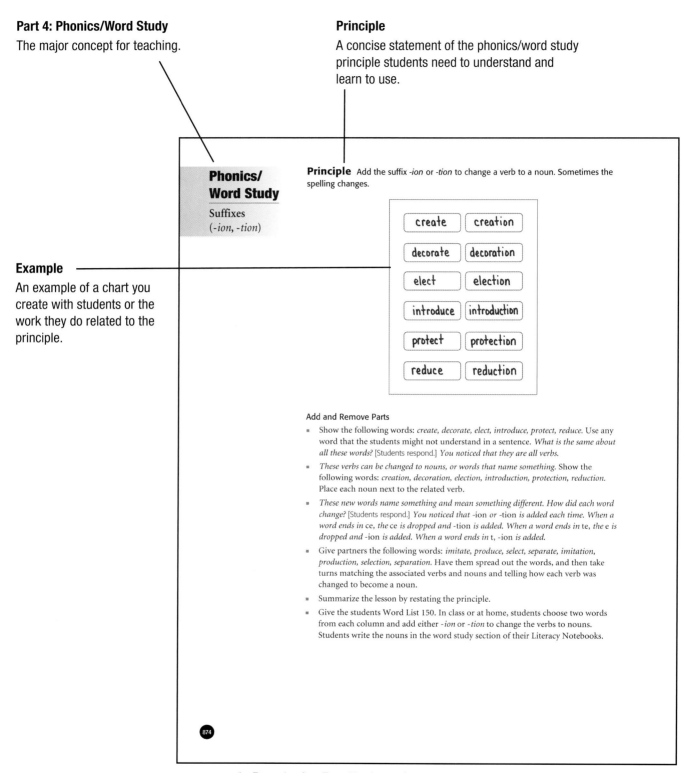

Phonics/ Word Study

Suffixes
(*-ion*, *-tion*)

Principle Add the suffix *-ion* or *-tion* to change a verb to a noun. Sometimes the spelling changes.

create	creation
decorate	decoration
elect	election
introduce	introduction
protect	protection
reduce	reduction

Example
An example of a chart you create with students or the work they do related to the principle.

Add and Remove Parts

- Show the following words: *create, decorate, elect, introduce, protect, reduce.* Use any word that the students might not understand in a sentence. *What is the same about all these words?* [Students respond.] *You noticed that they are all verbs.*
- *These verbs can be changed to nouns, or words that name something.* Show the following words: *creation, decoration, election, introduction, protection, reduction.* Place each noun next to the related verb.
- *These new words name something and mean something different. How did each word change?* [Students respond.] *You noticed that* -ion *or* -tion *is added each time. When a word ends in* ce, *the* ce *is dropped and* -tion *is added. When a word ends in* te, *the* e *is dropped and* -ion *is added. When a word ends in* t, -ion *is added.*
- Give partners the following words: *imitate, produce, select, separate, imitation, production, selection, separation.* Have them spread out the words, and then take turns matching the associated verbs and nouns and telling how each verb was changed to become a noun.
- Summarize the lesson by restating the principle.
- Give the students Word List 150. In class or at home, students choose two words from each column and add either *-ion* or *-tion* to change the verbs to nouns. Students write the nouns in the word study section of their Literacy Notebooks.

874

FIGURE 3.3D An Example of an Even-Numbered Standard Lesson (Page 4 of 6)

Part 5: Reading a New Book

Suggestions for supporting students' proficient reading of a new independent level text.

Genre Focus

A statement indicating the key genre characteristics of the new book.

Reading a New Book

Suggested Language

NEW BOOK
The Old Knife, Level Q

GENRE FOCUS This historical fiction text represents what many farm families endured during the Great Depression. The descriptions of the many challenges of running a farm without a male adult at home help the story come alive for readers.

Introducing the Text

- *Your new book today is* The Old Knife *by Sharon Fear. Listen while I read some information the author provides.* Read the material on the inside back cover to the students. Then, have them read the back cover of the book and share their thinking.

- *What's the genre of this book?* [Students respond.] *It's historical fiction. What do you know about this genre?* [Students respond.] *The story is not real, but it could have happened, and the setting is in the past. So you need to think about the times that these characters lived in and what their lives were like.*

- *Look at pages 2 and 3. There's Alex and his father and mother. Read this first page to yourself, and then let's talk about what Alex is like.* [Students read and respond.]

- *We know that Alex sometimes just doesn't think. You will learn that that's how he broke his knife's handle. A knife was a very important tool on the farm at that time.*

- *Look at page 6. You can see that Alex has a basin—a bowl—in his room to wash his face in the morning. They don't have an indoor bathroom.*

- *Look at page 7 and read the words in italics. Then, talk about what you are thinking.* [Students read and respond.]

- *Go to page 10. Here the writer says that they have enough food for the winter, but Alex has never had to worry about that before. He feels a stab of resentment toward his dad. What does that mean?* [Students respond.] *It's almost like he feels real pain because he is angry at his dad.*

- Have students turn to page 13 and locate the word *drudgery*. Clarify the meaning.

- *As you read, think about why Alex feels so resentful, and also think about what he hopes for his birthday. He wants a new knife. He feels he deserves a new knife because of all his hard work. Some interesting things happen to Alex. As you read, notice whether his feelings change.*

Introducing the Text

Suggestions to orient readers to new ideas, language, and text features for the independent level book.

PROMPTING GUIDE, PART 1
Refer to pages 15 and 18 as needed

Reading the Text

- Students begin to read the text silently if there is time.

- Sample oral reading and prompt, as needed, for initiating problem-solving actions and phrased reading that reflects understanding. Use *Prompting Guide, Part 1* for precise language.

Reading the Text

Suggestions for sampling oral reading and selecting prompts from the *Prompting Guides, Part 1* and *Part 2*

875

FIGURE 3.3E An Example of an Even-Numbered Standard Lesson (Page 5 of 6)

Classroom and Homework

A summary of work for students to do in the classroom or at home (e.g., finish the book, phonics/word study, or game).

Assessing Reading and Writing Behaviors

A list of reading and writing behaviors to notice as you observe student behavior. Some may not be applicable, depending upon which option you chose for revisiting the text.

Supporting English Language Learners

Important considerations for supporting English language learners in this particular lesson.

Professional Development Links

Suggestions for accessing other professional resources, connected to the concepts and teaching in this lesson.

Classroom and Homework

- Finish reading *The Old Knife*.
- Use Word List 150 to practice reading and writing words that end with *-ion* and *-tion* (optional).

Assessing Reading and Writing Behaviors

Observe to find evidence that readers can:

- understand and discuss the organization of a nonfiction text.
- think critically about and discuss the organization of a text.
- understand and describe characteristics of the genre of historical fiction.
- use knowledge of the setting to comprehend a historical fiction text and discuss aspects of the setting.
- infer and state a character's feelings and notice change.

- derive the meaning of a word from context and connect with other words.
- understand how to change a verb into a noun by adding *-ion* or *-tion*.
- read aloud with appropriate phrasing.
- identify important information, put it in a brief summary, and organize it in paragraphs.
- compare two stems to identify similarities and differences.

Supporting English Language Learners

To support English Language Learners, you can:

- **be sure** students understand prompts used to support and extend phrased reading.
- **encourage** students to note evidence from the text as they reread.
- **have** students use their notes to expand oral language prior to writing.
- **check** for understanding of the meanings of the root words and suffixes in Phonics/Word Study.
- **define** quickly *pry* and *whittle* before having students read the italicized words on page 7.
- **help** students hear and repeat new, unfamiliar vocabulary before reading (e.g., *stoking, kindling, drudgery, seething, agitation, plummeted*).

- **have** students find evidence in the text of Alex changing as they read.
- **be explicit** in teaching literary language (e.g., *Like a flea on a hot griddle, do his dad proud, think before you jump*).
- **model** inferring vocabulary meanings where possible (e.g., *stock tank, manger, butchered, mucking out*).
- **help** students understand the different uses of italics, including within a character's thoughts and for emphasis.

Professional Development Links

Professional Development and *Tutorial* DVDs, *LLI Gold System*
View "Instructional Procedures for Writing About Reading: Independent Writing" on the *Professional Development DVD*.

Genre Study: Teaching with Fiction and Nonfiction Books
Read Chapter 10, "Nonfiction Texts: Purpose, Organization, and Audience."

Teaching for Comprehending and Fluency: Thinking, Talking, and Writing About Reading, K–8
Read pages 183–189 of Chapter 13, "Understanding the Demands of Nonfiction Texts."

Leveled Literacy Intervention System Guide, LLI Gold System
Read "Teaching Standard Lessons (Even-Numbered)" in Section 4.

876

FIGURE 3.3F An Example of an Even-Numbered Standard Lesson (Page 6 of 6)

45-Minute Standard Lesson Framework

Standard Lesson (Odd-Numbered)	Standard Lesson (Even-Numbered)
Discussing Yesterday's New Book *5 minutes*	**Revisiting Yesterday's New Book** Choose one: • Comprehension • Vocabulary • Fluency *5 minutes*
Revisiting Yesterday's New Book Choose one: • Comprehension • Vocabulary • Fluency *5 minutes*	**Rereading and Assessment** *5 minutes*
Phonics/Word Study *10 minutes*	**Writing About Reading** *15 minutes*
Reading a New Book (Instructional Level) • Introducing the Text • Reading the Text • Discussing and Revisiting the Text • Teaching Points *25 minutes*	**Phonics/Word Study** *10 minutes*
	Reading a New Book (Independent Level) • Introducing the Text • Reading the Text *10 minutes*

FIGURE 3.4 45-Minute Standard Lesson Framework

Overview of Novel Study Lesson Sequence Framework

Figure 3.5, which follows, shows an overview of Day 1 of the Novel Study Lesson sequence framework, with notes about the modifications for Days 2–4 .

Lesson Information

The lesson number, level, the system, new book title, and genre.

Materials

A list of materials for the lesson and the cover of the novel students read during the sequence.

Goals

The specific goals for the lesson. Choose the goals that apply to comprehension, vocabulary, or fluency, depending on the needs of your students.

How the Book Works

A statement to help you think about the overall structure of the text—the way the writer has organized and presented the information. Consider it as you introduce the text and invite students to notice features of the text.

Text Analysis

An analysis of the new book separated into the ten characteristics that are used to analyze books.

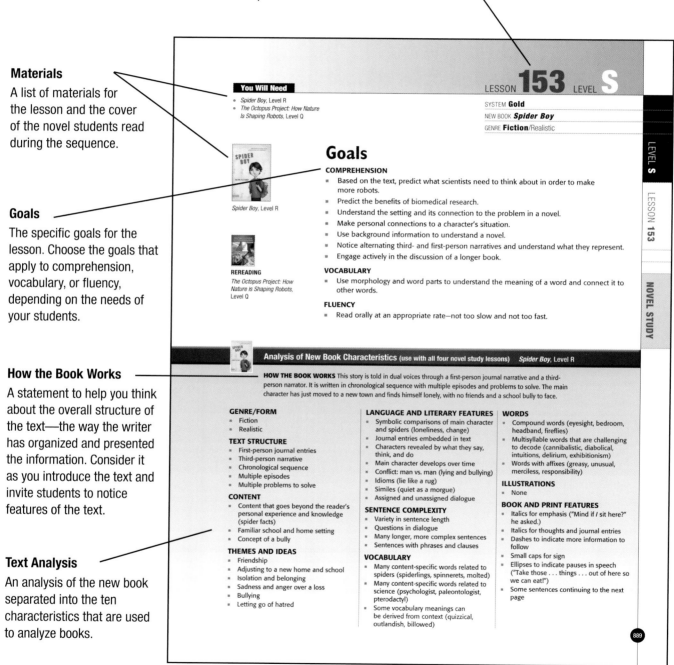

You Will Need
- Spider Boy, Level R
- The Octopus Project: How Nature Is Shaping Robots, Level Q

LESSON **153** LEVEL **S**

SYSTEM **Gold**
NEW BOOK **Spider Boy**
GENRE **Fiction**/Realistic

Spider Boy, Level R

REREADING
The Octopus Project: How Nature is Shaping Robots, Level Q

Goals

COMPREHENSION
- Based on the text, predict what scientists need to think about in order to make more robots.
- Predict the benefits of biomedical research.
- Understand the setting and its connection to the problem in a novel.
- Make personal connections to a character's situation.
- Use background information to understand a novel.
- Notice alternating third- and first-person narratives and understand what they represent.
- Engage actively in the discussion of a longer book.

VOCABULARY
- Use morphology and word parts to understand the meaning of a word and connect it to other words.

FLUENCY
- Read orally at an appropriate rate—not too slow and not too fast.

Analysis of New Book Characteristics (use with all four novel study lessons)   *Spider Boy*, Level R

HOW THE BOOK WORKS This story is told in dual voices through a first-person journal narrative and a third-person narrator. It is written in chronological sequence with multiple episodes and problems to solve. The main character has just moved to a new town and finds himself lonely, with no friends and a school bully to face.

GENRE/FORM
- Fiction
- Realistic

TEXT STRUCTURE
- First-person journal entries
- Third-person narrative
- Chronological sequence
- Multiple episodes
- Multiple problems to solve

CONTENT
- Content that goes beyond the reader's personal experience and knowledge (spider facts)
- Familiar school and home setting
- Concept of a bully

THEMES AND IDEAS
- Friendship
- Adjusting to a new home and school
- Isolation and belonging
- Sadness and anger over a loss
- Bullying
- Letting go of hatred

LANGUAGE AND LITERARY FEATURES
- Symbolic comparisons of main character and spiders (loneliness, change)
- Journal entries embedded in text
- Characters revealed by what they say, think, and do
- Main character develops over time
- Conflict: man vs. man (lying and bullying)
- Idioms (lie like a rug)
- Similes (quiet as a morgue)
- Assigned and unassigned dialogue

SENTENCE COMPLEXITY
- Variety in sentence length
- Questions in dialogue
- Many longer, more complex sentences
- Sentences with phrases and clauses

VOCABULARY
- Many content-specific words related to spiders (spiderlings, spinnerets, molted)
- Many content-specific words related to science (psychologist, paleontologist, pterodactyl)
- Some vocabulary meanings can be derived from context (quizzical, outlandish, billowed)

WORDS
- Compound words (eyesight, bedroom, headband, fireflies)
- Multisyllable words that are challenging to decode (cannibalistic, diabolical, intuitions, delirium, exhibitionism)
- Words with affixes (greasy, unusual, merciless, responsibility)

ILLUSTRATIONS
- None

BOOK AND PRINT FEATURES
- Italics for emphasis ("Mind if *I* sit here?" he asked.)
- Italics for thoughts and journal entries
- Dashes to indicate more information to follow
- Small caps for sign
- Ellipses to indicate pauses in speech ("Take those . . . things . . . out of here so we can eat!")
- Some sentences continuing to the next page

889

FIGURE 3.5A   An Example of Day 1 of a Novel Study Lesson Sequence Framework (Page 1 of 6)

Part 1: Discussion of Yesterday's New Book

Covers showing yesterday's new book and suggestions for discussion. (This section only appears on the first day of a novel study sequence and is designed to bring closure to the reading of the book in the previous standard lesson.)

Key Understandings

Statements of key understandings from the text. Use these to help you guide the discussion and to observe for evidence of comprehension.

Messages

A statement conveying the "big" idea of the text. (In the next three novel study lessons, the statement applies to the entire text. Students work to develop the idea over the four days of reading.)

Part 2: Revisiting Yesterday's New Book

Suggestions for three choices: comprehension, vocabulary, and fluency. In the next three Novel Study Lessons, options are to revisit sections of the book the previous day or for homework.

Discussing Yesterday's New Book

REREADING
The Octopus Project: How Nature Is Shaping Robots. Level Q

PROMPTING GUIDE, PART 2
Refer to pages 15–17 as needed

Revisiting Yesterday's New Book

Options and Suggested Language

✓ *Choose one:*
- ○ Comprehension
- ○ Vocabulary
- ○ Fluency

REREADING
The Octopus Project: How Nature Is Shaping Robots. Level Q

890

▪ Invite students to share their thinking about *The Octopus Project: How Nature Is Shaping Robots.* Some key understandings they may express:

Thinking **Within** the Text	Thinking **Beyond** the Text	Thinking **About** the Text
▪ Scientists want to imitate octopuses because they are smart and can fit in small places. ▪ To make an octopus robot, scientists study robots and the behavior of real octopuses. ▪ The robotic octopus and other kinds of robots are being designed to do things people can't easily do.	▪ It is a long and complicated process to make a robot that mimics an octopus. ▪ Observing nature can enhance scientists' and engineers' understandings of ways to help humans.	▪ The illustration on page 10 gives readers an idea of the many things scientists need to consider when making an octopus robot. ▪ The sidebar on page 9 that shows how cats drink adds to the reader's understanding of how complicated animals can be.

MESSAGES Nature has brilliant designs. By copying these designs, scientists can create robots that can change our lives. The Octopus Project is an example of how nature can inform science.

Comprehension Predict

Let's look back at your reading from yesterday to talk about your thinking.

- **Close Reading** *Read pages 10 to 15. As you read, notice what the scientists had to think about to produce a robot octopus that could do some of the things a real octopus can do. Then, look at the chart titled "What Will They Think of Next?" Think about what the different types of robots would need to be able to do in order to be successful in doing what scientists want them to do. When you finish reading, let's talk about what the robots would need in order to perform the tasks that scientists would want them to do.* [Students read and respond.]

- **Confirm Thinking** *You predicted that most of the robots would need some kind of skin to keep them dry or to withstand high temperatures. Some would need cameras to take photos from a long distance away. Some would need to move easily over rough surfaces. Some would need to move underwater. Some would need powerful joints and engines to run fast. Stu... think in new ways abou...*

Vocabulary Use Morphology and Word Parts: *biomimetics*

Let's look back at your reading from yesterday to think together about word meaning.

- Have the students find the word *biomimetics* in bold on page 2 or in the glossary. *Let's look at the parts of this word,* biomimetics. Write the word on the whiteboard and ask students to take it apart by syllables (*bi/o/mi/met/ics*). They can write the word in the word study section of their Literacy Notebooks.

- Then, ask students to write the word *mimic* and talk about the connections between that word and *biomimetics. The word part* bio *means "life." Something that is mimetic imitates things. So what does biomimetics have to do with?* [Students respond.]

- Write *mimic, mime, mimicry,* and *mimetic. What part of the words is the same?* [Students respond.] *A mime is a performance that imitates or mocks someone. There are no words but really dramatic gestures. It's an old art form. The word mime can also mean "a performer, someone who does mime." A mimic is someone who makes fun of people by imitating them, or doing mimicry. All of these words have something to do with imitating or mimicking.*

PROMPTING GUIDE, PART 1
Refer to page 17 as needed

Fluency Rate Mover: Rate

Let's look back at your reading from yesterday to think about how your reading sounds.

- *Turn to page 15 and listen while I read the first paragraph. This paragraph is exciting because it describes the potential value of the Octopus Project. Notice how it sounds when I read it the first time. Then, I'm going to read it a little faster and you can comment on how my reading sounds. I won't read too fast—just the right speed to sound like talking.*

- Read the paragraph slowly. Then, follow by reading it at a good rate. *How did my reading sound?* [Students respond.]

- Then, have students read to a partner.

891

FIGURES 3.5B AND 3.5C
An Example of Day 1 of a Novel Study Lesson Sequence Framework (Pages 2 and 3 of 6)

Part 3: Reading a New Book

Suggestions for supporting students in proficient reading and rich discussion of the novel.

Genre Focus

A statement indicating the key genre characteristics of the new book.

Reading a New Book

Suggested Language

NEW BOOK
Spider Boy, Level R

GENRE FOCUS This story is realistic fiction because, although it didn't actually happen, it could have happened in real life. Bobby and his family have moved to New York from Illinois, and he is having trouble adjusting to his new life. Over time, he learns to be himself again while making new friends, rekindling old interests, and offering forgiveness to a bully.

Introducing the Text

- *For the next four days, you are going to read a chapter book. The title is* Spider Boy *and the author is Ralph Fletcher. There's Bobby on the cover. His nickname is Spider Boy. Can you guess why?* [Students respond.] *Bobby and his family have just moved to a place called New Paltz, New York. He is going to a new school. Have you ever experienced that or do you know someone who has? What's it like?* [Students respond.]

- Read the last paragraph on page 6 aloud to the students. *Does Ralph Fletcher seem to understand how Bobby feels? What are some words and phrases that the writer uses to express the feeling of being new?* [Students respond.]

- *Bobby misses Naperville, Illinois, where he used to live, and he misses his best friend. He has a sister named Brianna who wants everyone to call her Breezy. He has a pet tarantula named Thelma. What do you think of that?* [Students respond.]

- *You are going to read the first three chapters today, pages 1 to 34. You'll read how Bobby feels about Thelma and also about a boy at school called Chick Hall, who is kind of a bully.*

- *An important thing to remember as you read is that all over the world there are different time zones.* Give an example from your own region to clarify time differences for the students. *Notice how time differences affect Bobby.*

- *There are two kinds of writing in this book. Look at page 1 and read the first two paragraphs. Then, talk with a partner about who is telling the story.* [Students read and respond.] *This is Bobby's journal, so he is doing the writing. Notice how he has dated it. Now, read the text at the bottom of page 2. Who is telling the story here?* [Students read and respond.]

- *Most of the book is written as a third-person narrative. The writer is telling about the characters and using words like* he, she, *and* they, *as if the action is happening and there is another person, a "third" person telling about it.*

- *The entire book is told from the perspective of Bobby. He is the main character. The story is about him and how he feels and what he does. You will find pieces from his journal and some of the writing he does in school in just about every chapter. Those pieces of writing will be in first person, when Bobby is telling the story and how he feels. For these sections, the writer uses words like* I, me, my, *and* we.

- *Read through page 34. Notice the setting and the problem.* Have students use stick-on notes to mark places that they would like to come back to during the discussion.

Introducing the Text

Specific suggestions to help orient readers to new ideas, language, and text features in the section of the book they will read today. (On the fourth day of this sequence, students may finish the book. They have a concluding discussion and then write about the book.)

Reading the Text

Suggestions for sampling oral reading of a section of the book and selecting prompts from *Prompting Guides, Part 1* and *Part 2*.

PROMPTING GUIDE, PART 1
Refer to page 20 as needed

Reading the Text

- Students read Chapters One, Two, and Three silently.

- Sample oral reading and prompt, as needed, for integrating all dimensions of fluency in a manner that reflects understanding. Use *Prompting Guide, Part 1* for precise language.

FIGURE 3.5D An Example of Day 1 of a Novel Study Lesson Sequence Framework (Page 4 of 6)

Discussing and Revisiting the Text

Guidelines for engaging students in a book club discussion, including questions or prompts to move toward a deeper understanding of the text.

Key Understandings

Statements of key understandings from the text. Use these to help you guide the discussion and to observe for evidence of comprehension.

Messages

A statement conveying the main or "big" ideas of the text.

Part 4: Introduction to and Assignment of Reading

A brief statement about what students will be expected to read at home, with additional information if needed, and a prompt for thinking. (This does not appear on Day 4 when book is finished.)

PROMPTING GUIDE, PART 2
Refer to pages 66–69 as needed

Discussing and Revisiting the Text

- *Turn and talk to a partner and share your first thoughts about this book.* [Students respond.]
- *Who can start us off by sharing something you and your partner talked about?* [Students respond.]
- To encourage thinking and talking, you may want to select from the following questions/prompts:
  - *Is the setting important in this book? Why or why not?*
  - *What have you learned so far about what Bobby is like as a character? Talk about his journal and what he says and does.*
  - *I'm wondering about Bobby's story about the silk farm. Do you think it's true?*
  - *Do you think Thelma will be important in the story? Why?*
- If the discussion gets too far away from the text, redirect the discussion with prompts such as *We were discussing _____. I'd like to return to our discussion of _____. Does anyone have any comments about what _____ just said?*
- Continue the discussion, guiding students toward the key understandings and the main message of the text. Some key understandings students may express:

Thinking *Within* the Text	Thinking *Beyond* the Text	Thinking *About* the Text
▪ Bobby and his family move to New York from Illinois. ▪ Bobby writes in his journal about spiders and is worried about his pet tarantula, Thelma. ▪ Some boys tease Bobby at school and call him Spider Boy. ▪ Bobby meets Butch who warns him about Chick Hall, the bully.	▪ Bobby feels angry about having to move. ▪ Bobby is lonely in the new school and can't figure out how to fit in. ▪ Butch befriends Bobby because he understands about being teased. ▪ Bobby has an active imagination.	▪ The writer introduces conflicts (bullying, telling stories) early in the story to capture the reader's interest. ▪ The writer chooses to give two points of view—from the first-person journal and the third-person narrator—to make the story more interesting.

MESSAGE Moving to a new place can present many challenges.

Introduction to and Assignment of Reading

- *Tonight, you are going to read Chapters Four and Five of* Spider Boy, *pages 35 to 55. As you read, notice how the writer reveals Bobby's feelings about Naperville, where he used to live. You'll also begin to realize that there are some interesting science facts in this book.*

893

FIGURE 3.5E An Example of Day 1 of a Novel Study Lesson Sequence Framework (Page 5 of 6)

LEVEL S   LESSON 153   NOVEL STUDY

Classroom and Homework

A list of student responsibilities (often reading but sometimes taking notes or writing).

Assessing Reading and Writing Behaviors

A list of reading and writing behaviors to notice as you observe student behavior. Some may not apply, depending on your choice for revisiting the text.

Supporting English Language Learners

Some important considerations for supporting English language learners in this particular lesson.

Professional Development Links

Suggestions for accessing other professional resources, connected to the concepts and teaching in this lesson.

Classroom and Homework

- Read Chapters Four and Five of *Spider Boy*.

Assessing Reading and Writing Behaviors

Observe to find evidence that readers can:

- based on the text, predict what scientists need to think about in order to make more robots.
- predict the benefits of biomedical research.
- understand and discuss the setting and its connection to the problem in a novel.
- engage actively in the discussion of a longer book.
- share personal connections to a character's situation.
- share background information with others to understand a novel.

- notice alternating third- and first-person narratives and discuss what they represent.
- use morphology and word parts to understand the meaning of a word and connect it to other words.
- read orally at an appropriate rate—not too slow and not too fast.

Supporting English Language Learners

To support English Language Learners, you can:

- **define** *mimicry* also as "the act of copying" during Vocabulary work, demonstrating if possible.
- **restate** the meaning of *potential value* during Fluency work.
- **define** *dawdle* briefly after reading the last paragraph on page 6 in *Spider Boy* to students.
- **point out** how the story begins with comparisons of spiders to killers (e.g., *serial killers, Jack-The-Ripper, bloodthirsty vampires*).

- **model** explicitly how to infer the meaning of idiomatic language (e.g., *Shake a leg, A creature of habit, That's my exit cue*).
- **notice** if students are not using italics to differentiate the journal from the narrative.
- **demonstrate** how to derive new vocabulary meanings from context when applicable.

Professional Development Links

 Professional Development and *Tutorial* DVDs, *LLI Gold System*
View "Sample *LLI* Lessons: Novel Study Lesson" on the *Professional Development DVD*.

 Genre Study: Teaching with Fiction and Nonfiction Books
Read Chapter 14, "Thinking and Talking About Genre: Interactive Read-Aloud and Literature Discussion."

 Teaching for Comprehending and Fluency: Thinking, Talking, and Writing About Reading, K–8
Read pages 284–287 of Chapter 19, "Deepening Comprehension: Engaging Students in Small-Group Literature Discussion."

 Leveled Literacy Intervention System Guide, LLI Gold System
Read "Teaching the Novel Study Lesson Sequence: The Four-Day Novel Study Sequence" in Section 4.

 894

FIGURE 3.5F An Example of Day 1 of a Novel Study Lesson Sequence Framework (Page 6 of 6)

45-Minute Novel Study Lesson Framework

Day 1	Day 2	Day 3	Day 4
Discussing Yesterday's New Book *5 minutes*	**Revisiting Yesterday's Reading** Choose one: • Comprehension • Vocabulary • Fluency *5 minutes*	**Revisiting Yesterday's Reading** Choose one: • Comprehension • Vocabulary • Fluency *5 minutes*	**Revisiting Yesterday's Reading** Choose one: • Comprehension • Vocabulary • Fluency *5 minutes*
Revisiting Yesterday's New Book Choose one: • Comprehension • Vocabulary • Fluency *5 minutes*	**Reading a New Section** • Introducing the Text • Reading the Text • Discussing and Revisiting the Text • Introduction to and Assignment of Reading *40 minutes*	**Reading a New Section** • Introducing the Text • Reading the Text • Discussing and Revisiting the Text • Introduction to and Assignment of Reading *40 minutes*	**Concluding Discussion** • Reflections on the Book *10 minutes*
Reading a New Book • Introducing the Text • Reading the Text • Discussing and Revisiting the Text • Introduction to and Assignment of Reading *35 minutes*			**Writing About Reading** *30 minutes*

FIGURE 3.6 45-Minute Novel Study Lesson Framework

Overview of Test Preparation Lesson Framework

Figure 3.7, which follows, shows an overview of Day 1 of a Test Preparation Lesson, with notes about modifications for Days 2–4.

Lesson Information
The lesson number and level.

Materials
A list of materials for the lesson.

Goals
Specific teaching goals for the lesson.

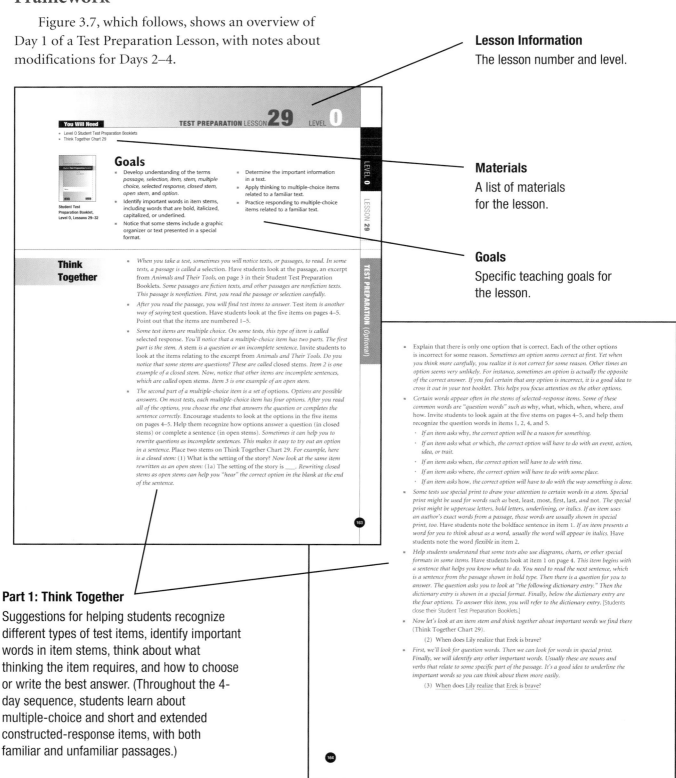

Part 1: Think Together
Suggestions for helping students recognize different types of test items, identify important words in item stems, think about what thinking the item requires, and how to choose or write the best answer. (Throughout the 4-day sequence, students learn about multiple-choice and short and extended constructed-response items, with both familiar and unfamiliar passages.)

FIGURE 3.7A AND 37B An Example of Day 1 of Test Preparation Lesson Framework (Pages 1 and 2 of 5)

Part 2: Have a Try

Suggestions for helping students work with a partner to discuss multiple-choice or constructed-response items.

Critical Thinking

Descriptions of the kind of thinking each item requires (matched by number).

Student Test Preparation Booklet Page

Shows a sample of the page from the Student Test Preparation Booklet, including correct responses to multiple-choice items and well-written, thoughtful sample responses to constructed-response items.

Part 3: On Your Own

Suggestions for having students read one or more passages and respond independently, followed by group review.

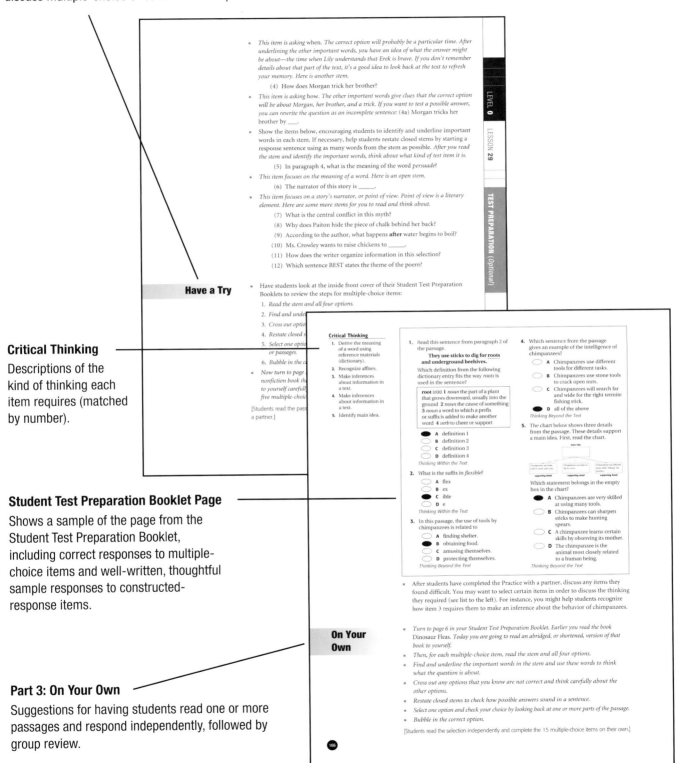

FIGURE 3.7B AND 3.7C An Example of Day 1 of Test Preparation Lesson Framework (Pages 3 and 4 of 5)

Critical Thinking

Descriptions of the kind of thinking each item requires (matched by number).

Student Test Preparation Booklet Page

Shows a sample of the page from the Student Test Preparation Booklet, including correct responses to multiple-choice items and well-written, thoughtful sample responses to constructed-response items.

Critical Thinking

1. Derive the meaning of a word from context.
2. Derive the meaning of a word from context and recognize its antonym.
3. Identify correct pronunciation and understand syllables.
4. Recognize affixes and understand how a prefix changes the meaning of a word.
5. Synthesize important information from a text.
6. Identify important information in a text.
7. Make predictions based on information in a text.
8. Synthesize important information from a text.
9. Make inferences about information in a text.
10. Make inferences about information in an illustration and a text.

---

1. Read these sentences from paragraph 1 of the passage.

   Have you ever seen a cat or dog driven crazy by an itch? If so, the animal was probably tormented by teeny, tiny, sneaky, blood-sucking fleas.

   The *tormented* animal was
   - A frightened.
   - B given relief.
   - C entertained.
   - ● D made miserable.

   Thinking Within the Text

2. Read these sentences from paragraph 6 of the passage.

   Fleas continue to thrive today. How? In order to survive, fleas have had to take on new adaptations.

   Which word is an antonym for *thrive*?
   - A live
   - B swarm
   - ● C weaken
   - D pounce

   Thinking Within the Text

3. The word *adaptation* in paragraph 3 is spoken with extra stress on the
   - A first syllable
   - B second syllable
   - ● C third syllable
   - D fourth syllable

   Thinking Within the Text

4. Reread the third sentence in paragraph 3. What does the prefix in *unnoticed* mean?
   - ● A not
   - B near
   - C again
   - D before

   Thinking Within the Text

5. How were ancient fleas like fleas today?
   - A They had sharp claws.
   - ● B They sucked in blood for food.
   - C They were about one inch long.
   - D They had strong legs perfect for jumping.

   Thinking Within the Text

6. Insects have survived for millions of years because they can
   - A jump well.
   - B hide in leaves.
   - C go without food for months.
   - ● D adapt to changing conditions.

   Thinking Within the Text

7. From reading this passage, you can predict that millions of years from now
   - A fleas will live mostly in cities.
   - B people will outnumber fleas.
   - ● C fleas will still be tormenting animals.
   - D the flea's saliva will no longer make an animal sick.

   Thinking Beyond the Text

8. Which word BEST represents how dinosaurs are presented in this passage?
   - ● A victims
   - B hunters
   - C tricksters
   - D companions

   Thinking Beyond the Text

9. What might have happened if an ancient flea lacked sharp claws?
   - A A dinosaur would have felt the insect sooner.
   - ● B A dinosaur could have easily gotten rid of the insect.
   - C The insect would not have been able to jump very high.
   - D The insect would not have been able to draw out blood from the dinosaur.

   Thinking Beyond the Text

10. From the illustration and the passage, you can infer that
    - A the Stegosaurus never ate insects.
    - ● B the Stegosaurus was not a meat-eater.
    - C fleas scrambled onto a dinosaur one at a time.
    - D fleas preferred the Stegosaurus over other dinosaurs.

    Thinking Beyond the Text

167

FIGURE 3.7D An Example of Day 1 of Test Preparation Lesson Framework (Page 5 of 5)

45-Minute Test Preparation Lesson Framework			
Day 1 (familiar text)	**Day 2** (unfamiliar text)	**Day 3** (familiar text)	**Day 4** (unfamiliar text)
Think Together • multiple-choice items *5 minutes*	**Think Together** • multiple-choice items *5 minutes*	**Think Together** • constructed-response items *5 minutes*	**Think Together** • constructed-response items *5 minutes*
Have a Try *10 minutes*	**Have a Try** *10 minutes*	**Have a Try** *10 minutes*	**Have a Try** *10 minutes*
On Your Own *30 minutes*	**On Your Own** *30 minutes*	**On Your Own** *30 minutes*	**On Your Own** *30 minutes*

FIGURE 3.8 45-Minute Test Preparation Lesson Framework

Teaching with the *LLI Gold System*

In the previous section, we provided an overview of the four types of lesson frameworks:

❏ Standard Lessons (Odd-numbered)

❏ Standard Lessons (Even-numbered)

❏ Novel Study Lesson Sequence

❏ Optional Test Preparation Lessons

In this section, we provide a detailed description of each type of lesson and the instructional procedures and tools that are incorporated into the lessons.

▶ Teaching Standard Lessons (Odd-Numbered)

On the first day of a standard lesson (such as 11, 13, 15, etc.), a new instructional level book is introduced. The focus is on reading, discussion of meaning, vocabulary, fluency, phonics/word study.

The first and last pages of each lesson may be likened to bookends (see Figure 4.1). The first page provides an overview of lesson goals, materials, and an analysis of the new book text characteristics. The last page provides work to be done in class or at home, suggestions for assessing reading and writing behaviors, considerations for ELL students, and professional development links.

The framework for the standard lessons (odd- and even-numbered) is presented in Figure 3.4 on p. 45. There are four main parts to the odd-numbered standard lesson (see Figures 4.2 and 4.3):

Part 1. Discussing Yesterday's New Book (5 minutes)

Students share their thinking about the independent level book read the day before. Use the chart for Thinking Within, Beyond, and About the Text to guide the discussion toward the key understandings.

A "Messages" statement below the chart provides insight into the "big," or important ideas of the text.

Part 2. Revisiting Yesterday's New Book (5 minutes)

Revisiting a previously read text is a powerful way to deepen students' understanding and give them opportunities to reflect on the meanings of words and on how the reading should sound. Three choices are provided for teaching through revisiting. You choose the option that best meets the needs of your students and provide extra attention to that area.

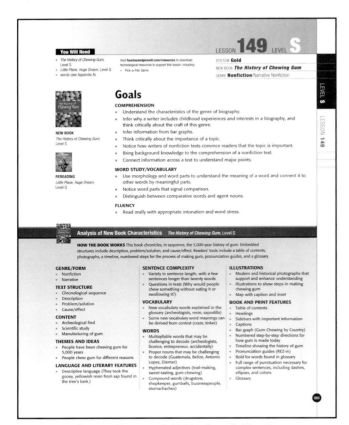

FIGURE 4.1A Standard Lesson (Odd-Numbered), First Page

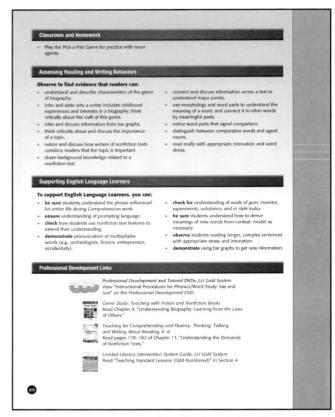

FIGURE 4.1B Standard Lesson (Odd-Numbered), Last Page

Choose one:

○ Comprehension—Students reread a portion of the text. Guide their discussion after reading and confirm their thinking. Close reading is directed toward one or more strategic actions, which are indicated in the title of the section.

○ Vocabulary—Students reflect on a word within the previously read text and often expand word knowledge by connecting related words.

○ Fluency—Students look back at a text in a way that helps them develop awareness about how their oral reading should sound. They have the opportunity to practice all dimensions of fluency.

Part 3. Phonics/Word Study (10 minutes)

In the phonics/word study part of the lesson, a specific principle is listed at the top of the chart. These principles are drawn from *The Continuum of Literacy Learning*. They have been systematically selected and sequenced to support student learning of the critical phonics and word structure understandings required to read proficiently at levels O through T.

Specific language is included to make each principle clear to students, and explicit teaching is suggested. Students are involved in an inquiry process and "hands-on" work with words and their parts. A comprehensive list of the words for each lesson can be found in the back of the *Lesson Guide*. Much of the work is done with a partner using whiteboards, word magnets, and the word study section of their Literacy Notebooks. Magnetic letters are an option when greater kinesthetic learning is needed.

Part 4. Reading a New Book (25 minutes)

There are four steps in reading the new instructional level book (see Figures 4.4 and 4.5).

INTRODUCING THE TEXT

Engage students in a conversation that supports their proficient processing of a new text at the

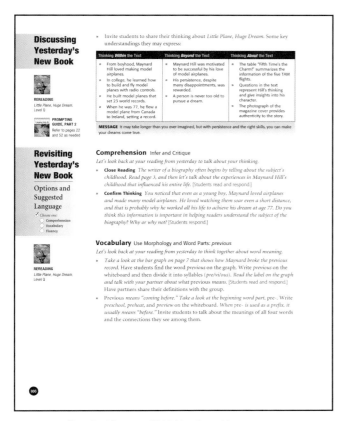

FIGURE 4.2 Standard Lesson (Odd-Numbered)

FIGURE 4.3 Standard Lesson (Odd-Numbered)

instructional level, keeping the genre statement in mind when introducing the text. The introduction may include:

- ❏ Statements about the overall structure of the text or "how it works."

- ❏ Suggested language to invite students to talk about what they know or what they are thinking.

- ❏ Attention to key information that will help students understand the text (background information, similar texts, known or similar characters, types of problems).

- ❏ Attention to particular words and concepts that students need to know to read the text with understanding.

- ❏ Demonstration or discussion of a particular language or sentence structure that may be difficult for students to read.

- ❏ Attention to particular words that students may need help in decoding.

- ❏ Prompts to think about something specific while reading.

Not all elements described above need to be included in every introduction. Guidance is provided in each lesson, but you should think about your own students' needs and select from and add to the introductory conversation. Students should participate rather than just listen; each time the lesson suggests "Students Respond," you are inviting conversation. Remember that the introduction is not long, so keep attention focused on the text rather than expanding to wider topics.

READING THE TEXT

After students begin to read the text silently, sample oral reading by tapping a student's hand or calling on one and have the student read in a soft voice. Observe reading behaviors, and also take the opportunity to interact briefly with individuals to support the use of strategic interactions for processing texts if needed. *Prompting Guides, Part 1* and *Part 2* are useful tools for selecting prompts to support problem solving in oral reading. One suggestion is provided, but you can select any prompts that meet your students' specific needs.

FIGURE 4.4 Standard Lesson (Odd-Numbered)

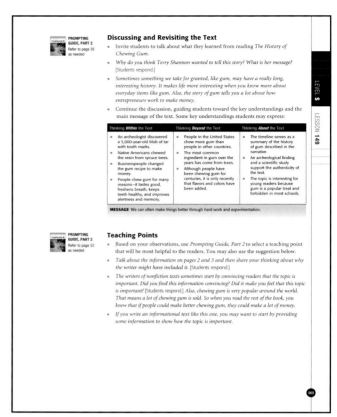

FIGURE 4.5 Standard Lesson (Odd-Numbered)

DISCUSSING AND REVISITING THE TEXT

Invite students to share their thinking about the book. Their comments are important and you want the discussion to be a conversation. Help them listen and talk to each other. Guide the discussion toward the expression of the key understandings. A suggestion is provided for discussion in this section.

Sometimes students recall important information and even infer some of the important ideas in a text, but miss the larger, overarching messages. A "Message" statement below the chart helps you support students in thinking about the bigger, important ideas in the text.

SELECTING A TEACHING POINT

Based on your observations in this lesson (as well as ongoing knowledge of the students), select a teaching point that will be most helpful to readers. Use *Prompting Guide, Part 1* or *Part 2* to help in selecting points. One suggestion is provided in the lesson.

Teaching points are meant to be concise and direct. They usually require some demonstration as well as action.

▶ Teaching Standard Lessons (Even-Numbered)

The second day of the standard lesson sequence is an even-numbered lesson (such as 12, 14, 16, etc.), which introduces a new independent level book. The focus is on writing about reading, vocabulary, fluency, reading, phonics, and word study. The even-numbered standard lessons vary slightly in their structure from the odd-numbered standard lessons.

The first and last pages of each lesson serve as bookends. The first page provides an overview of lesson goals, materials, and an analysis of the new book text characteristics (see Figure 3.3A, p. 39). The last page provides work to be done in class or at home, suggestions for assessing reading and writing behaviors, considerations for ELL students, and professional development links (see Figure 3.3F, p. 44).

There are five main parts to the even-numbered standard lesson.

Part 1. Revisiting Yesterday's New Book (5 minutes)

Revisiting a previously read text is a powerful way to deepen students' understanding and give them opportunities to reflect on the meanings of words and on how their reading should sound. Three choices are available for teaching through revisiting a text that has been read once before (see Figure 4.6). Choose the option that best fits the needs of your students and provide extra attention to that area.

Choose one:

○ Comprehension—Students reread a portion of the text to examine it closely. Guide their discussion after reading and confirm their thinking. Close reading is directed toward one or more strategic actions, which are indicated in the title

of the section. Then you invite them to share their thinking and confirm it.

○ Vocabulary—Students reflect on the meaning of a word within the previously read text and often expand word knowledge by connecting related words.

○ Fluency—Students look back at a text in a way that helps them develop an awareness of how their oral reading should sound. They have the opportunity to practice all dimensions of fluency.

Part 2. Rereading and Assessment (5 minutes)

For the even-numbered standard lessons, select one student, and using the Recording Form, take a reading record on a short selected passage from the instructional level book they read the day before (see Figure 4.7) . Engage the student in a brief comprehension conversation and make a teaching point that will be most helpful to the reader.

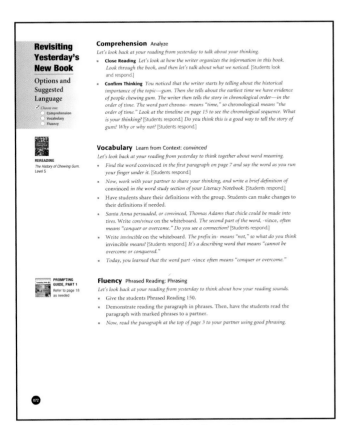

FIGURE 4.6 Standard Lesson (Even-Numbered)

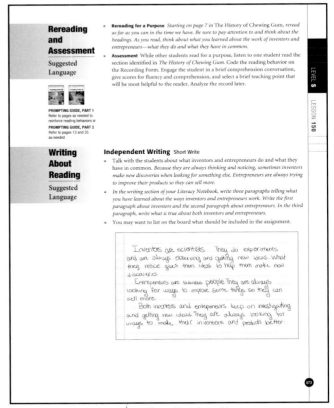

FIGURE 4.7 Standard Lesson (Even-Numbered)

Assess what the student has learned recently and what she can do as a result of your teaching. The reading records provide a picture of ongoing progress. By comparing from week to week and month to month, you can detect difficulties and note increasing strengths.

While you are assessing one student, have the other students reread a portion of the same book for a purpose, which is provided in the lesson. The purpose is related to the writing about reading activity they do later in the lesson.

Part 3. Writing About Reading (15 minutes)

In this part of the lesson, engage students in a conversation to support and extend their thinking about the book introduced and read in yesterday's lesson (see Figure 4.7). They use the Writing About Reading section of their Literacy Notebooks to engage in a particular form of writing about reading with support and teaching. Three types of writing are used in *LLI* lessons:

❏ *Shared Writing*—As you talk with students about the book, guide the conversation to produce a text that you write, acting as scribe. This involves students in composition without the constraint of having to write the words. At the same time, involve them in thinking about the construction of the words. Students may glue a copy of the text in the writing section of their Literacy Notebooks the next day.

❏ *Dictated Writing*—After having a brief discussion about the portion of the book, read aloud a series of sentences, which the students write with your support in the Literacy Notebooks. Some words will be known; help students construct others using the whiteboard or the back of the previous page to work out words as needed. Dictated writing gives students an opportunity to experience a well-constructed message with a clear concept, one that they can read again several times and revisit to think about the text, if time allows.

❏ *Independent Writing*—After a brief discussion, students compose and write their own sentences in the writing section of their Literacy Notebooks. Support them as needed in composing several sentences that reflect their thinking and constructing challenging words, using the whiteboard or back of previous pages.

There are three genres for writing about reading in *LLI* lessons:

❏ *Functional Writing*—Functional writing is about communication. Students write to remember information, get something done, or bring analytic thinking to bear on a text. Functional writing may include using graphic organizers of all kinds as well as letters to the teacher about texts.

❏ *Narrative Writing*—Narrative writing is used when writers produce a story or sequential account of something that happened in a narrative text. It also includes a summary that might be written of a narrative text.

❏ *Informational Writing (including persuasive)*— Informational writing requires readers and writers to gather facts and to organize them in a logical way. It also includes the writing they do to persuade an audience. They may use underlying structures such as compare/contrast, description, cause/effect, time sequence, and problem/solution. The writing about reading activity is short, so students do not write long reports but instead write short segments that demonstrate informational writing.

Part 4. Phonics/Word Study (10 minutes)

In the phonics/word study part of the lesson a specific principle is listed at the top of the chart (see Figure 4.8). These principles are drawn from *The Continuum of Literacy Learning*. They have been systematically selected and sequenced to support student learning of the critical phonics and word structure understandings required to read proficiently at levels O through T.

For each principle, specific language is included to make the principle clear to students, and explicit teaching is suggested. Students are involved in inquiry and in "hands-on" work with words and their parts. Much work is done with a partner. They use whiteboards, word magnets, and the Word Study section of their Literacy Notebooks.

Part 5. Reading a New Book (10 minutes)

In the even-numbered standard lessons, because students are reading an independent level text, a shorter introduction is usually recommended;

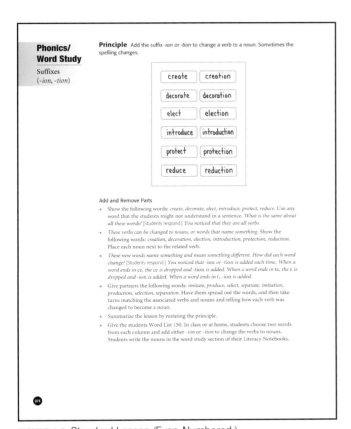

FIGURE 4.8 Standard Lesson (Even-Numbered)

FIGURE 4.9 Standard Lesson (Even-Numbered)

nevertheless, they do need an introduction (see Figure 4.9) . As with the odd-numbered standard lessons, engage students in a conversation during the introduction and draw attention to key concepts, information, and words that they need to process the text smoothly.

If time permits, have students begin to read the text silently while you sample oral reading and prompt for strategic actions. Before the end of the lesson, ask students to finish reading the text in class or at home.

▶ Teaching the Novel Study Lesson Sequence

At the end of each level, students spend four days reading a longer chapter book, one that has been carefully selected for its potential in helping students think deeply about texts and build stamina by reading a text over several days. The novel is at a lower level than the students' instructional level because:

- ❑ They must sustain memory, interest, and engagement over several days.

- ❑ They need to comprehend concepts for a longer text.

- ❑ The problems are more complex and there is more character development than in a shorter text.

FIGURE 4.10 Novel Study Titles for *LLI Gold System*

The major difference between teaching a Novel Study Lesson and a standard lesson is that students continue reading the same text over four days. So, with the exception of the first day, the Revisiting Text choices will refer to a previous chapter or chapters of the longer book. The framework for novel study lessons is presented in Figure 3.6 on p. 51. Notice that phonics/word study is not present in the novel study lesson to allow for maximum time to read and discuss the longer book.

As with the standard lessons, the first and last pages of each novel study lesson are like bookends (see Figure 4.11). The first page provides an overview of lesson goals, materials, and an analysis of the new book text characteristics. The last page provides work to be done in class or at home, subsections for assessing reading and writing behaviors, considerations for ELL students, and professional development links.

The Four-Day Novel Study Sequence

The lesson sequence for the novel study is slightly different from day to day, as you see in Figures 4.11 and 4.12. If students are unable to complete the assigned reading during the time alloted on a given day, you may choose to have them finish reading, during independent reading time, or at home. Each lesson has these main parts:

DAY 1 OF NOVEL STUDY LESSON SEQUENCE

The first day of the sequence begins in a similar manner to the standard lesson with "Part 1, Discussion of Yesterday's New Book," and "Part 2, Revisiting Yesterday's New Book." Students discuss and revisit the independent level book read on the previous day. This is followed by "Part 3, Reading a New Book" where the novel is introduced and a book group discussion takes place.

DAYS 2–3 OF NOVEL STUDY LESSON SEQUENCE

The second and third days of the sequence are the same. The lesson begins with Part 1, "Revisiting Yesterday's Reading," during which you revisit the first section of the novel and choose a focus on comprehension, vocabulary, or fluency based on the area your students need the most. In Part 2, "Reading a New Section," the next section of the novel is introduced, students read silently, then discuss what was read. This is followed by an introduction to and assignment of reading for the next day.

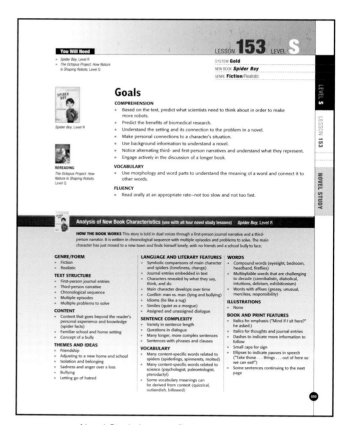

FIGURE 4.11A Novel Study Lesson, first page

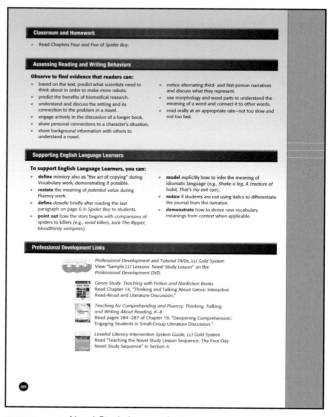

FIGURE 4.11B Novel Study Lesson, last page

FIGURE 4.12A — Novel Study Lesson, Day 1

Discussing Yesterday's New Book

REREADING
The Octopus Project: How Nature Is Shaping Robots, Level Q

PROMPTING GUIDE, PART 2
Refer to pages 15–17 as needed

Revisiting Yesterday's New Book

Options and Suggested Language

Choose one:
- ☑ Comprehension
- ○ Vocabulary
- ○ Fluency

REREADING
The Octopus Project: How Nature Is Shaping Robots, Level Q

■ Invite students to share their thinking about *The Octopus Project: How Nature Is Shaping Robots*. Some key understandings they may express:

Thinking *Within* the Text	Thinking *Beyond* the Text	Thinking *About* the Text
■ Scientists want to imitate octopuses because they are smart and can fit in small places. ■ To make an octopus robot, scientists study robots and the behavior of real octopuses. ■ The robotic octopus and other kinds of robots are being designed to do things people can't easily do.	■ It is a long and complicated process to make a robot that mimics an octopus. ■ Observing nature can enhance scientists' and engineers' understandings of ways to help humans.	■ The illustration on page 10 gives readers an idea of the many things scientists need to consider when making an octopus robot. ■ The sidebar on page 9 that shows how cats drink adds to the reader's understanding of how complicated animals can be.

MESSAGES Nature has brilliant designs. By copying these designs, scientists can create robots that can change our lives. The Octopus Project is an example of how nature can inform science.

Comprehension Predict

Let's look back at your reading from yesterday to talk about your thinking.

■ **Close Reading** *Read pages 10 to 15. As you read, notice what the scientists had to think about to produce a robot octopus that could do some of the things a real octopus can do. Then, look at the chart titled "What Will They Think of Next?" Think about what the different types of robots would need to be able to do in order to be successful in doing what scientists want them to do. When you finish reading, let's talk about what the robots would need in order to perform the tasks that scientists would want them to do.* [Students read and respond.]

■ **Confirm Thinking** *You predicted that most of the robots would need some kind of skin to keep them dry or to withstand high temperatures. Some needed cameras to take photos from a long distance away. Some needed to move easily over rough surfaces. Some need to move underwater. Some would need powerful joints and engines to run fast. Studying and thinking about how animals function help scientists think in new ways about machinery.*

FIGURE 4.12B — Novel Study Lesson, Day 1

Vocabulary Use Morphology and Word Parts: *biomimetics*

Let's look back at your reading from yesterday to think together about word meaning.

■ Have the students find the word *biomimetics* in bold on page 2 or in the glossary. *Let's look at the parts of this word, biomimetics. Write the word on the whiteboard* and ask students to take it apart by syllables (*bi/o/mi/met/ics*). They can write the word in the word study section of their Literacy Notebooks.

■ Then, ask students to write the word *mimic* and talk about the connections between that word and *biomimetics. The word part bio means "life." Something that is mimetic imitates things. So what does biomimetics have to do with?* [Students respond.]

■ Write *mimic, mime, mimicry,* and *mimetic. What part of the words is the same?* [Students respond.] *A mime is a performance that imitates or mocks someone. There are no words but really dramatic gestures. It's an old art form. The word mime can also mean "a performer, someone who does mime." A mimic is someone who makes fun of people by imitating them, or doing mimicry. All of these words have something to do with imitating or mimicking.*

PROMPTING GUIDE, PART 1
Refer to page 17 as needed

Fluency Rate Mover: Rate

Let's look back at your reading from yesterday to think about how your reading sounds.

■ *Turn to page 15 and listen while I read the first paragraph. This paragraph is exciting because it describes the potential value of the Octopus Project. Notice how it sounds when I read it the first time. Then, I'm going to read it a little faster and you can comment on how my reading sounds. I won't read too fast—just the right speed to sound like talking.*

■ *Read the paragraph slowly. Then, follow by reading it at a good rate. How did my reading sound?* [Students respond.]

■ Then, have students read to a partner.

LEVEL **S** | LESSON 153 | NOVEL STUDY

FIGURE 4.12C — Novel Study Lesson, Day 1

Reading a New Book

Suggested Language

NEW BOOK
Spider Boy, Level R

GENRE FOCUS This story is realistic fiction because, although it didn't actually happen, it could have happened in real life. Bobby and his family have moved to New York from Illinois, and he is having trouble adjusting to his new life. Over time, he learns to be himself again while making new friends, rekindling old interests, and offering forgiveness to a bully.

Introducing the Text

■ *For the next four days, you are going to read a chapter book. The title is* Spider Boy *and the author is Ralph Fletcher. There's Bobby on the cover. His nickname is Spider Boy. Can you guess why?* [Students respond.] *Bobby and his family have just moved to a place called New Paltz, New York. He is going to a new school. Have you ever experienced time zones before? What's it like?* [Students respond.]

■ *Read the last paragraph on page 6 aloud to the students. Does Ralph Fletcher seem to understand how Bobby feels? What are some words and phrases that the writer uses to express the feeling of being new?* [Students respond.]

■ *Bobby misses Naperville, Illinois, where he used to live, and he misses his best friend. He has a sister named Brianna who wants everyone to call her Breezy. He has a pet tarantula named Thelma. What do you think of that?* [Students respond.]

■ *You are going to read the first three chapters today, pages 1 to 34. You'll read how Bobby feels about Thelma and also about a boy at school called Chick Hall, who is kind of a bully.*

■ *An important thing to remember as you read is that all over the world there are different time zones. Give an example from your own region to clarify time differences for the students. Notice how time differences affect Bobby.*

■ *There are two kinds of writing in this book. Look at page 1 and read the first two paragraphs. Then, talk with a partner about who is telling the story.* [Students read and respond.] *This is Bobby's journal, so he is doing the writing. Notice how he has dated it. Now, read the text at the bottom of page 2. Who is telling the story here?* [Students read and respond.]

■ *Most of the book is written as a third-person narrative. The writer is telling about the characters and using words like he, she, and they, as if the action is happening and there is another person, a "third" person telling about it.*

■ *The entire book is told from the perspective of Bobby. He is the main character. The story is about him and how he feels and what he does. You will find pieces from his journal and some of the writing he does in school in just about every chapter. Those pieces of writing will be in first person, when Bobby is telling the story and how he feels. For these sections, the writer uses words like I, me, my, and we.*

■ *Read through page 34. Notice the setting and the problem.* Have students use stick-on notes to mark places that they would like to come back to during the discussion.

PROMPTING GUIDE, PART 1
Refer to page 20 as needed

Reading the Text

■ Students read Chapters One, Two, and Three silently.

■ Sample oral reading and prompt, as needed, for integrating all dimensions of fluency in a manner that reflects understanding. Use *Prompting Guide, Part 1* for precise language.

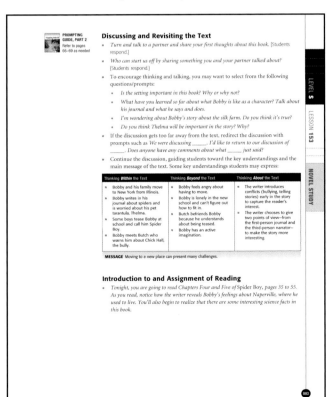

FIGURE 4.12D — Novel Study Lesson, Day 1

PROMPTING GUIDE, PART 2
Refer to pages 66–69 as needed

Discussing and Revisiting the Text

■ *Turn and talk to a partner and share your first thoughts about this book.* [Students respond.]

■ *Who can start us off by sharing something you and your partner talked about?* [Students respond.]

■ To encourage thinking and talking, you may want to select from the following questions/prompts:
   ■ *Is the setting important in this book? Why or why not?*
   ■ *What have you learned so far about what Bobby is like as a character? Talk about his journal and what he says and does.*
   ■ *I'm wondering about Bobby's story about the silk farm. Do you think it's true?*
   ■ *Do you think Thelma will be important in the story? Why?*

■ If the discussion gets too far away from the text, redirect the discussion with prompts such as *We were discussing _____. I'd like to return to our discussion of _____. Does anyone have any comments about what _____ just said?*

■ Continue the discussion, guiding students toward the key understandings and the main message of the text. Some key understandings students may express:

Thinking *Within* the Text	Thinking *Beyond* the Text	Thinking *About* the Text
■ Bobby and his family move to New York from Illinois. ■ Bobby writes in his journal about spiders and is worried about his pet tarantula, Thelma. ■ Some boys tease Bobby at school and call him Spider Boy. ■ Bobby meets Butch who warns him about Chick Hall, the bully.	■ Bobby feels angry about having to move. ■ Bobby is lonely in the new school and can't figure out how to fit in. ■ Butch befriends Bobby because he understands about being teased. ■ Bobby has an active imagination.	■ The writer introduces conflicts (bullying, telling stories) early in the story to capture the reader's interest. ■ The writer chooses to give two points of view—from the first-person journal and the third-person narrator—to make the story more interesting.

MESSAGE Moving to a new place can present many challenges.

Introduction to and Assignment of Reading

■ *Tonight, you are going to read Chapters Four and Five of Spider Boy, pages 35 to 55. As you read, notice how the writer reveals Bobby's feelings about Naperville, where he used to live. You'll also begin to realize that there are some interesting science facts in this book.*

LEVEL **S** | LESSON 153 | NOVEL STUDY

DAY 4 OF NOVEL STUDY LESSON SEQUENCE

The last day of the sequence begins again with Part 1, "Revisiting Yesterday's Reading," during which you revisit the section read on the previous day and choose a focus on comprehension, vocabulary, or fluency. Since this is the last day, Part 2 is called "Concluding Discussion," where students reflect on the book that they have now finished reading. In Part 3, "Writing About Reading," students write about their reflections. Since all of the full-length books are fictional, the prompts for writing focus on thinking deeply about characters and how they change, plot (problem/resolution), and the author's message. They may also involve looking at the craft of writing.

▶ Teaching Test Preparation Lessons

A sequence of four optional Test Preparation Lessons is included at the end of each level for schools interested in helping students prepare for standardized testing. These lessons can be taught after the novel study sequence and before starting the next level. Alternatively, you can work with students on these lessons at another time of day.

These lessons are designed to support students' reading and writing competencies on standardized tests. They include attention to narrative, expository, persuasive, and procedural test selections and multiple-choice and constructed-response items. Consumable Student Test Preparation Booklets, which are provided with the *LLI Gold System*, are used for student work throughout this lesson sequence (see Figure 4.13). Test items in

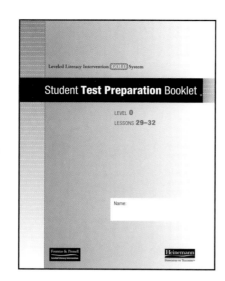
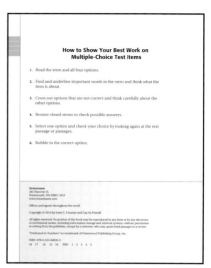
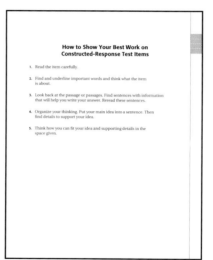
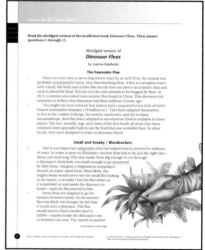
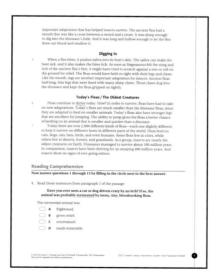
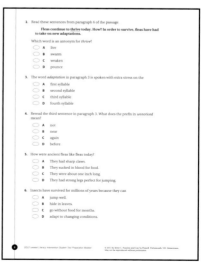

FIGURE 4.13 Student Test Preparation Booklet

the student booklets were written after analyzing a variety of state and national tests in order to reflect the best practices in testing language and format.

These lessons take advantage of the sequence of texts students have just read in the standard lessons. Selected instructional level texts from the fiction and nonfiction books for the level have been abridged to create passages for some parts of the lessons. Students apply test-taking strategies first to these familiar texts that have been read and discussed before. Then, they apply the same strategies to unfamiliar reading material—excerpts modeled on typical test passages. Each lesson moves from thinking together to trying out the thinking and, finally, to engaging in the thinking independently. Students learn the language and format of testing and how to respond in a way that meets the expectations of a wide variety of standardized assessments. (See Figure 3.8, on p. 55 for a review of the Test Preparation Lesson sequence framework.)

There are three main parts to the Test Preparation Lessons:

FIGURE 4.14 Test Preparation Lesson, Day 1

Part 1. Think Together (5 minutes)

In the first part of the lesson, you and your students think together about recognizing different types of test items (including those related to vocabulary, literary elements, text organization and type, and interpretation of ideas), identifying important words in item stems, and determining what students need to think about to complete the item successfully (see Figure 4.14). You help them look back at the passage and locate and reread the important information there. You guide students in restating questions to check possible answers and in using strategies to eliminate incorrect options in multiple-choice items. Each lesson contains a Think Together chart, in which you may give examples of item stems for students to see and discuss. You also help students organize their thinking in order to state and support main ideas in constructed-response items. In the interest of time, you may wish to select examples related to the needs of your students.

Part 2. Have a Try (10 minutes)

In the second part of the lesson, after reading the passage or passages, students work with a partner to discuss each item, choosing the best multiple-choice option or writing a short or extended constructed response (see Figure 4.15). You will still support and teach as needed. Keep in mind this is an instructional, not a testing, situation. Then the group reviews the items and responses together.

Part 3. On Your Own (30 minutes)

In the last part of the lesson, students try reading a selection and responding as independently as possible. Based on your observations, you may support and teach individual students, as needed. The group reviews the items along with correct answers and well-written responses (see Figure 4.16).

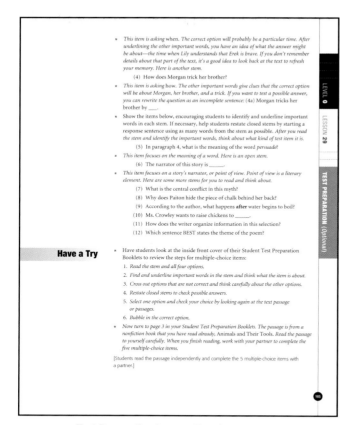

- *This item is asking when. The correct option will probably be a particular time. After underlining the other important words, you have an idea of what the answer might be about—the time when Lily understands that Erek is brave. If you don't remember details about that part of the text, it's a good idea to look back at the text to refresh your memory. Here is another stem.*

    (4) How does Morgan trick her brother?

- *This item is asking how. The other important words give clues that the correct option will be about Morgan, her brother, and a trick. If you want to test a possible answer, you can rewrite the question as an incomplete sentence: (4a) Morgan tricks her brother by ___.*

- Show the items below, encouraging students to identify and underline important words in each stem. If necessary, help students restate closed stems by starting a response sentence using as many words from the stem as possible. *After you read the stem and identify the important words, think about what kind of test item it is.*

    (5) In paragraph 4, what is the meaning of the word *persuade*?

- *This item focuses on the meaning of a word. Here is an open stem.*

    (6) The narrator of this story is ___.

- *This item focuses on a story's narrator, or point of view. Point of view is a literary element. Here are some more stems for you to read and think about.*

    (7) What is the central conflict in this myth?

    (8) Why does Paiton hide the piece of chalk behind her back?

    (9) According to the author, what happens **after** water begins to boil?

    (10) Ms. Crowley wants to raise chickens to ___.

    (11) How does the writer organize information in this selection?

    (12) Which sentence BEST states the theme of the poem?

Have a Try

- Have students look at the inside front cover of their Student Test Preparation Booklets to review the steps for multiple-choice items:

    1. *Read the stem and all four options.*

    2. *Find and underline important words in the stem and think what the item is about.*

    3. *Cross out options that are not correct and think carefully about the other options.*

    4. *Restate closed stems to check possible answers.*

    5. *Select one option and check your choice by looking again at the text passage or passages.*

    6. *Bubble in the correct option.*

- Now turn to page 3 in your Student Test Preparation Booklets. The passage is from a nonfiction book that you have read already, Animals and Their Tools. Read the passage to yourself carefully. When you finish reading, work with your partner to complete the five multiple-choice items.

[Students read the passage independently and complete the 5 multiple-choice items with a partner.]

FIGURE 4.15 Test Preparation Lesson, Day 1

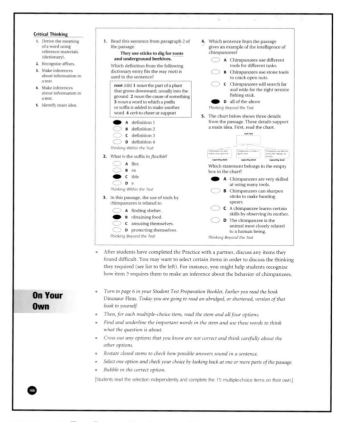

Critical Thinking

1. Derive the meaning of a word using reference materials (dictionary).

2. Recognize affixes.

3. Make inferences about information in a text.

4. Make inferences about information in a text.

5. Identify main idea.

1. Read this sentence from paragraph 2 of the passage.

    They use sticks to dig for roots and underground beehives.

    Which definition from the following dictionary entry fits the way *roots* is used in the sentence?

    root (rüt) 1 *noun* the part of a plant that grows downward, usually into the ground 2 *noun* the cause of something 3 *noun* a word to which a prefix or suffix is added to make another word 4 *verb* to cheer or support

    ○ A definition 1
    ○ B definition 2
    ○ C definition 3
    ○ D definition 4
    Thinking Within the Text

2. What is the suffix in *flexible*?
    ○ A flex
    ○ B ex
    ● C ible
    ○ D e
    Thinking Within the Text

3. In this passage, the use of tools by chimpanzees is related to
    ○ A finding shelter.
    ● B obtaining food.
    ○ C amusing themselves.
    ○ D protecting themselves.
    Thinking Beyond the Text

4. Which sentence from the passage gives an example of the intelligence of chimpanzees?
    ○ A Chimpanzees use different tools for different tasks.
    ○ B Chimpanzees use stone tools to crack open nuts.
    ○ C Chimpanzees will search far and wide for the right termite fishing stick.
    ● D all of the above
    Thinking Beyond the Text

5. The chart below shows three details from the passage. These details support a main idea. First, read the chart.

    Which statement belongs in the empty box in the chart?
    ● A Chimpanzees are very skilled at using many tools.
    ○ B Chimpanzees can sharpen sticks to make hunting spears.
    ○ C A chimpanzee learns certain skills by observing its mother.
    ○ D The chimpanzee is the animal most closely related to a human being.
    Thinking Beyond the Text

- After students have completed the Practice with a partner, discuss any items they found difficult. You may want to select certain items in order to discuss the thinking they required (see list to the left). For instance, you might help students recognize how item 3 requires them to make an inference about the behavior of chimpanzees.

On Your Own

- Turn to page 6 in your Student Test Preparation Booklet. Earlier you read the book Dinosaur Fleas. Today you are going to read an abridged, or shortened, version of that book to yourself.

- Then, for each multiple-choice item, read the stem and all four options.

- Find and underline the important words in the stem and use these words to think what the question is about.

- Cross out any options that you know are not correct and think carefully about the other options.

- Restate closed stems to check how possible answers sound in a sentence.

- Select one option and check your choice by looking back at one or more parts of the passage.

- Bubble in the correct option.

[Students read the selection independently and complete the 15 multiple-choice items on their own.]

FIGURE 4.16 Test Preparation Lesson, Day 1

Review will allow you to help students analyze the stem, the correct answer, and the three incorrect options in any multiple-choice item. In this way, students may reinforce their understanding of how to identify important words in the stem; how to locate sentences in the passage or passages that relate to the item; as well as how to recognize the reasons why various options are not the best answer.

As the group reviews constructed-response items, you might focus students' attention on how well they identified key words; found sentences in the passage or passages with relevant information; organized their thinking by stating a main idea; and developed their main idea by supporting it with examples and other details from one or more texts. Students may also compare and contrast their writing with the well-written sample responses to see how clearly they expressed their ideas.

Instructional Procedures and Tools for *LLI*

In this section, we provide an explanation of several instructional procedures and tools that are used throughout *LLI* lessons:

- ❏ Support students in reading a new text that has opportunities to extend comprehension, vocabulary, and processing strategies.

- ❏ Provide options for close reading to extend comprehension, vocabulary learning, and fluency practice that are specific to a text as well as help students think across texts through series books, fiction, and nonfiction.

- ❏ Develop fluency and phrasing through explicit instruction.

- ❏ Help students learn about how words work.

- ❏ Help students learn to apply knowledge of phonics to word solving while reading continuous text.

- ❏ Extend comprehension through discussion and specific instruction.

- ❏ Help students learn how to demonstrate and extend understanding through writing about reading.

- ❏ Display new understandings in classroom work.

- ❏ Develop the habit and joy of home reading.

▶ Instructional Procedures for *LLI*

Instructional Procedures for Comprehension

Throughout the *LLI* lessons, you work to support and teach students to construct the twelve systems of strategic actions shown in Figure 5.1. In proficient reading, all twelve processing systems work together simultaneously in the head.

INTRODUCTION TO THE TEXT

As you introduce new books to students, provide the kind of support they need to process them with excellent comprehension. Talk with students during the book introduction to gain information about their ability to make connections, inferences, and predictions. Select language examples from *Prompting Guide, Part 2* to support the introductory conversation about the text. For example:

- ❏ "What are you thinking about this character?" [Infer]

- ❏ "How do you think this character will feel about that?" [Infer]

- ❏ "What might happen?" [Predict]

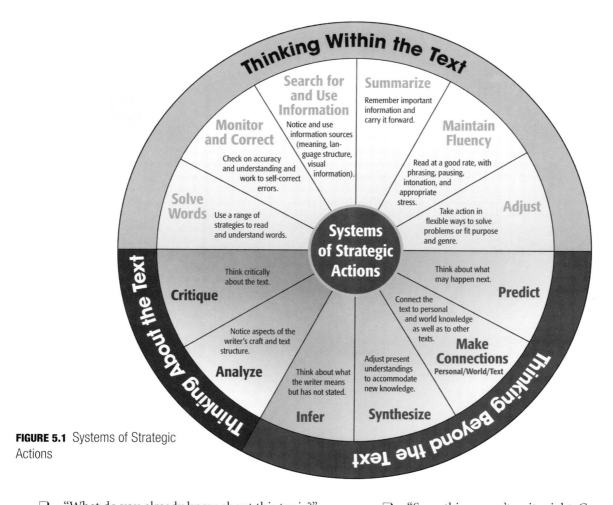

FIGURE 5.1 Systems of Strategic Actions

❏ "What do you already know about this topic?" [Make Connections]

❏ "What is this problem making you think about?" [Make Connections]

❏ "Has anything like that ever happened to you?" [Make Connections]

READING THE TEXT

As students read the book, sample oral reading. Your observations will provide helpful information about the readers' abilities to solve words, monitor and correct, search for and use information, maintain fluency, and adjust reading to solve problems. You can interact briefly with students to support strategic actions. Refer to *Prompting Guide, Part 1* for helpful language to support your students' problem solving as they work through the text. For example:

❏ "What can you try?" [Solve Words]

❏ "Do you know a word like that?" [Solve Words]

❏ "Try that again." [Monitor and Correct]

❏ "Something wasn't quite right. Can you fix it?" [Monitor and Correct]

❏ "Were you right?" [Monitor and Correct]

❏ "Try that again, and look at (point to information)." [Search for and Use Information]

❏ "Try that again, and think how it should sound." [Search for and Use Information]

❏ "You can slow down to figure it out and then move on." [Adjust]

❏ "Did you find yourself reading faster during the exciting part?" [Adjust]

❏ "Make your own reading sound interesting." [Maintain Fluency]

DISCUSSING THE TEXT

Using effective teaching helps students expand their processing power. The discussion after reading is another time to gather evidence about students' abilities to use strategic actions and extend their thinking about the text. In the talk, you can see evidence of their abilities to summarize, predict, make connections, synthesize, infer, analyze, and critique. Use *Prompting Guide, Part 2* to assist you in selecting language that expands students' thinking. For example:

- ❑ "What are the most important ideas?" [Summarize]

- ❑ "Tell what you know so far." [Summarize]

- ❑ "When did you know . . . ?" [Predict]

- ❑ "Talk about the new information you learned from this book." [Synthesize]

- ❑ "The real message of this book is . . . " [Infer]

- ❑ "What did the writer do to make the story funny? Interesting? Sad?" [Analyze]

- ❑ "What makes this a good ___ (biography, fantasy, etc.)?" [Critique]

TEACHING POINT

At the end of the odd-numbered standard lesson, after students read and discuss the new book, there is an opportunity to make a very specific teaching point directed toward the systems of strategic actions. Choose this teaching point based on your observation of students and your analysis of their needs. One suggestion is included in each lesson, but you should notice the way the readers process the text and tailor your teaching point to these precise needs.

REREADING FOR DEEP COMPREHENSION

When students revisit the text the next day, you have an opportunity to deepen their understanding. A paragraph, page, or several pages are selected for rereading. Ask students to think about or notice something in particular. This questioning prompts them to use strategic actions. A discussion follows. Two key actions are involved:

1. *Close Reading*: You may want to say, "Let's look back at your reading from yesterday and talk about your thinking." Then invite students to reread a portion of the text, but prompt their thinking. For example:

    - *The Boy Who Saves Camels* is narrative nonfiction. It's written like a story, so it is a narrative, but it is a true story so it is a nonfiction or informational text. It centers on Cameron, but the real story is about the danger of pollution

and the idea of saving animals. When a person accomplishes something, a writer likes to give readers information so they can infer why the person makes decisions. Read page 6, and then let's talk about why Cameron became so interested in saving camels. [Infer/Critique]

- When you interview someone, you prepare some of the questions in advance. But also, you need to really listen to your subject. Sometimes the answer to a question will help you think of another question. Read page 5. Why do you think the interviewer asked the second question? [Infer]

The discussion that follows is an open one, but guide students to address your original prompt. If students do not bring out major points, demonstrate the thinking yourself.

2. *Confirm Thinking*: At the end of the discussion, confirm students' thinking in a way that summarizes the learning. You may want to take the opportunity to expand thinking further. Some examples of confirming thinking are:

    - You noticed that the writer provides information about Cameron before he came to Abu Dhabi. She shows how a person's early life can influence what he does later. The wildlife in South Africa made Cameron love and want to protect animals, and those feelings transferred to the camels in the desert. Do you think telling Cameron's story helps to persuade readers to protect the camels and other wildlife? Why or why not?

    - You noticed that Jeff's answer to the first question on the page raised the topic of a drive to create. The interviewer then asked Jeff why he thinks he has the drive to create. That's called a follow-up question. The interviewer probably didn't think of it in advance, but was listening carefully to the subject. We don't know that for sure, but it seems likely. Some questions are probably prepared in advance, but when you do an interview, you always want to be quick to follow up by asking another question to get more information.

The particular system of strategic actions addressed for each lesson is named in the title of the instructional procedure. Very often, the prompt requires a combination of strategic actions, but the teacher's primary goal is named. These suggestions are there along with some suggested language for confirming thinking, but you may find some surprises in your students' conversation, and that is a good thing!

Instructional Procedures for Vocabulary Development

Vocabulary refers to an individual's knowledge of words and their meanings, including those recognized and used in speaking, listening, reading, and writing. Individuals add to their vocabularies throughout their lives, and there is no more powerful way to expand word knowledge than through reading and talking about books. In fact, the amount of time students spend reading is a great predictor of vocabulary size. At the same time, instruction to build vocabulary contributes greatly to reading comprehension. One of the most enduring findings in reading research is the extent to which students' vocabulary knowledge relates to their reading comprehension.

Students who are lagging behind in reading almost always have deficits in vocabulary, so they must expand word knowledge even more rapidly than their higher-progress classmates. Students who lag behind need to accelerate vocabulary learning. To make this kind of progress in vocabulary learning, students need explicit instruction.

This means that students, especially those who are struggling in reading or are taking on vocabulary in a language different from that in their homes and communities, need both explicit instruction and rich engagement in texts, supported by oral language. They need to *learn how to learn vocabulary from reading and talking* so that they can continue to add to their vocabularies independently. The vocabulary procedures in *LLI* include intentional teaching of new vocabulary that students encounter in context. Additionally, students are involved in conversation about word parts.

You can help students become acquainted with some key words through the text introduction, reading, and discussion. But in revisiting a text, the entire context is better known, so the support for intentional instruction and learning is very strong. In the following section, we describe the *LLI* instructional procedures for revisiting texts to learn vocabulary. The procedures are designed to engage readers in learning about words and word parts; all involve the combination of explicit teaching and vocabulary expansion through using context and connecting words. First, we discuss the underlying principles on which *LLI* vocabulary instruction is based. Specific instructional procedures can facilitate vocabulary learning.

A set of easy-to-use instructional procedures help students take an active approach to vocabulary learning. The procedures become automatic and routine, thus allowing the students' full attention to be devoted to word meaning and structure. Over time, students learn to apply the routines in a rapid and unconscious way while reading. In this way, they learn to add to their reading, speaking, and writing vocabularies automatically as they encounter texts.

INSTRUCTIONAL PROCEDURES FOR REVISITING THE TEXT TO EXPAND VOCABULARY

We have said that revisiting a previously read text is a highly supportive context for the reader to use strategies for learning the meaning of words. Vocabulary is developed across all the reading and word study components of *LLI* lessons. Very specific vocabulary teaching is one option for revisiting the text, so you may want to choose one of the other options (comprehension or fluency) on any given day. Your decisions will be based on an analysis of your students' skills and needs. Vocabulary is one option for revisiting the text. See the lesson framework shown in Figure 5.2.

In this section, we describe the particular procedures used in revisiting a text that students have previously read. Teach students to use four procedures, which are named within the lesson framework. You should modify or vary them as needed. Sometimes, more than one, or a slight variation, is embedded in the suggestions for the lesson, but the primary procedure is listed. These are suggestions only; after you have used them for a while, you may want to vary your choices based on your students' responses.

Learn from Context

There are five steps for teaching students to use context to derive the meaning of words. They are:

1. *Identify.* Read the sentence with the word aloud (or read the entire paragraph, if it is important). Ask students to say the word and to think what

FIGURE 5.2 Revisiting the Text with Vocabulary

it means in the story or book. As students become more sophisticated (or if the text is easy for them), ask them to say the word and then read the sentence or paragraph themselves. In this case, use the word in a sentence with the meaning stated in the story.

2. *Hypothesize.* Have students hypothesize the meaning from context. Alternatively, provide a student-friendly meaning, and clarify their understanding if needed.

3. *Expand.* Discuss the word in this context and others so that students begin to understand that word meaning may stay constant or vary across contexts. Ask students to give their own examples of the word in a sentence or provide at least two other contextualized examples. Multiple contexts are needed to construct a meaningful and memorable representation of the word. If appropriate, expand understanding by connecting the word with related words—for example, *detain, detention; obsess, obsession.*

4. *Interact.* Invite students to interact with the word. For example, ask: "Which of these two things would make you gleeful? Which would be more incredible? When are times you are exhausted?"

5. *Summarize.* Have students repeat the word they learned. Provide a brief summary of the words learned, relating to each other if appropriate.

You may find that some steps are not necessary if the word is "almost familiar" to students and the learning seems solid, but the basic process will still be valuable to students. Remember that the goal of the procedure is to enable students to learn words from context in other texts that they read. As they learn words "on the run" while reading, they won't necessarily follow the five steps described in a methodical manner. In fact, you hope that the process will become quick, streamlined, and largely unconscious.

Use Morphology and Word Parts

If students know how to examine root and base words and understand how affixes (prefixes and suffixes) create words that are different but related in meaning, then they do not have to learn each word in isolation. The process becomes much more complex, of course. Some affixes change the function of a word in a sentence (e.g., noun to adjective or verb to noun) and others change the tense (of verbs). Use everyday language to talk about the word parts, what they mean, and how they change the word.

Using morphology and word parts means helping students notice prefixes, suffixes, root words or base words, and connected words (words sharing common elements such as *courage* and *courageous*).

There are six steps for teaching students how to use morphology:

1. *Identify.* Students know that they do not understand the word (or have only partial understanding).

2. *Analyze.* Students analyze the word for parts that are recognizable. They think about the meaning and whether an affix requires a change in sound or spelling.

3. *Hypothesize.* Students hypothesize the meaning of the word based on their analysis of word parts.

4. *Check.* Students check their understanding of the meaning by using the context of the sentence, the paragraph, or a larger part of the text.

5. *Expand.* Expand understanding of the word by asking students to use the word in a sentence or provide their own examples. Provide clarifying examples yourself as needed. You can also expand understanding by showing students words that are related in some way—for example, having the same base or root word, or the same affixes.

6. *Summarize.* Summarize the learning to make it explicit.

Think, Pair, Share

The Think, Pair, Share (adapted from Lyman 1981) procedure brings students together to rehearse their understanding of words before sharing them with the group (see Figure 5.3). In doing so, they use a combination of context and word parts and morphology. They may also combine their background experiences to bring more meaning to the word. There are six basic steps in the Think, Pair, Share procedure:

1. *Identify.* Call students' attention to a paragraph (or sentence) containing one or two vocabulary words. You may want to have students say the word or, if needed, use it in a sentence that gives them a little more support.

2. *Hypothesize.* Ask each student to read the sentence or paragraph and think about the meaning of the word. You may want them to make a note about the word in the word study section of their Literacy Notebooks.

3. *Define with a partner.* Students talk with a partner. They share their thinking and construct a brief definition. They can write the definition in the word study section of their Literacy Notebooks.

4. *Share.* Pairs share their definitions with the group. They explain their rationales and identify the context clues or word parts that helped them.

Vocabulary Think, Pair, Share: *commence, capitulate*

Let's look back at your reading from yesterday to think together about word meaning.

- *Ms. Mallow is a pretty smart teacher. She uses some big words, too, and Nick doesn't understand them. Read what she said in the last sentence on page 6, and then talk with your partner about what she was really saying. Try to think of a synonym for* commence *and one for* capitulate. [Students read and respond.]

- Have students talk in pairs and then have pairs share their thinking with the group.

- Commence *means "begin" and* capitulate *means "give in or give up." So Ms. Mallow is really saying, "Get started or give up." Why do you think the writer has Ms. Mallow use big words like that instead of just saying "get started or give up"?* [Students respond.]

- *One of the ways a writer makes characters interesting is by having them use words in unusual ways. It makes the story more interesting and sometimes funny. Those words are a clue that Ms. Mallow knows what she is doing and Nick doesn't.*

FIGURE 5.3 Think, Pair, Share Activity

5. *Expand.* Add information and clarify understanding as necessary. You may want to expand understanding by showing students some related words, if appropriate.

6. *Summarize.* Summarize the learning to make it explicit.

Use Reference Tools

When the text does not provide enough information to learn the meaning of a word, help students use reference tools including the glossary, a dictionary, thesaurus, or others. Increasingly, these tools are available electronically via the Internet. Because of time limitations (and possibly technological access), in this guide the suggestions for use of outside resources in the *LLI Gold System* are limited to the use of the glossary or Dictionary Definitions, which can be downloaded from the Online Resources site. There are six steps in using reference tools:

1. *Identify.* Call students' attention to a sentence that includes the word and have them say it. For the *LLI Gold System*, glossaries appear at the end of nonfiction books. Point out that if the word is in bold, it is defined in the glossary. Some lessons also suggest using Dictionary Definitions, which are available on the Online Resources site.

2. *Search and Read.* Students search for the word in the glossary or Dictionary Definitions. Point out that the words are in alphabetical order if needed. Have students read the definition and think about the meaning of the word. Alternatively, have students hypothesize the meaning from context and check their understanding with the glossary or Dictionary Definitions.

3. *Share.* Students talk about the word, expressing their own understanding.

4. *Check.* Students go back to the text to confirm the meaning of the word within the context.

5. *Expand.* Invite students to use the word in a sentence or give their own examples of experience with the word. If appropriate, show them the examples of one or two related words (by morphology or meaning).

6. *Summarize.* Summarize the learning to make it explicit.

As you work with your students in the *LLI Gold System*, the instructional procedures will become automatic, but remember to vary them in response to student needs.

Instructional Procedures for Fluency

Fluency is an important aspect of reading. By reading fluently, students display their proficiency. Historically, research has shown an important relationship between fluency and comprehension. In recent times, the emphasis has increasingly been on speed, but the connection between speed and comprehension is tenuous. An over-emphasis on increased scores on speed tests can lead students to skip and scan—skipping important key words without working on them—and forget to monitor for understanding. The rates of reading (speed) seem to have increased in recent years, but that increase has not been accompanied by an increase in comprehension scores.

Fluency is not determined solely by rate, certainly not "words per minute" or even "accurate number of words per minute." Working to increase rate without recognizing other dimensions of fluency can undermine fluency. In *LLI* lessons, we consider six dimensions of fluency (Fountas and Pinnell 2001):

1. *Pausing.* Pausing refers to the way the reader's voice is guided by punctuation. For example, readers take a short breath at a comma and a longer pause at a dash, a period, a question mark, or an exclamation point. Pausing requires that readers notice and use punctuation.

2. *Phrasing.* Phrasing is related to pausing but requires more processing of the language of the text. When students read orally (and possibly mentally as they read silently) they put words together in groups to represent the meaningful units of language. The writer has mapped out the meaning of the language in the grammatical structure, and the reader is required to *parse* the sentences in a way that reflects meaning. Sometimes phrases are cued by punctuation, but often they are not. Phrased reading sounds like oral language, although it is more formal. (Except for very skilled orators, you can usually tell when people are reading even if you can't see them.)

3. *Word Stress.* In oral renditions, readers emphasize particular words (slight punch or stronger tone) to reflect the meaning as speakers would do in oral language. Word stress may vary according to the reader's interpretation, but there are acceptable and unacceptable ways to stress words.

4. *Intonation*. Intonation refers to the way the oral reader varies the voice in tone, pitch, and volume to reflect the meaning. Intonation is sometimes called "expression," but in fact, expression involves all of the dimensions of fluency. Readers' interpretation may vary, but it is important that it is present.

5. *Rate*. Rate refers to the pace at which the reader moves through the text—not too fast and not too slow. The reader moves along steadily with few slow-downs, stops, or pauses to solve words. Another way to describe the rate is *momentum*. The momentum keeps the reader from bogging down, struggling, and losing comprehension of the text, so it is very important. Yet, note that rate is not synonymous with speed. And all readers may stop and reflect, go back to reread, ponder interesting ideas, and spend time examining illustrations. There are wide ranges of acceptable rates for processing texts. Sometimes people read very quickly; sometimes they read slowly for very good reasons. Rate must be considered within the situation, and we need to encourage students to read with phrasing and pausing, as well as to move on at an acceptable rate.

6. *Integration*. Proficient readers consistently integrate all of the five dimensions of fluency listed and defined above. You can teach very specifically for each of the dimensions, and that is important, but ultimately, integrated reading is the goal.

TEACHING FOR FLUENCY IN *LLI* LESSONS

Within *LLI*, fluency is supported in many ways. Students are reading at the instructional or independent level so there is maximum opportunity to read with fluency. They are not struggling to read texts that are so difficult for them that there is no chance of fluent reading. But struggling students need more than text selection and support to sound like proficient readers.

Fluency is closely related to comprehension. In fact, it is impossible to read with integration of all dimensions of fluency if you do not understand the meaning of the text. The text introduction prepares students for reading with high accuracy, making fluency possible. Even more important, as you introduce the text you direct readers' attention to the new ideas, language, and text features that contribute to the readers' understanding. This support allows the reader to process the whole text with a forward momentum, thinking about the meaning and language structure while reading the text at a good rate.

While students are reading a text, you have the opportunity to sample oral reading so that you can evaluate fluency. Also, you can interact briefly with students using explicit language that supports reading fluency. Refer to the section on maintaining fluency in *Prompting Guide, Part 1*. For example:

- ❏ "Take a short breath when you see a comma." [Pausing]
- ❏ "Read it like this [model phrase units]." [Phrasing]
- ❏ "Make this word sound important." [Word Stress]
- ❏ "Make your voice go down at the period. Then stop." [Intonation]
- ❏ "Can you read this quickly?" [Rate]
- ❏ "Make your voice show what you think the author meant." [Integration]
- ❏ "How do you think your reading sounds?" [Integration]

When you ask students to revisit a text they have previously read, you have an excellent opportunity to do some effective teaching for fluency. The content of the entire text is available to readers, and they have already thought about and talked about the meaning. They have processed the language structure once before and worked out the unfamiliar words. Now their attention can go to how the reading should sound.

REVISITING THE TEXT TO IMPROVE FLUENCY

In *LLI* lessons, you use five instructional procedures to support fluency as you guide students to revisit texts. The goal is to help students reconstruct the meaning of the text as they read (the expressive interpretation of the text). You want to help students develop an internal understanding of fluency—a "feel" for it. As students gain proficiency in oral reading fluency, their silent reading will also improve.

Phrased Reading

Here you help students develop a sense of the text as language. When people talk, they use phrases, and when they read orally, they reflect meaning with phrases. Reading should have a "language rhythm" to it rather than sounding robotic. If students need to learn phrasing, it helps to read texts with marked phrase units. Students can work with a partner to read a paragraph or page on which phrase units are lightly marked. Students read the text silently. Then, they take turns reading it orally to each other, putting together the phrases as marked. You will need to demonstrate the action the first few times students attempt it. For each lesson that suggests marked phrase units, a copy of the paragraph or page of text is printable from the Online Resources site.

Echo Reading

This instructional procedure provides another way to demonstrate fluent oral reading. Read a sentence and then have students read it in unison immediately afterward. As an alternative, read a whole paragraph, and then have students read to a partner, echoing your reading. The paragraphs may include dialogue and/or complex punctuation. Before reading, say, "Listen to how my reading sounds." Invite students to discuss the reading either right after you read or after the echo reading is completed.

- ❏ "Did you notice how I read that, or did you notice how that sounded?"
- ❏ "What did you notice about my reading? Why do you think I did that with my voice?"
- ❏ "How did my reading help you think what the writer meant?"

Assisted Reading

To help students experience the feel of fluent reading, use assisted reading (Shany, Biemiller 1995). First, read a paragraph or sentence with fluency. Then, have the student read the same text fluently with you or a partner chorally. If students have difficulty tracking the print and keeping up, have them slide a finger under the print while reading. You can vary the procedure by starting to read the passage fluently, and then let your voice drop off while the student continues to read.

Rate Mover

It is often necessary to help students increase their reading rate. Some students, even when reading with high accuracy, tend to move along slowly. Select a paragraph and read it several times to students, modeling how to get a little faster each time. Be sure to control the reading so that it is not too fast and also to use all other dimensions of fluency. Sometimes when students try to read fast, they become robotic and expressionless. Have students read the paragraph two or three times to a partner, attempting to read it a little faster each time, but never too fast. If time allows, have students reverse roles. It may be necessary to help the reader's eyes move across the text by moving a small card across the text to speed up tracking. Afterward, you can ask to read the text again quickly and smoothly without the card.

Readers' Theater

Readers' theater offers an enjoyable and authentic reason to read aloud. Some *LLI* books include a play, or readers' theater script, at the end. For others, a readers' theater has been written and can be printed from the Online Resources site. Some readers' theater scripts take the form of choral reading (reading in unison as a whole group or in subgroups) and use the voice as an instrument to communicate the meaning and mood of the text. The readers' theater will be short, sometimes focusing on a scene from the book and sometimes offering a summarized version. Assign parts and ask students to read the script silently. Have them perform the voices. You can move the process along a bit by taking the part of the narrator. We do not advise making a "production" of the readers' theater (for example, standing in a line while performing or using props). The enjoyment and value is in the reading. An example of readers' theater is shown in Figure 5.4.

Instructional Procedures for Phonics/Word Study

Every reader needs to develop efficient, flexible strategic actions for recognizing words and taking them apart as they read. In *LLI* lessons you will help your students develop strong control of six critical areas of word learning so they can demonstrate strong visual processing (see Figure 5.5).

In *LLI* lessons, there are six, easy-to-learn instructional procedures to develop readers' knowledge of words and how they work that address these six key areas. Each procedure engages students in inquiry and generating an important principle. In each lesson students search for common features in a group of words and construct principles that help them read and write those words and others like them. Over time, students learn to apply the

Readers' Theater 23
Readers (4): Nick, Fergus, Erin, Narrator

NICK: I am not weak! I'm at least as strong as you are.

FERGUS: Prove it.

NICK: I challenge you to a . . . a . . . tug-of-war!

FERGUS: You got it. After school today, and don't chicken out.

ERIN: You can't win, you know. Your arm isn't that much bigger than a twig on this tree.

NICK: This tree.

NARRATOR: Nick looked at her kind of funny for a second. Then he started to smile.

NICK: I'm going to need one long rope.

NARRATOR: After school, Nick and Fergus stood facing each other. They both held onto a long rope. It stretched all the way across the schoolyard and around the corner of the school building. Lots of students stood around, watching. Nobody would bet on Nick.

ERIN: (loud) I can't watch!

NARRATOR: Erin covered her face with her hands and ran off, past Nick and around the corner of the school. She tied the rope around the trunk of the big tree.

NICK: Are you ready to lose? All right. Pull on the count of three. One . . . Two . . .

ERIN: This is never going to work.

NICK: . . . Three!

NARRATOR: Fergus gave a mighty heave and staggered back two steps. The rope went tight and stopped Fergus cold. All the kids gasped in disbelief. They were thinking, "Nick can't really beat Fergus, can he?"

NICK: (to himself) How long can the rope hold where I cut halfway through it?

NARRATOR: All at once, the rope broke with a snap. Fergus went flying head over tail, and Nick was left holding half a broken rope.

NICK: Wow, too bad the rope broke. Want to try it again tomorrow?

FERGUS: No, no. That's fine. We'll call it a draw.

NICK: We could still arm wrestle to see who is strongest.

NARRATOR: Fergus scrambled to his feet and ran.

ERIN: You got lucky this time.

NICK: I was clever.

ERIN: Only if clever suddenly means foolish.

NICK: If I'm so foolish, how do I get myself out of these messes?

ERIN: If you're so smart, why do you get yourself into them?

NICK: Because life isn't any fun till you're at the end of your rope.

FIGURE 5.4 Readers' Theater: *The Great Tug-Of-War*

procedures in an unconscious way. They learn to solve words automatically as they encounter texts.

SAY AND SORT

1. Show words that have a common feature [*counter, around, amount, coward, powder, drowsy*].

2. Students search for patterns, both visual and phonological. [They all have a unique vowel pattern.]

3. Help students to articulate the principle. [Some multisyllable words have a unique vowel pattern.]

4. Students work with partners to apply the principle. [Students sort word magnets by spelling patterns.]

5. Summarize the learning by restating the principle.

BREAK WORDS

1. Break words into parts to read them or write them. [*book/case, fire/place, down/stairs*]

2. Students search for a reason for the way these words are broken. [Students may say that they are compound words and are divided between the two smaller words.]

3. Help students articulate the specific principle. [Some words are made up of two smaller words.]

4. Students work with partners to apply the specific principle. [Students write a list of words in the word study section of their Literacy Notebooks or on a whiteboard and show where to break each word into parts.]

5. Summarize the learning by restating the principle.

Six Areas of Word Learning	
Letter-Sound Relationships (Phonics)	The sounds of oral language are related in both simple and complex ways to the twenty-six letters of the alphabet. Learning the connections between letters and sounds is basic to understanding written language. Students tend to learn the "regular" connections between letters and sounds (*b* for the first sound in *bat*) first. But they also must learn that often letters appear together; for example, it is efficient to think of the two sounds at the beginning of *black* as being together. Sometimes a sound like /sh/ is connected to two letters; sometimes a cluster of letters is connected to one sound, for example /a/ in *freight*. Students learn to look for and recognize these letter combinations as units, which make their word solving more efficient. A few students may need some work with learning the sounds in words (phonemic awareness), then connecting the sounds with individual letters.
Spelling Patterns	Efficient word solvers look for and find patterns in the way words are constructed. Knowing spelling patterns helps students notice and use larger parts of words, thus making word solving faster and easier. Patterns are also helpful to readers in writing words, because they can quickly write down the patterns rather than laboriously working with individual sounds and letters.
High-Frequency Words	A core of high-frequency words is a valuable resource as students build their reading and writing processing systems. We can also call them "high-utility" words because they appear often and can sometimes be used to help solve other words. Making recognition of high-frequency words automatic frees attention to understand meaning as well as solve other new words. In general, readers learn the simpler words, and in the process develop efficient systems for learning more words; the process accelerates. They continuously add to the core of high-frequency words they know. Lessons on high-frequency words can develop automaticity and help readers look more carefully at their features.
Word Meaning/ Vocabulary	Vocabulary refers to the words one knows as part of language. For comprehension and coherence, students need to know the meaning of the words in the texts they read and write. It is important for them to constantly expand their listening, speaking, reading, and writing vocabularies and to develop more complex understandings of words they already know (e.g., words may have multiple meanings or be used figuratively).
Word Structure	Words are built in rule-governed ways. Looking at the structure of words will help students learn how words are related to one another and how they can be changed by adding letters, letter clusters, and larger word parts. Readers who can break down words into syllables and can notice categories of word parts can apply their word-solving strategies efficiently.
Word-Solving Actions	Word solving is related to all the categories of learning previously described, but we have also created a separate category for it that focuses on the strategic moves readers and writers make when they use their knowledge of the language system while reading and writing continuous text. These strategies are "in-the-head" actions that are invisible, although we can often infer them from overt behaviors.

FIGURE 5.5 The Six Areas of Word Learning from *The Continuum of Literacy Learning*

Principle Add a prefix to a word to change its meaning. Add *non-* to mean "not" and *pre-* to mean "before."

Add and Remove Parts

- Show the following words in two columns: *nonfat, nonstick, prepay, prerecord.* Use any word that the students might not understand in a sentence.
- *What do you notice about all of the words?* [Students respond.]
- *What does the beginning word part, or prefix, mean?* [Students respond.]
- Lead students to determine that the prefix *non-* means "not," and the prefix *pre-* means "before."
- Give partners the following words turned facedown on the table: *fiction, heat, sense, school, toxic, test.* In turn, students take a word, add the prefix *non-* or the prefix *pre-* to make a real word, and use it in a sentence.
- Summarize the lesson by restating the principle.
- Give the students the Make It Match Game to play in class or at home.

FIGURE 5.6 Example of Add and Remove Parts

MATCH PAIRS

1. Show students pairs of words that have common features or meanings. Pairs can be matched on any kind of connection. [*cymbal/symbol, whether/weather, aloud/allowed, miner/minor*]

2. Students search for connections between words in pairs. [Students may notice that they sound alike.]

3. Help students articulate the principle. [Some multisyllable words sound alike but are spelled differently and have different meanings.]

4. Students work with partners to apply the principle. [Play a match words game with homophones.]

5. Summarize the learning by restating the principle.

ADD AND REMOVE PARTS

1. Show students word groups with common word parts. [*pretest, preschool, preheat, nonsense, nontoxic, nonfiction*] (See Figure 5.6)

2. Students search for connections between the words. [Students may notice that they all have prefixes.]

3. Help students articulate the principle. [Add a prefix to a word to change its meaning. Add *non-* to mean "not" and *pre-* to mean "before."]

4. Students work with partners to apply the principle. [Students work with base words on word magnets or in their Literacy Notebooks, adding prefixes and using each new word in a sentence.]

5. Summarize the learning by restating the principle.

NOTICE PARTS

1. Show students a group of words with common features. [*dreary, earthquake, fertile, reindeer, serpent, yearly*]

2. Students look at the words to determine the common features. [Students may notice that they all have *er* or *ar*.]

3. Help students understand the principle. [Some multisyllable words have a syllable with a vowel pattern and *r*. Some have an *r*-influenced vowel pattern that sounds like long *e*.]

4. Students work with partners to practice using these spelling patterns. [Students use word magnets and underline the vowel and *r* pattern.]

5. Summarize the learning by restating the principle.

WORDS TO KNOW

1. Show students a group of high-frequency words. [*because, people, though, their, they're, these*]

2. Students look at each word and determine what features will help them remember each word. [Students may notice the *o* in *people*.]

3. Help students understand the principle. [Some multisyllablewords appear frequently in reading and writing.]

4. Students work with partners to practice high-frequency words. [Students use high-frequency words in sentences and write them in the word study section of their Literacy Notebooks or on a whiteboard.]

5. Summarize the learning by restating the principle.

Notice on the Map for Phonics/Word Study (see Appendix B) that every four lessons, the focus of phonics/word study alternates between syllabic and morphemic principles. The syllabic principles include letter-sound relationships, spelling patterns in words, and word-solving actions. Readers learn how to notice and use phonics principles and spelling patterns in single syllable and multisyllable words. They learn how to break multisyllable words and think about the syllable that is emphasized or stressed.

The second major category relates to morphemic principles. This category includes word structures such as plurals, inflectional endings, roots, prefixes, and suffixes as well as word-solving actions. Morphemes are units of meaning. When readers learn how to attend to the morphemes or meaningful parts of words, they learn the building blocks of words.

Instructional Procedures for Writing About Reading

There is a strong relationship between reading and writing. When students write about reading in a way that is meaningful to them, they select, organize, and integrate information. Writing enhances reading comprehension and it also helps students to see text structure and think about aspects of the writer's craft.

Writing about reading involves students in expanding their understanding of the text through writing. All writing is in conventional form as it becomes a text for reading. Students use lined paper in the Literacy Notebook, which also contains a variety of useful resources. They use pencils or ballpoint pens, and teachers use correction tape for student errors.

WRITING IN THE LITERACY NOTEBOOK

To avoid correcting student errors, teach students to use scrap paper or the back of the previous page in the Literacy Notebook or one-inch correction tape:

- ❏ Students can try words they are uncertain about. ["Try it out, and see if it looks right."]

- ❏ Students can copy hard words, like proper names, previously written by the teacher. [*Jill Heinerth*]

- ❏ To help students construct multisyllable words, draw letter boxes for each syllable, and have students say or clap the parts. [Example: *remember*. Teacher says, "Say or clap *remember*." Teacher says, "What is the first part?" Student says, "*re*." Teacher draws two boxes. Teacher says, "Next part?" Student says, "*mem*." Teacher draws three boxes. Teacher says, "Last part?" Student says, "*ber*." Teacher draws three boxes.]

Instead of students erasing their errors, they can use white correction tape so they don't waste time. The finished product should be spelled correctly so it can be revisited at a later time. However, you may choose not to attend to every spelling error.

FORMS OF WRITING

There are several forms of writing used in *LLI* lessons.

1. *Character Sketch*
   Students write a brief description of one of the main characters, citing evidence that supports their thinking. [Choose a character, tell why, and briefly describe what the person is like.]

2. *Persuasive Paragraph*
   In a paragraph, students state their opinion of an issue presented in the text in a way that would persuade others to agree with them. [State opinion about a decision made in the book and convince others to agree with you.]

3. *Interview Questions*
   Students write questions they would like to ask the subject of a biographical text. [Compose questions to ask the subject of a biography.]

4. *Argument*
   Students describe the problem and its causes presented in a text. Then they write an argument in support of solutions, citing evidence from the text. [Describe the problem presented and tell why it needs to be resolved.]

5. *Outline*
   Students use the headings, subheadings, and sub-subheadings in an informational text to create an outline of the book. [Use heading, subheadings, and sub-subheadings from the informational text.]

6. *Short Write*
   Students write briefly on a specific aspect of a book. [Take a position on a book with multiple perspectives, empathize with a specific character.]

7. *Two-Column Writing*
   Students record information in two columns in the word study section of their Literacy Notebooks, often citing evidence for their thinking. [Compare and contrast two characters, state the cause/effect of an issue presented in a text.]

8. *Three-Column Writing*
   Students record information in three columns in the word study section of their Literacy Notebooks, often citing evidence for their thinking. [Describe the different characteristics of two characters in the right and left column and then how they are the same in the middle column.]

9. *List*
   Students use words or phrases related to the information in a book. [Make a list of what scientists learned about certain animals.]

10. *Letter*
    Students write letters to the teacher, either taking a position or writing from a character's perspective. You always respond in writing, but it is not necessary to provide a long response. [Write a letter stating personal opinion related to a problem stated in a text.]

11. *Summary*
    Students write a summary of the whole story or the big idea in a few sentences. [Summarize the events from a character's point of view; three- or four-sentence summary telling what is important in the book.]

12. *Graphic Organizer*
    Students use a graphic organizer to present specific information from a text in an organized way. The graphic organizer will be created on a page or glued into the writing section of their Literacy Notebooks [Character Analysis, Character Web, Story Map, Four Square, Timeline, Venn Diagram].

TYPES OF WRITING

There are three kinds of writing in *LLI* lessons. Before writing about reading you will always engage students in a conversation to encourage and extend their thinking and talking about a portion of the book reread in the lesson. There is a suggested type of writing in every even-numbered standard lesson; however, at any point you should choose the type of writing based upon the needs of your students. For example, early on in lessons you may want to choose shared and dictated writing to demonstrate how to compose and problem solve before asking for independent writing.

Shared Writing

In shared writing, talk with students about the book and compose a response to the reading. Contribute to the conversation in a way that deepens their thinking and expands their language. Their ideas are written on a chart:

1. There is conversation throughout the process that helps reveal the writing about reading process.

2. With your support, students negotiate the response sentence by sentence.

3. You write the response on a chart that everyone can see.

4. Students read what has been written.

5. The response students have produced becomes a resource. Students may copy all or part of the response into the writing section of their Literacy Notebooks if time allows. Or you can write or type the response for the students to glue into their Literacy Notebooks for the next day.

The value of shared writing is that it engages students in every aspect of the writing about reading process in a highly supportive way.

Dictated Writing

In dictated writing, talk with students about an aspect of the book.

1. You dictate three or four sentences to the students. Read the whole message and then read it sentence by sentence, repeating as needed.

2. Students write the dictated sentences with your support in the writing section of their Literacy Notebooks. You keep the writing moving along.

3. Some of the words will be known. For unknown words, help students engage in word solving, using word parts and letter sequences or syllables by quickly drawing Elkonin boxes on the back of the previous page. You can also write a word for a student. For common unknown words, like proper nouns, write the words on a whiteboard for the students to copy.

4. Students read their writing once or several times.

5. Suggested sentences are provided in the lessons, but you may want to use sentences that were generated from the conversation. You can revisit the text for a particular teaching point if time allows.

The value of dictated writing is that it gives students an opportunity to write and reread a well-constructed response with a clear concept.

Independent Writing

In independent writing, you talk with students about the book using specific ideas and vocabulary (see Figure 5.7).

1. Students compose their responses. You may need to help individuals shape or extend the language through conversation. You may also need to help them remember their compositions.

2. Students write their responses in the writing section of their Literacy Notebooks.

3. Some of the words will be known. For unknown words, help students engage in word solving, using word parts, letter sequences, and syllables. Make use of Elkonin boxes on the practice page to facilitate the word solving if needed. For especially difficult words, show the words on a whiteboard or paper.

4. Students reread their writing to monitor for content and spelling.

5. Students reread their writing to you or a partner.

The value of independent writing is that students develop independent control over all aspects of composition and recording of writing about reading. They learn to monitor for content and spelling and capitalization.

USING ELKONIN BOXES TO SUPPORT WORD CONSTRUCTION

D. B. Elkonin, a Russian psychologist, developed a tool for helping students think about the sounds and letters in words. The technique has also been used by Marie Clay and other researchers and educators.

We have not specified in the lessons where to use the scaffold of sound or letter boxes. You will need to decide when they will be helpful to individual students. You will model by drawing the boxes and support students in using them.

Below are descriptions of different Elkonin boxes.

1. *Sound Boxes with Letters (sound analysis)*
   For sound boxes with letters, students say the word slowly and write the letters that represent the sounds in sequence. Make one box for every sound (not letter) in every word.

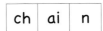

2. *Letter Boxes (visual analysis)*
   Students say the word slowly and write letters in the boxes. They learn to think about how words look. Make one box for each letter. Knowing that the boxes for sounds and letters don't necessarily match, helps students attend to spelling patterns.

p	l	e	a	s	e

3. *Working without Boxes (single syllable words)*
   Students use sound analysis while writing new words. They say words slowly to hear the sounds and write letters and letter clusters.

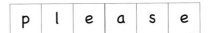

Writing About Reading

Suggested Language

Independent Writing Letter

- *In the writing section of your Literacy Notebook, write a letter to me about this story and what it makes you think. Be sure to include what you think the writer's message is.*
- You may want to list on the board what should be included in the assignment.

Dear Ms G,

I think that Bobby was just so miserable because he had to move that he wouldn't unpack and he didn't really want to get to know any new friends. I can understand that because when I went to visit my grandmother I was the same way. But he was lucky because he had Thelma, even though he was worried about her, and he had his interest in spiders.

He felt more at home because of his friendship with Lucky and the science teacher helping him. One thing that was important was the conflict with Chick. This helped him come out of his shell and stand up for himself. He did that.

In the end, Bobby felt at home in New York. He had friends and Thelma was still alive. She had molted. He had a new tarantula. It didn't replace Monk, but it was a good spider. Bobby got more into things like football, and he had a good time at the dance. But he didn't completely change. He still played the trick of the fake tarantula on Butch.

The message of this story is that you have to use what you like and know to help you when you are in a new place that isn't very good. Also, you should try to make new friends. Bobby didn't ever give up his interest with spiders and that helped him. He loved his tarantulas. If I moved, I would still keep thinking about my dog.

Sincerely,
Dirk

FIGURE 5.7 Example of Independent Writing Letter

4. *Letter Boxes (multisyllable words)*
Students say or clap the syllables in a multisyllable word as you make the boxes for one syllable at a time. They work syllable by syllable, recording the letters in a sequence.

r	e	m	e	m	b	e	r

5. *Working without Boxes (multisyllable words)*
Students say words in syllables, write the sounds they hear, and think about how they look.

▶ Instructional Tools for *LLI*

The following are instructional tools that are used throughout *LLI* lessons to support your instruction.

The Continuum of Literacy Learning

See Figure 5.8 for an example of *The Continuum of Literacy Learning* material that is included at the end of each level in the *Lesson Guide*. It lists specific behaviors and understandings that are required for students to read successfully at the level. These behaviors and understandings are cumulative across the levels. They include important competencies students need to think within, beyond, and about texts. In other words, the reader is taking on a variety of new demands as the texts grow more challenging. The reader will also be applying the same strategic actions but in more sophisticated ways to more complex texts. For example, a student reading at level Q and successfully meeting the demands of the text is also able to meet the demands of texts at levels O and P. The understandings include much more than simply reading the words accurately. This section also includes additional suggestions for word work. If your students have good control of the principles in the Phonics/Word Study part of the lessons, you might substitute one of the options. Or, you may want to offer some of the suggestions to the classroom teacher.

All *LLI* lessons are designed to help you accomplish the goals listed in *The Continuum of Literacy Learning* for the level. Your goal is to help readers meet the demands of successive levels of text and in the process, expand their systems of strategic actions.

Refer regularly to this section to monitor student progress and guide your teaching.

The following suggestions may contribute to greater effectiveness in teaching in your lessons:

❑ Read each new book carefully with *The Continuum of Literacy Learning* goals in mind. Think about what your students can do, and then find behaviors and understandings that they control, partially control, or do not yet control.

❑ Read the introduction to the text and teaching points for the lesson, keeping in mind the processing needs of your students. Make any adjustments you think are necessary to meet the needs of your particular students.

❑ Look at the Phonics/Word Study part of the lesson and the suggestions for word work at that level in *The Continuum of Literacy Learning*. Make any adjustments you think are necessary to meet the needs of your particular students.

❑ As you near the end of a series of 28 lessons (including 24 standard lessons and 4 novel study lessons), look at *The Continuum of Literacy Learning* to see what your students now control and what they need to know to successfully process texts easily at this level.

❑ As students grow more proficient and reading becomes easy at the level, look at the behaviors and understandings for the next higher level. You'll find many of the same strategies for which you've been teaching because the reading process is built by applying the same set of complex strategies to increasingly more difficult texts. You may find new understandings or more complex versions of the same understandings. Start to look toward this next level.

Prompting Guides, Part 1 and *Part 2*

Prompting Guide, Part 1 is a tool for you to use to support students as they read or write. It contains precise language that can be used to teach for, prompt for, and reinforce effective strategic actions in oral reading and writing. *Prompting Guide, Part 1* is also available as an app from the Apple iTunes App Store.

The prompts are a call for the reader to take some quick action so as not to interrupt the reader's continuous processing of meaning. A prompt requires the reader to problem solve with your support.

Readers at **Level S:**

At level S, readers automatically read and understand a full range of genres, including biographies on less well-known subjects, more complex fantasy, and hybrid texts that blend more than one genre in a coherent whole. They read both chapter books and shorter informational texts; also, they read special forms such as mysteries, series books, books with sequels, short stories, diaries, and logs. Fiction narratives are straightforward but have elaborate plots and many complex characters who develop and change over time. As readers, they understand perspectives different from their own as well as settings and people far distant in time and space. They can process sentences (some with more than fifteen words) that are complex, contain prepositional phrases, introductory clauses, lists of nouns, verbs, or adjectives, and they solve new vocabulary words, some defined in the text and others unexplained. Most reading is silent; fluency and phrasing in oral reading are well established. Readers are challenged by many longer descriptive words and by content-specific and technical words that require using embedded definitions, background knowledge, and readers' tools, such as glossaries. They can take apart multisyllable words and use a full range of word-solving skills. They read and understand texts in a variety of layouts as well as fonts and print characteristics and consistently search for information in illustrations and increasingly complex graphics.

Thinking **Within** the Text

Solving Words

- Notice new and interesting words, record them, and actively add them to speaking or writing vocabulary
- Determine the meaning of academic and topic-related words in a text
- Demonstrate knowledge of flexible ways to solve words (noticing word parts, noticing endings and prefixes)
- Solve multisyllable words (many with three or more syllables) using vowel patterns, phonogram patterns, affixes, and other word parts
- Solve content-specific words and technical words using graphics and definitions embedded in the text as well as background knowledge
- Solve some undefined words using background knowledge
- Use readers' tools such as glossaries, dictionaries, and pronunciation guides to solve words, including difficult proper nouns and technical words
- Understand connotative meaning and figurative use of words
- Use the context of a sentence, paragraph, or whole text to determine the meaning of a word
- Develop deeper understanding of words that have been encountered before but are not fully known
- Identify words with multiple meanings, discuss alternative meanings, and select the precise meaning within the text
- Apply problem-solving strategies to technical words or proper nouns
- Understand words with multiple meanings
- Understand words that represent abstract concepts
- Use illustrations in graphic texts to derive meaning of words
- Notice unusual use of words in graphic texts (e.g., onomatopoetic words)

Monitoring and Correcting

- Continue to monitor accuracy and understanding, self-correcting when errors detract from meaning

Searching for and Using Information

- Search for information in graphics (simple diagrams, illustrations with labels, maps, charts, captions under pictures)
- Use a full range of readers' tools to search for information (table of contents, glossary, headings and subheadings, call-outs, pronunciation guides, index, references)
- Process long sentences (fifteen or more words) that are carried over several lines or to the next page
- Process sentences with embedded clauses (parenthetical material, prepositional phrases, introductory clauses, series of nouns, verbs, or adverbs)
- Process a wide range of complex dialogue, some unassigned
- Process texts with a variety of complex layouts and with some pages of dense print
- Remember the details of complex plots with many episodes
- Form implicit questions and search for answers while reading
- Process long stretches of descriptive language and remember pertinent information
- Respond to plot tension by reading to seek problem resolutions
- Sustain attention to a text read over several days, remembering details and revising interpretations as new events are encountered
- Notice details in illustrations that provide insight into characters' feelings or motives in graphic texts or convey action

Summarizing

- Follow and remember a series of events and the story problem and solution over a longer text in order to understand the ending
- Remember information in summary form over chapters, a series of short stories, or sequels in order to understand larger themes
- Identify important ideas in a text (including some longer and more complex narratives) and report them in an organized way, either orally or in writing
- Explain events, procedures, ideas, or concepts in a historical, scientific, or technical text (including what happened and why) based on specific information in the text
- Summarize a text at intervals during the reading of a longer text

Maintaining Fluency

- Read dialogue with phrasing and expression that reflects understanding of characters and events
- Demonstrate appropriate stress on words, pausing and phrasing, intonation, and use of punctuation while reading in a way that reflects understanding

Adjusting

- Change style and pace of reading to reflect purpose
- Adjust reading to process texts with difficult and complex layout
- Reread to solve words or think about ideas and resume good rate of reading
- Change purpose and aspects of processing to reflect understanding of genre
- In graphic texts, simultaneously follow illustrations and print

927

FIGURE 5.8A An Example of *The Continuum of Literacy Learning* pages from the *Lesson Guide* (Page 1 of 3)

Thinking **Beyond** the Text

Predicting

- Make a wide range of predictions based on personal experiences, content knowledge, and knowledge of similar texts
- Search for and use information to confirm or disconfirm predictions
- Justify predictions using evidence
- Change predictions as new information is gathered from a text
- Make predictions based on illustrations in graphic texts

Making Connections

- Make connections between the reader's real-life experiences and people who live in diverse cultures, distant places, and different times
- Bring background knowledge to the understanding of a text before, during, and after reading
- Bring knowledge from personal experiences to the interpretation of texts, particularly content related to preadolescents
- Make connections between the text and other texts that have been read or heard (particularly texts with diverse settings) and demonstrate in writing
- Use knowledge from one text to help in understanding diverse cultures and settings encountered in new texts
- Make connections between characters in different texts (similar setting, type of problem, type of person)
- Specify the nature of connections (topic, content, type of story, writer)

Synthesizing

- Mentally form categories of related information and revise them as new information is acquired across the text
- Demonstrate learning new content from reading
- Express changes in ideas or perspective across the reading (as events unfold) after reading a text
- Acquire new content and perspectives through reading both fiction and nonfiction texts about diverse cultures, times, and places
- Incorporate new knowledge to better understand characters and plots from material previously read when reading chapters, connected short stories, or sequels
- Draw conclusions from information
- Integrate information from two texts on the same topic in order to discuss or write about it

Inferring

- Infer cause and effect in influencing characters' feelings or motives
- Infer characters' feelings and motivations through reading their dialogue and what other characters say about them
- Follow multiple characters in different episodes, inferring their feelings about and influence on each other
- Infer setting, characters' traits and feelings, and plot from illustrations in graphic texts
- Demonstrate understandings of characters (their traits, how and why they change), using evidence to support statements
- Take perspectives that may be unfamiliar in interpreting characters' motives, causes for action, or themes
- Apply inferring to multiple characters and complex plots, with some subplots
- Infer the big ideas or themes of a text (some texts with mature themes and issues) and discuss how they are applicable to people's lives today
- Speculate on alternative meanings that the text may have
- Infer the meaning of symbols that the writer is using
- Infer causes of problems or of outcomes in fiction and nonfiction texts
- Identify significant events and tell how they are related to the plot

Thinking Beyond the Text

Involves bringing one's own thinking to the text to go beyond the literal meaning.

928

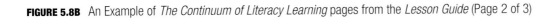

FIGURE 5.8B An Example of *The Continuum of Literacy Learning* pages from the *Lesson Guide* (Page 2 of 3)

Thinking About the Text

Involves awareness of writer's craft and the ability to analyze and critique the text.

LEVEL **S** **Behaviors** and **Understandings** to Notice, Teach, and Support

Thinking About the Text

Analyzing

- Notice and discuss aspects of genres (realistic and historical fiction, fantasy, biography, autobiography, memoir and diaries, and other nonfiction)
- Notice combined genres in hybrid texts
- Understand and talk about the overall text structure and underlying organizational structures (description, compare/contrast, temporal sequence, problem/solution, cause/effect)
- Demonstrate the ability to identify how an informational text is organized (categories, sequence, etc.)
- Identify and evaluate arguments and conclusions in persuasive texts
- Notice how the author or illustrator has used pictures and other graphics to convey meaning or create mood
- Notice and interpret figurative language and discuss how it changes a text
- Notice descriptive language and how it adds to enjoyment or understanding
- Recognize the use of figurative or descriptive language (or special types of language such as irony) and talk about how it adds to the quality (enjoyment and understanding) of a text

- Understand the role of setting in realistic and historical fiction as well as fantasy
- Notice how the writer built interest and suspense across a story
- Analyze complex plots and sometimes represent in diagrams or drawings
- Notice aspects of a writer's craft (style, language, perspective, themes) after reading several texts by him/her
- Notice writer's use of symbolism
- Identify similarities and differences across texts
- Identify author's implicitly stated purpose
- Identify main ideas and supporting details
- Identify elements such as setting, plot, resolution, and conflict
- Identify multiple points of view
- Notice how illustrations and text work together in graphic texts
- Notice aspects of the writer/illustrator's style in graphic texts
- Compare and contrast the points of view from which different stories are narrated including the difference between first and third person narration

Critiquing

- Evaluate the text in terms of readers' own experience as preadolescents
- Assess how graphics add to the quality of the text or provide additional information
- Notice and talk about the author's qualifications to write nonfiction
- Hypothesize how characters could have behaved differently
- Assess whether a text is authentic and consistent with life experience or prior knowledge (for example, in historical fiction)
- Express tastes and preferences in reading and support choices with specific descriptions of text features (plots, language, characters, genres)

Additional Suggestions

These suggestions are based on the kinds of word-solving strategies readers need to take words apart efficiently at this level.

Additional Suggestions for Letter/Word Work

Letter/Word Work One- to three-minute demonstrations with active student engagement using a chart or easel, whiteboard, or pencil and paper can develop fluency and flexibility in visual processing. Plan for explicit work in specific visual processing areas that need support.

- Add, delete, change letter clusters to make or take apart words (*giver/shiver/shivered/shivery*)
- Read words with a full range of plurals, including irregular plurals (*cactus/cacti*) and plurals that require spelling changes (*spy/spies*)
- Work flexibly with base words, making new words by changing letters and adding prefixes and suffixes (*ordinary/ordinarily/extraordinary*)
- Recognize and understand words that have multiple meanings, homographs (look the same, sound different: *address, address*), and homophones (sound the same, look different: *wade, weighed*), sound and look the same (*story*)
- Take apart words with complex phonograms and long vowel patterns, including vowel patterns with *r* (VVCC (*faint*), VVCe (*praise*), VCCe (*lunge*), VCCC (*crunch*), VVCCC (*straight*))

- Take apart and understand words with several syllables (*mis-rep-re-sen-ta-tion*)
- Read frequently appearing syllable patterns in multisyllable words (*-er-* in *other, service*)
- Use what is known about words to read new words (*path, sympathy*)
- Recognize words in which several different letters or clusters represent a single sound (/k/ = *ck* in *duck*, *que* in *unique*, *k* in *kayak*, *ch* in *choir*)
- Read words using open (ending in a vowel: *ri-val*) and closed (ending in a consonant: *riv-er*) syllables

929

FIGURE 5.8C An Example of *The Continuum of Literacy Learning* pages from the *Lesson Guide* (Page 3 of 3)

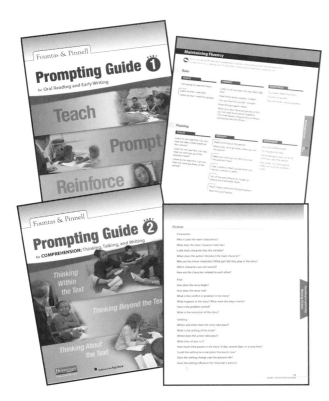

FIGURE 5.9 *Prompting Guides, Part 1* and *Part 2* sample pages

- ❑ Commonly Misspelled Words
- ❑ Graphic Organizers
- ❑ Fiction Text Structure
- ❑ Nonfiction Text Structure
- ❑ Rules for Capitalization
- ❑ Rules for Punctuation

Word Study (Figure 5.10B)

- ❑ Initial Consonant Clusters and Digraphs
- ❑ Final Consonant Clusters and Digraphs
- ❑ Sound of *k* Chart
- ❑ Silent Letters
- ❑ Vowel Sounds Charts
- ❑ Types of Syllables
- ❑ Breaking Multisyllable Words
- ❑ Affixes Charts
- ❑ Word Roots
- ❑ Plurals
- ❑ Homophones and Homographs Charts
- ❑ Multiple-Meaning Words
- ❑ Synonyms and Antonyms Charts
- ❑ High-Frequency Words

Prompting Guide, Part 2 is a tool for teaching readers to focus or expand their thinking. These prompts can be used during discussion, after the reading, and when revisiting the text and are designed to deepen understanding. Use these prompts to engage students in expanding their thinking about the meaning of the text. *Prompting Guides, Part 1* and *Part 2* are also available in Spanish, and as eBooks from the Apple iTunes App Store.

The Literacy Notebook

The Literacy Notebook is a place for students to work out words and to share their thinking about texts. One 72-page Literacy Notebook is provided per level. The notebooks are two-way books, including one section for word study, and one for writing about reading. Students open the book in one direction and then flip it over to find the other section. Each of the two sections includes several pages of tools and resources, followed by blank, lined pages. The resources include the following:

Writing About Reading (Figure 5.10A)

- ❑ Guidelines for Checking Your Writing
- ❑ Friendly Letter Form

Word Games, Sorts, and Classroom/Home Activities

Word and phonics games are additional tools for helping students practice some foundational concepts about how words work. The games are fun and interesting and require students to look carefully at words and parts of words, while giving them multiple exposures to them.

All game directions and game boards are printable from the Online Resources site. In the *Gold System*, there are seven basic games, word sorts, and word lists.

1. Stress Me Out!
2. Make It or Break It
3. Word Slap!
4. Pick-a-Pair
5. Lotto
6. Make It Match
7. Draw 3
8. Practice Sort
9. Word List

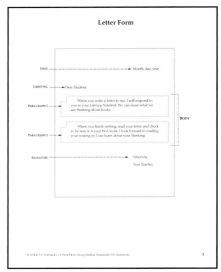

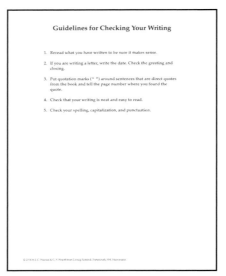

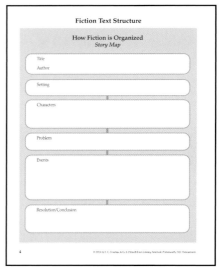

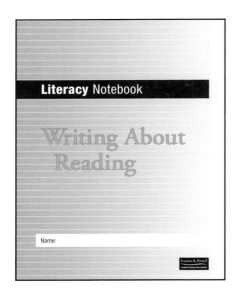

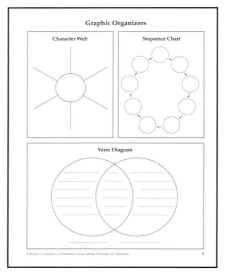

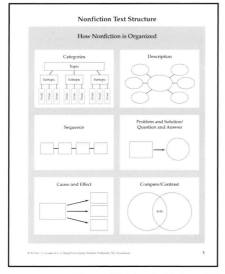

FIGURE 5.10A Literacy Notebooks Tools and Resources for Writing About Reading

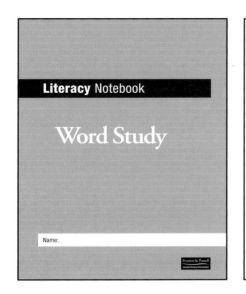

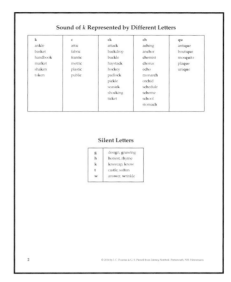

FIGURE 5.10B Literacy Notebooks Tools and Resources for Word Study

Homophones

ant – aunt	cymbal –symbol	patience – patients
assistants – assistance	flew – flu	peddle – pedal
ate – eight	flower – flour	plane – plain
board – bored	hanger – hanger	presence – presents
boarder – border	heard – herd	principal – principle
bolder – boulder	higher – hire	some – sum
break – brake	hoarse – horse	stair – stare
capital – capitol	hole – whole	sundae – Sunday
ceiling – sealing	knows – nose	their – there
cellar – seller	lessen – lesson	threw – through
cents – scents	miner – minor	waist – waste
cereal – serial	missed – mist	way – weigh
choral – coral	morning – mourning	weather – whether
close – clothes	muscle – mussel	wood – would

Homographs

batter	hamper	pupil
compact	husky	racket
console	invalid	refuse
content	lighten	second
converse	lumber	sewer
counter	meter	stable
cricket	minute	staple
desert	pitcher	story
dresser	poker	swallow
flounder	present	temple

9

Multiple-Meaning Words

back	court	fall	land	patient	sink	star
bed	deck	foot	letter	program	skip	watch
block	draw	glass	notice	roll	space	wave
blue	face	handle	organ	season	sheet	stamp

Synonyms

answer – response	faithful – loyal
clever – intelligent	gentleness – tenderness
competence – ability	grateful – thankful
couple – duo	important – significant
defend – uphold	mislead – deceive
delete – remove	mistake – error
deny – reject	occur – happen
divide – separate	praise – compliment
evil – malicious	surprise – amazement
expensive – valuable	truthful – honest

Antonyms

abundant – scarce	identical – different
allow – forbid	increase – decrease
answer – question	nervous – unafraid
appear – vanish	organized – messy
benefit – disadvantage	partial – complete
boring – exciting	preserve – destroy
clever – foolish	release – retain
confident – fearless	request – reply
fantasy – reality	simple – difficult
gigantic – miniscule	tardy – early
guilty – innocent	unusual – common

10

High-Frequency Words

about	children	heard	possible	thousand
against	clothes	heart	probably	through
already	complete	hundred	problem	together
although	could	important	question	toward
always	country	instead	really	trouble
among	different	knowledge	reason	usually
animal	difficult	large	said	walk
another	direction	learn	scared	want
around	early	listen	second	watch
beautiful	enough	live	several	were
because	every	many	simple	what
been	except	nothing	solve	where
believe	favorite	once	somewhere	whether
between	finally	one	special	which
brother	found	only	suddenly	while
brought	frequently	other	their	would
caught	friend	people	these	written
center	from	perhaps	they're	wrong
certain	happened	picture	though	young
change	happily	piece	thought	yourself

11

© 2014 by I. C. Fountas & G. S. Pinnell from *Literacy Notebook*. Portsmouth, NH: Heinemann.

FIGURE 5.10B Literacy Notebooks Tools and Resources for Word Study, *cont.*

STRESS ME OUT!

Cut apart the word cards. Use the game board and a game piece for each player. The objective is for players to pick a word card, decide whether the stress is on the first or second syllable of the word, and move their game pieces along the game board.

Game Directions:

1. Shuffle the cards, and create a draw pile.

2. Have players begin at the START circle on the game board.

3. Taking turns, each player turns over one card.

4. If the card is a word card, the player determines whether the stress is on the first or second syllable.

5. If the player correctly identifies the stressed syllable, she moves her game piece ahead to the nearest 1 if the first syllable is stressed or to the nearest 2 if the second syllable is stressed.

6. If the player is unable to identify correctly the stressed syllable, she remains on her spot until her next turn.

7. If the player draws a direction card, she moves her piece according to the direction on that card.

8. Players put the used cards in a discard pile. If the draw pile runs out of cards before someone wins, the players shuffle the cards in the discard pile and place them facedown, creating a new draw pile.

9. The first player to reach the WIN circle wins.

MAKE IT OR BREAK IT

Cut apart the word cards. The objective is for players to select a word card and, based on the card they choose, decide whether they need to make or break a word using the lesson principle.

Game Directions:

1. Shuffle the word cards, and lay all the cards facedown.

2. Taking turns, each player turns over one card.

3. Based on the lesson principle, the player decides whether he should make or break the word on the card. For example, if the card shows the whole word *welcome*, he would tell where to break the word into syllables—*wel/come*. If the card shows the word divided into syllables, *den/tist*, he would put the parts together and say the whole word, *dentist*.

4. If the player is able to correctly make or break a word based on the lesson principle, he keeps the word card. If the player is unable to make or break a word, he returns the card facedown.

5. The player with the most word cards at the end wins.

WORD SLAP!

Cut apart the word cards. The objective is for players to identify whether two word cards match based on the lesson principle (e.g., same vowel pattern, same beginning or ending sound).

Game Directions:

1. Deal the cards facedown, one at a time, creating a draw pile for each player.

2. At the same time, two players each turn over one card.

3. If the players turn over word cards that match, the first player to slap her own pile and say, "Slap!" takes both cards and puts them aside in a match pile. If the words do not match, players place the cards in a discard pile. When players have no more cards in their draw piles, they shuffle the discard pile and deal each player a draw pile.

4. Players continue to draw cards until all the cards are gone. The player with the most sets of matched word cards at the end wins.

PICK-A-PAIR

Cut apart the word cards. The objective is for players to gather matching pairs of word cards (e.g., homophones, antonyms, synonyms).

Game Directions:

1. Shuffle the cards and lay them facedown in rows.

2. Taking turns, each player turns over two cards.

3. If the words match, the player takes the pair and turns over two more cards. The player continues turning over two cards at a time until the words do not match.

4. If the words do not match, the player turns both cards back over, ending her turn.

5. If the first card a player turns over is a WILD card, the player keeps the WILD card and turns over two more cards in search of a match. If the second card a player turns over is a WILD card, the player turns over one more card to try to find a matching pair. If a match is made, the player keeps the WILD card and the pair. If no match is made, the player keeps the WILD card and turns the other two cards back over, ending her turn.

6. The player who has the most cards at the end wins.

LOTTO

Cut apart the word cards. Use a different game board and 16 plastic chips or pennies per player. The objective is for players to match the word cards with the words on the game boards.

Game Directions:

1. Each player should cover his FREE space with a chip or penny.

2. Players take turns drawing word cards and reading the cards.

3. If any player has a match to the word card, the player covers the space on his game board with a chip or penny.

4. The first player to cover all the words on his game board wins.

MAKE IT MATCH

Cut apart the word cards. The objective is for players to collect pairs of word cards, each pair making a match or creating a new word (e.g., plurals, prefixes, suffixes).

Game Directions:

1. Shuffle the word cards, and divide them to create two draw piles.

2. The first player selects a card from each draw pile.

3. If a player can make a match or new word with the two cards drawn from the piles, she keeps both cards and puts them aside in a match pile.

4. If a player cannot make a match or new word with the two cards drawn from the piles, she chooses one card to keep and returns the other card to the bottom of either draw pile.

5. Players take turns drawing from both piles. Players can make a match using the two cards they draw or using one of the cards they draw and one of the cards they kept from a previous turn.

6. The first player who makes five matches or new words wins.

DRAW 3 (GO FISH VARIATION)

Cut apart the word cards. The objective is to collect as many sets of three words as possible (e.g., *heavy heavier, heaviest*).

Game Directions:

1. Shuffle the word cards, and create a draw pile. Each player draws three cards from the pile. Then in turn, players either draw a card from the pile or ask another player for a word that can be used to make a set. For example, if a player has the word *heavy*, he might ask, "Do you have *heavier*?"

2. If the player has the word that was asked for, he gives it away. If the player does not have the word, he says, "draw," and the player who asked for the word draws a card from the pile.

3. The game continues as players try to make complete sets. When a player has a complete set of three words, he places it aside. The game ends when all cards in the pile have been drawn.

4. The player with the most complete sets at the end wins.

PRACTICE SORT

In this activity, students will be given a set of words that they will sort or categorize based on shared features or principles. For example, students sort words that share a common vowel sound or words that share the same spelling rule when adding a suffix.

WORD LIST

In this activity, students apply a phonics or word study principle using words chosen from a list. For example, students write pairs of homographs in sentences to show the different meanings of the words. Students complete this work in the word study section of the Literacy Notebook.

Graphic Organizers for Writing About Reading

Graphic organizers including a Character Web, Timeline, and Story Sequence Chart can be printed from the Online Resources site. They can be used to help students organize their thinking about their writing (see Figure 5.11).

Maps for Phonics/Word Study and Vocabulary

See Appendices B and C of this book for the Phonics/Word Study and Vocabulary Maps. These plans show the sequence of teaching in these two areas, across the *Gold System*. Using *The Continuum of Literacy Learning* pages in the *Lesson Guide* for each level, you may choose to vary the principles, spending more or less time on them.

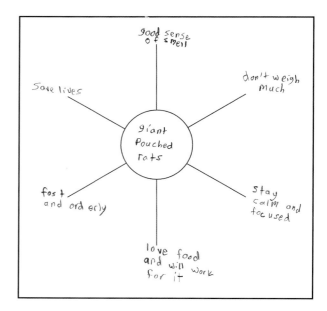

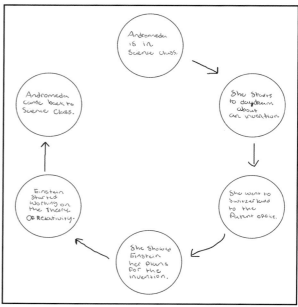

Cause	Effect	Cause	Effect	Cause	Effect
Roman custom of bathing spread	People started to bathe.	Black Death	People stopped bathing.	Discovery that germs cause disease.	People take lots of baths.
500 B.C.E to 1300 C.E.	Before 1350 C.E	1350 C.E.	1350 to 1800 C.E.	1800s	1800s to today

FIGURE 5.11 Graphic Organizers for Writing About Reading

section 6

Assessment and Record Keeping in the *LLI System*

▶ Ongoing Assessment

Assessment is the act of collecting information or data about the learners you teach. When you assess your students for the start of the intervention, you collect important information about each student's reading level, comprehension, fluency, and processing strategies. This information is critical for beginning instruction at an appropriate level and with appropriate emphases, but students will change rapidly. You will collect more valuable information from your daily informal observations of the students as they read and write during lessons. You will also take a reading record on each student approximately every two weeks. This standardized assessment will capture the reading behaviors the reader controls independently. Over time, you can use these reading records to monitor progress. This section of the

System Guide provides suggestions, examples, and forms to collect, analyze, and organize the formal and informal data that you will need to guide your instruction.

▶ Administering the Reading Record Using the Recording Form

A reading record is a systematic tool used to code, score, and analyze a student's precise reading behaviors. You use a standardized system to gain an objective assessment of the student's reading *without* your teaching support. You learn what students can do independently at their levels.

Take a reading record on one student during the "Rereading and Assessment" section of the standard even-numbered lessons. You will have a reading record on every student in the group about every two weeks (See Figure 6.1).

We have provided a Recording Form for each new instructional level book read in the standard (odd-numbered) lessons; forms can be printed from the Online Resources site. During the second part of each even-numbered standard lesson (Rereading Books and

Page 1 (form)

Student: Angelia Grade: 4 Date: _____
Teacher: Mrs. Ha School: _____

Recording Form
Part One: Oral Reading

Excerpt is taken from pages 7–9

Running words: 296

Summary of Scores:	
Accuracy	97%
Self-correction	1
Fluency	3
Comprehension	8

Teacher: Chicle is a sticky substance that comes from sapodilla trees in Central America. Read this section to find out how one entrepreneur and inventor turned a mistake into a successful business.

Sources of Information Used

Page	Text	E	SC	E (M S V)	SC (M S V)
7	Oops!				
	Then, one man's mistake produced a better chewing gum.				
	A Mexican general named Antonio Lopez de Santa Anna				
	needed money. He decided he could make it by selling *(would)*				
	chicle, and he convinced an American inventor named				
	Thomas Adams that chicle could be made into tires.	1		(M) (S) (V)	
	It was 1869 and people needed tires for their carriages.				
	Chicle was cheap and the rubber usually used to make				
	tires was very expensive. Santa Anna and Adams thought				
	they would make a fortune if Adams could make a rubber				
	substitute out of chicle.				
	Subtotal	2 0 1 1 1 0 0 0			

Fountas & Pinnell Leveled Literacy Intervention 1

Page 2 (form)

Part One: Oral Reading *continued*

Sources of Information Used

Page	Text	E	SC	E (M S V)	SC (M S V)
8	Santa Anna handed Adams a knob of gray chicle				
	covered in bark and rocks. Soon after, Adams bought about *(James/SC)* *(Adam)*	1	m (S) v	(m) (S) (V)	
	a ton more of chicle to use in experiments. Adams and his	1		(M) (S) (V)	
	family tried for a year to make something like rubber from				
	the chicle. They had no luck. Chicle, it turned out, was not *(a)*	1		(m) (S) (V)	
	a good material to use to make tires.				
	Then one day Adams was in a drugstore. He watched a				
	girl buy a penny's worth of chewing gum. The shopkeeper				
	told Adams the gum he sold was made of paraffin wax, *(was)* *(from para v)*	2		(M) (S) (V)	
	and that it was not good to chew. Adams immediately *(Adam)*	1		(M) (S) (V)	
	thought of all the chicle he had left at home from his	1		(m) (S) v	
	failed tire experiments. Perhaps he could use the chewy				
	substance to make and sell a better type of gum.				
	Subtotal	6 1 5 6 2 1 0 1			

2 *Fountas & Pinnell Leveled Literacy Intervention*

Page 3 (form)

Part One: Oral Reading *continued*

Sources of Information Used

Page	Text	E	SC	E (M S V)	SC (M S V)
9	Adams began to experiment with the chicle once again.				
	Soon, he found that the dried resin would not dissolve in				
	water, which meant it wouldn't dissolve inside a person's				
	mouth, either. He molded pieces of chicle into balls—the				
	first gumballs—and began selling them. *(gumball)*	1		(m) (S) (v)	
	Soon drugstores wanted more. This time, Adams molded *(added/Adam)*				
	the gum into sticks and wrapped them in tissue paper. His				
	gum business was ready to take off.				
	Subtotal	1 0 1 0 1 0 0 0			
	End Time ___ min. ___ sec. **Total**	9 1 7 7 4 1 0 1			

Fountas & Pinnell Leveled Literacy Intervention 3

Page 4 (form)

Accuracy Rate	Errors	17 or more	14–16	11–13	8–10	5–7	2–4	0–1
	%	Below 95%	95%	96%	(97%)	98%	99%	100%

Self-Corrections 1

Fluency Score 0 1 2 (3)

Fluency Scoring Key

0 Reads primarily word-by-word with occasional but infrequent or inappropriate phrasing; no smooth or expressive interpretation, irregular pausing, and no attention to author's meaning or punctuation; no stress or inappropriate stress, and slow rate.

1 Reads primarily in two-word phrases with some three- and four-word groups and some word-by-word reading; almost no smooth, expressive interpretation or pausing guided by author's meaning and punctuation; almost no stress or inappropriate stress, with slow rate most of the time.

2 Reads primarily in three- or four-word phrase groups; some smooth, expressive interpretation and pausing guided by author's meaning and punctuation; mostly appropriate stress and rate with some slowdowns.

3 Reads primarily in larger, meaningful phrases or word groups; mostly smooth, expressive interpretation and pausing guided by author's meaning and punctuation; appropriate stress and rate with only a few slowdowns.

4 *Fountas & Pinnell Leveled Literacy Intervention*

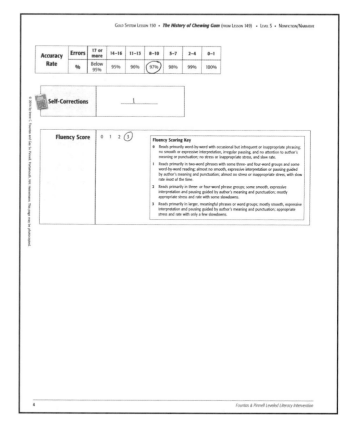

FIGURE 6.1 Completed Reading Record

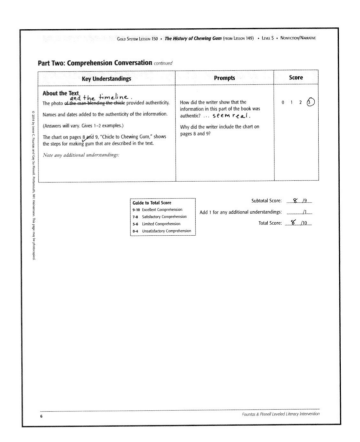

FIGURE 6.1 Completed Reading Record (*cont.*)

Assessment), listen to one student read an excerpt from yesterday's new book, code the reading behavior on the Recording Form, give a score for fluency, have a brief comprehension conversation, and make a teaching point that you think will be most helpful to the reader. The other students will be reading an excerpt from yesterday's new book silently.

You read the title and introduction statement to the student and ask her to begin reading the excerpt orally. While you are coding the student's reading behavior on the Recording Form, it is important to observe what the student can do without your support. Do not help or interfere in any way, verbally or nonverbally, except to say "You try it" when the student appeals for help or give a "told" when the reader has tried something and/or will not move on. Say "You try it" if the reader has not tried something, and then wait no more than three seconds before you give a "told" so as not to allow the meaning to be lost. A "told" is counted as an error.

▶ Learning How to Assess, Monitor Progress, and Guide Teaching

In this guide, we provide a brief overview of the systematized process for coding, scoring, and analyzing reading behaviors. The Tutorial DVD provides in-depth information and as much practice as you need to become skilled in all aspects of using reading records and linking the information to instruction.

The professional book *When Readers Struggle, L–Z: Teaching That Works* (in press) provides detailed descriptions of reading behaviors as well as numerous examples for analysis. In these resources, you will learn what each type of behavior tells about the "in-the-head" systems the student is likely using or neglecting as she processes a text. This analysis will help you determine the emphasis for your teaching.

► Oral Reading

Coding Reading Behaviors on a Recording Form

In this section we briefly describe coding conventions. Use the Tutorial DVD and work at your own rate to learn how to code. Using the DVD, you have many opportunities to practice and become skilled in using this powerful tool.

As the student reads, observe the precise behaviors and mark on the typed text using the coding system shown in Figure 6.2. Be sure to use the standardized coding system so your coding can be read by any person and the information will be consistent.

Evaluating Fluency

As you are coding the reading record, pay attention to how the reading sounds. Make quick notes during the reading. Immediately after the student finishes reading orally, rate the fluency by circling the score on the fluency rubric (see Figure 6.3). Consider the phrasing, intonation, pausing, stress, and reading rate as well as the integration of all dimensions of fluent processing.

Calculating Accuracy

When you take a record of reading behavior, you get many different kinds of information. First, you are able to determine the *accuracy*, that is, the percent of total words that were read correctly. Accuracy is important, and it is a key factor in effective processing. Students may read a text with high accuracy but understand it only superficially. They may read a text with lower accuracy but remember enough details to get the gist. But in general, there is a relationship between accuracy and understanding. Count up the number of uncorrected errors. A chart specific to the text appears on each form to help you determine the accuracy rate as a percentage (see Figure 6.4).

Recording Self-Correction Rate

Self-correction behavior is an indication that the student is monitoring his reading behavior and attempting to search for multiple sources of information to make sense of the text. In young, beginning readers this behavior is observable, resulting in a high ratio of errors to self-corrections. In older, more proficient problem solvers most of this behavior seems to be taking place "in the head" and may not result in many noticeable self-corrections. Nevertheless, you want to make note of the number of self-corrections. If a student makes an error and then corrects it, you have powerful evidence of what that reader is attending to and using. Think about how often the reader notices an error and corrects it or attempts to correct it. Notice what information the reader uses to correct the error (see Figure 6.5).

► Talk About Reading

The Comprehension Conversation

Once the student has completed the oral reading, have a brief comprehension conversation with the student to gain evidence of understanding. In your conversation, consider the evidence that the student showed you yesterday. You may not need to use all the prompts or questions. Make decisions based on your observation of yesterday's reading and conversation and today's documentation of reading. Mark a score based on your overall analysis.

Begin with the general prompt to get the student talking about the book. You may want to check off each key understanding on the Recording Form the student demonstrates. Probe for further information using the prompts as needed. For some students it may be necessary to reword the prompt or probe for him to explain his thinking (i.e., "Say more about that"). Often just pausing a few seconds more to listen will also prompt the student to say more. Rewording, further probing, and providing extra "wait time" will not affect the score. Allow the student to look back in the text if he initiates it. If the student starts to read the book again, stop him by saying, "Just tell me in your own words." The questions will help you determine the student's thinking within, beyond, and about the text.

The comprehension conversation should not sound like an interrogation—more like a conversation between readers who are interested in the book. You will have evidence of comprehending even while the student is reading. He might make errors that do not make sense and then correct them to make the reading meaningful.

Coding and Scoring Errors at-a-Glance

Behavior	What the Reader Does	How to Code	Example	How to Score	
Accurate Reading	Reads words correctly	Do not mark *or* place check (✓) above word	**No mark** *or* ✓ environments		No error
Substitution	Gives an incorrect response	Write the substituted word above the word	worry / wonder	Substitution, not corrected	1 error
Multiple Substitutions	Makes several attempts at a word	Write each substitution in sequence above the word	speckles|spices|specials species	Multiple substitutions, not corrected	1 error for each incorrect word in text
			adept|adopt|SC adapted	Multiple substitutions, self-corrected (SC)	No error; 1 SC
			to|touch|teeth tooth	Multiple misreadings of the same word, not corrected	1 error for each incorrect word in text
			Attic Arctic	Multiple misreadings of names and proper nouns	1 error first time missed; no errors after that
			can not | they're can't | they are	Misreading contractions (reads contraction as two words or two words as contraction)	1 error each time
Self-correction	Corrects a previous error	Write the error over the word, followed by SC	use | SC usually		No error; 1 SC
Insertion	Adds a word that is not in the text	Write in the inserted word using a caret	very ∧		1 error per word inserted
Omission	Gives no response to a word	Place a dash (–) above the word	‾ only	Skipping a word / Skipping a line	1 error per word / 1 error per word
Repetition	Reads same word again	Write R after the word	R		No error

Coding system developed by Marie Clay as part of the running record system in An Observation Survey of Early Literacy Achievement, Revised Second Edition, 2006, Heinemann.

Fountas & Pinnell Leveled Literacy Intervention Red System

FIGURE 6.2A Coding and Scoring Errors at-a-Glance, page 1

section 6

Assessment and Record Keeping

Coding and Scoring Errors at-a-Glance (continued)

Behavior	What the Reader Does	How to Code	Example	How to Score	
Repeated Repetitions	Reads the same word more than once	Write R for the first repetition, then write a number for the additional repetitions	R₂ R₃		No error
Rereading	Returns to the beginning of sentence or phrase to read again	Write R with an arrow back to the place where rereading began	R		No error
	Rereads and self-corrects	Write R with an arrow back to the place where rereading began and a SC at point of self-correction	theirselves|sc R They can wrap themselves		No error; 1 SC
Appeal	Verbally asks for help	Write A above the word	A environments	Follow up with "You try it"	No error
"You Try It"	The child appeals, the teacher responds with "You try it"	Write Y after the word	A environments| Y	"You try it" followed by correct word	No error
				"You try it" followed by omission, incorrect word, or Told	1 error
Told	Child doesn't attempt a word even after "You try it"	Write T after the word or the Y	A environments| Y | T A environments| T		1 error
Spelling Aloud	Child spells word by saying the names of letters	Write the letters in all capital letters	E-V-E-R ever	Spelling followed by correct word	No error
				Spelling followed by incorrect word	1 error
Sounding Out	The child makes the sounds associated with the letters in the word	Write the letters in lower case with hyphens between them	o-n-l-y ✓ only	"Sounding out" followed by correct word	No error; no SC
			t-em-per|temper temperature	"Sounding out" followed by incorrect word or no word	1 error
			b-|SC polar	Sounding the first letter incorrectly and then saying the word correctly	No error; no SC

Coding system developed by Marie Clay as part of the running record system in An Observation Survey of Early Literacy Achievement, Revised Second Edition, 2006, Heinemann.

Fountas & Pinnell Leveled Literacy Intervention Red System

FIGURE 6.2B Coding and Scoring Errors at-a-Glance, page 2

Fluency Score	0 (1) 2 3	**Fluency Scoring Key**

Fluency Scoring Key

0 Reads primarily word-by-word with occasional but infrequent or inappropriate phrasing; no smooth or expressive interpretation, irregular pausing, and no attention to author's meaning or punctuation; no stress or inappropriate stress, and slow rate.

1 Reads primarily in two-word phrases with some three- and four-word groups and some word-by-word reading; almost no smooth, expressive interpretation or pausing guided by author's meaning and punctuation; almost no stress or inappropriate stress, with slow rate most of the time.

2 Reads primarily in three- or four-word phrase groups; some smooth, expressive interpretation and pausing guided by author's meaning and punctuation; mostly appropriate stress and rate with some slowdowns.

3 Reads primarily in larger, meaningful phrases or word groups; mostly smooth, expressive interpretation and pausing guided by author's meaning and punctuation; appropriate stress and rate with only a few slowdowns.

FIGURE 6.3 Fluency Rubric

Accuracy Rate	Errors	9 or more	7–8	6	4–5	3	1–2	0
	%	below 95%	(95%)	96%	97%	98%	99%	100%

FIGURE 6.4 Accuracy Chart

Self-Corrections	_2_

FIGURE 6.5 Self-Correction Chart

Scoring the Comprehension Conversation

You will also have evidence of comprehension from the first reading of the text in the previous lesson. If you use this evidence in combination with a brief conversation after reading, you are able to score the student's thinking in three categories. You may be thinking about some of these questions as you score the comprehension conversation after the reading.

Within the Text

❑ Is the reader gaining the literal meaning of the text through solving words, monitoring her own understanding, and accuracy?

❑ Can the reader tell what happened or report important facts?

❑ Is the reader searching for and using information and remembering information in summary form?

❑ Is the reader adjusting her reading to fit the form—and also sustaining fluency?

Beyond the Text

❑ Is the reader making predictions?

❑ Is the reader making connections with prior knowledge, personal experience, or other texts?

❑ Is there evidence that the reader is inferring what is implied but not stated in the text?

❑ Has the reader shown that he is synthesizing information by changing his own thinking?

About the Text

❏ Is the reader able to think about the literary elements of the text and recognize the writer's craft?

❏ Can the reader think critically about how the text was written?

Assign a score in all three areas. If the reader came up with one or more unique and valuable additional understandings not identified in the key understandings, give an extra point. Now calculate a total score of unsatisfactory, limited, satisfactory, or excellent. For a text to be appropriate, the student's comprehension must be satisfactory or excellent (see Figure 6.6).

Guide to Total Score

9-10 Excellent Comprehension

7-8 Satisfactory Comprehension

5-6 Limited Comprehension

0-4 Unsatisfactory Comprehension

FIGURE 6.6 Comprehension Rubric

Scoring the Oral Reading and Comprehension Conversation in the Reading Record: Summary

The following is a summary of the steps to score the reading record:

1. **Accuracy:** Circle the number of errors on the graph (or use the F&P Calculator/Stopwatch).

2. **Self-Corrections:** Record the number of self-corrections.

3. **Fluency:** Circle the fluency rating.

   0 = no phrasing or expression

   1 = minimal phrasing or expression

   2 = some phrasing or expression

   3 = mostly phrased and expressive reading

4. **Comprehension:**

   • Assign points in each category (Within, Beyond, About the Text), making a decision for each based on:

   0 = no understanding

   1 = little understanding

   2 = satisfactory understanding

   3 = excellent understanding

• Assign 1 extra point if appropriate for unique expression of understandings.

• Circle total comprehension score on the form. For levels L–Z:

   0–4 = unsatisfactory

   5–6 = limited

   7–8 = satisfactory

   9–10 = excellent

In *LLI* at levels L–Z, assess three areas of thinking—within, beyond, and about a text using a 10-point scoring scale. All three areas are essential to a complete understanding of the text. An extra point may be awarded to a student who expresses an additional understanding beyond the key understandings provided. Take the accuracy rate and the comprehension score into account to determine if the passage read was at the student's independent or instructional reading levels (see Figure 6.7).

Using the F&P Calculator/Stopwatch

The following are steps to administer the reading record using the F&P Calculator/Stopwatch. Although we don't recommend taking a reading rate on every student every time, occasionally you will want to measure the rate for individual students whose progress you are monitoring in that particular area of fluency. Remember that faster is not necessarily better. Many factors should be considered.

We recommend administering a reading record on one student every standard (even-numbered) lesson, which would give you a reading record every two weeks for a group of four. If you want to obtain a reading rate, you will need the F&P Calculator/Stopwatch. Follow steps 1–7 below.

1. Use yesterday's new book (the instructional level book from the odd-numbered lesson). Read the title and the introduction statement to the student, and ask her to begin reading the excerpt orally.

2. Press **RW**, and enter the number of running words (RW) in the text on the F&P Calculator/Stopwatch.

3. Press **Start Time** on the calculator as the student begins oral reading.

Finding the Levels, L–Z

Accuracy	Comprehension			
	Excellent 9–10	Satisfactory 7–8	Limited 5–6	Unsatisfactory 0–4
98–100%	Independent	Independent	Instructional	Hard
95–97%	Instructional	Instructional	Hard	Hard
Below 95%	Hard	Hard	Hard	Hard

FIGURE 6.7 Finding Independent, Instructional, and Hard Levels

4. **Code** the reading behavior on the Recording Form. Mark the typed text (see the Online Resources site), making a check for each word read accurately and using the coding conventions to record errors, self-corrections, and other behaviors. Make notes about how the reading sounded.

5. Press **End Time** when the reading is complete.

6. Press **#Errors**, and enter the number of errors on the calculator.

7. Press **Time** to get **Elapsed Minutes or Seconds**.

8. Press **WPM** to see **Words per Minute**.

9. Press **Accur.%** for the **Percentage of Accuracy**.

After the reading, assign a score for fluency. Have a comprehension conversation with the student about the text. Make notes about the student's understanding. Alternatively, check off items the student talks about. Use prompts, as needed, to stimulate discussion. Score each area, and decide on the additional point immediately after the conversation for a more systematized assessment. Circle the accuracy on the form. Select one or two teaching points to help the reader learn how to process more effectively.

▶ Analyzing Oral Reading Behaviors

The following explains how to analyze the reading record following the scoring process. You can also learn how to analyze the student's reading on the Professional Development and Tutorial DVDs. The DVDs allow you several opportunities to practice this analysis with thoughtful guidance. You will learn how to move from the coding and scoring of the reading record, to analyzing the information and using it to guide your teaching.

Sources of Information Used and Neglected

For each error, write **MSV** in the **E** column (whether self-corrected or not). For each self-correction, write **MSV** (all three letters) in the **SC** column. It is important to think about what led the reader to make the error and what the reader might have neglected. Circle one, two, or three letters for each error or self-correction, without reading beyond the error or self-correction. Don't bother to analyze omissions and substitutions for it is usually the reader's use of language structure that led to those errors. Think about the following as they apply to each error and self-correction:

❏ **Meaning.** Readers often make substitutions that indicate they are thinking about the meaning of the text. For example, a reader might say *dance* for *ballet*. Ask yourself the question: Did the meaning of the text influence the error? (Circle **M** in the column Sources of Information.)

❏ **Structure.** A powerful source of information for a reader is the structure or syntax of language. From our knowledge of oral language, we have implicit knowledge of the way words are put together to form phrases and sentences. It "sounds right" to us. Readers often substitute nouns for nouns or verbs for verbs, indicating an awareness of the syntactic rules of language. For example, a reader might say "We could probably come" for "We could possibly come." Ask yourself the questions: Does the error fit an acceptable English language structure? Did structure influence the error? (Circle **S** in the column.)

❑ **Visual Information.** Readers use the visual features of print—the letters and words—to read. They connect these features to phonetic information that exists in their heads. For example, a reader might say *every* for *very*. Ask yourself: Did the visual information from the print influence any part of the error (letter, part, word)? (Circle **V** in the column.)

Readers often use multiple sources of information as they process texts. For example, when the reader substituted *probably* for *possibly*, he attended to all three—meaning, language structure, and visual information. Here, you would circle or check **M**, **S**, and **V** in the error column.

Self-Correction Behavior

Analyze the self-corrections that the reader made. Here, you are hypothesizing *the additional information that the reader might have used to correct the error*. The self-correction, of course, indicates use of all three sources of information—meaning, language structure, and visual information—because it is the accurate word. But you are making a hypothesis about what the reader might have used as *additional* information to correct the error.

If the reader made the error *this* for *that* in the sentence, "He didn't understand that," for example, and then self-corrected, the error would be coded **M**, **S**, and **V**. The self correction would be coded **V** because the reader probably noticed more visual information at the end of the word to self correct.

The relationship between self-correction rate and progress in reading is not linear. As students progress, observable self-correction decreases and may become nonexistent. We assume that proficient readers are self-regulating both their oral and silent reading, but we will not be able to observe the behavior. If we find very high accuracy and also many self-corrections, we would notice it and work with the reader to get smoother processing.

These analyses will help you look quantitatively at the reader's use of different sources of information. Think about what the reader is noticing and what he is neglecting. You can help the reader attend to the information sources needed as you listen to him read orally or select teaching points after the reading. If readers in a group are neglecting to think about what might make sense, you can prompt them to do so. If they are not noticing the word parts that would be helpful, you can draw those parts to their attention. (Use *Prompting Guide, Part 1* for precise teaching language.)

Analyzing Strategic Actions

Now that you have completed your analysis of sources of information used and neglected, look at the behaviors you have recorded on the printed text. Think about the reader as a problem solver. Five areas will be helpful in your thinking:

❑ **Searching for and Using Information.** Effective readers *actively* search for the information they need to read with accuracy, fluency, and understanding. They make attempts that, even if not right, show you they are trying out what they know. You may notice that they reread to phrase a sentence appropriately or to use punctuation. You may also notice rereading to confirm an attempt. You can teach readers many ways to search.

❑ **Solving Words.** You want readers to have and use many ways to solve or analyze words. As they learn more, they will recognize many words automatically, but they also need to be able to use phonics and word analysis strategies so that they can learn many more words. Take note of how the reader is solving unknown words. Is it letter-by-letter or in larger units? Your teaching should support the reader using many different ways to solve words.

❑ **Self-Monitoring.** Rather than reading along and ignoring errors, you want the reader to *notice* when something doesn't fit. The reading may not make sense. Or it might not sound right or look right. Effective readers are constantly monitoring their own reading accuracy. Signs of monitoring can be rereading or pausing. If the reader does not show signs of self-monitoring, you can draw attention to mismatches and show her how to fix them.

❑ **Self-Correcting.** Self-correction is a sign that the reader is self-monitoring and working actively to make everything fit—meaning, visual information, and the way the reading sounds. You can prompt for self-correction. Keep in mind that even the most proficient readers will occasionally fail to correct small errors that do not affect comprehension (i.e., a/the) because they are placing a priority on reading fluently. You don't want to interrupt students every time they make an error like this because too much attention to these kinds of errors will slow down students and affect overall processing. But you do want high accuracy and attention to meaning.

❑ **Maintaining Fluency.** Effective readers put all sources of information together so that their reading sounds fluent and expressive. You can think about how the reading sounded. If the reader is not fluent and the text is easy enough, you can demonstrate fluent reading and show the reader how to put words together so that the reading sounds good. You can use the Six Dimensions of Fluency from the Online Resources site to guide your teaching.

As you think about each reader, you may find it useful to make notes using the Guide for Observing and Noting Oral Reading Behaviors (see Figure 6.8).

This guide will help you assess the student's behaviors for thinking within the text—the literal understandings the student controls. The guide is also available on the Online Resources site. Look at each category and think about the behavioral evidence you see in the Recording Form. Think about what the reader does at difficulty. Does he search for information—especially visual information? Notice what the reader does after an error. Is the error one that takes away from the meaning and the precise message? Make notes that will help you think about the student's strengths and needs and how the information can inform your teaching. Next, look at the student's responses to the comprehension conversation. What do they tell you about the student's thinking Within, Beyond, and About the text? How will your observations inform your teaching? Use *The Continuum of Literacy Learning* at the student's instructional level to select goals and next teaching moves. Then refer to *Prompting Guide, Part 1* and *Prompting Guide, Part 2* for precise language to teach for, prompt for, and

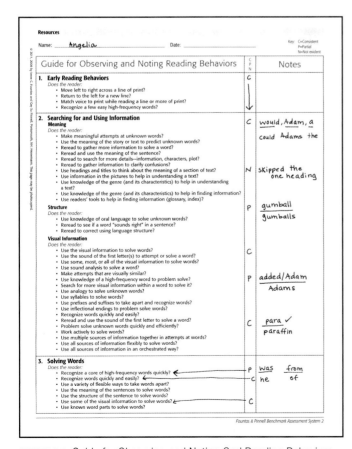
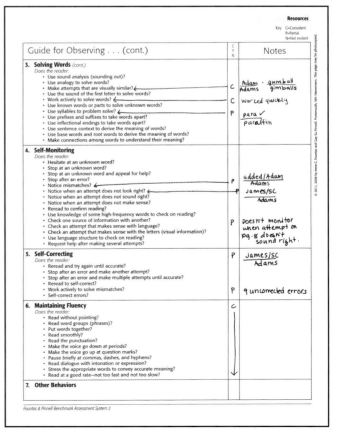

FIGURE 6.8 Guide for Observing and Noting Oral Reading Behaviors

reinforce effective processing strategies and for analytical and critical thinking.

Figure 6.1 is a completed reading record on Angelia's reading of a level S book, *The History of Chewing Gum*. Notice the accurate reading as well as the places where the student did some problem solving. The student read at an instructional level with satisfactory comprehension and fluency. Also notice that the teacher made notes and checked key understandings.

▶ Record Keeping

Collect information to inform your ongoing teaching. Keep your record keeping simple, efficient, and informative. We have provided a few forms for daily record keeping and/or keeping a record of each student's lessons. All of the record keeping forms can be printed from the Online Resources site.

Lesson Record Forms for Standard Lessons

In Figure 6.9 you see a sample of a completed form for Odd-Numbered and Even-Numbered Standard Lessons. This form shows parts of a lesson and spaces to make notes for four students. The two-page Even-Numbered Standard Lesson Record Form looks similar but is designed to include writing. If your groups are larger than the recommended four students, alternate versions of the Lesson Record Forms with spaces for six students are available from the Online Resources site.

Your notes should consist of specific details of behavioral evidence—what the student can do or what he needs to learn how to do. Evidence can be found of each reader's use of strategic actions through observing reading behavior and talk, and during the comprehension conversation. Make notes about significant writing behaviors that indicate a student's ability to construct words and compose sentences. You can then use your notes to plan what you will emphasize when you teach the next lesson. (See *When Readers Struggle, L–Z: Teaching That Works, Prompting Guide, Part 1* and *Prompting Guide, Part 2*.)

Lesson Record Forms for Novel Study Lessons

In Figure 6.10 you can see a completed Novel Study Lesson Record form showing parts of a lesson and notes for four students. If your groups are larger than the recommended four students, an alternate version of the Novel Study Lesson Record form with spaces to make notes for six students is also available from the Online Resources site.

Lesson Record Forms for Test Preparation Lessons

In Figure 6.11 you can see a completed Test Preparation Lesson Record form showing parts of a lesson and notes for four students. If your groups are larger than the recommended four students, an alternate version of the Test Preparation Lesson Record Form with spaces to make notes for six students is also available from the Online Resources site.

Intervention Record

The Intervention Record (Figure 6.12, p. 109) is designed for your use in documenting the lessons each student receives. This form is critical for monitoring the number of *LLI* lessons per week and the number of small-group lessons the student receives in the classroom each week. Accurate record keeping with this form will help you determine the effectiveness of *LLI* on student achievement.

Write the lesson number in the box, and use the appropriate code to indicate the reason the student missed a scheduled lesson. In addition, you will want to ask the classroom teacher how many times the student had small-group literacy instruction in the classroom so you have a complete record of the amount of reading instruction the student received each week. The form also allows you to record the data from the reading records you will have on each student about every two weeks. It provides a quick reference to monitor the student's accuracy, fluency, and comprehension (thinking within, beyond, and about the text). An explanation of the codes is at the bottom of each form. Print and keep this form in the student's folder. Alternately, you may want to record this information on the Online Data Management System (ODMS).

Odd-Numbered Lesson (Top Left Form)

Lesson Record: 4-Student Version   Odd-Numbered Lesson

Date: _____ Teacher: **Mrs. Ha** Grade: **4** Lesson **149**

GOALS:

Sothearith	Cynthia	Louly	Angelia
Learn and use new vocabulary.	Infer character traits and author's message.	Monitor reading for accuracy and understanding.	Participate actively in discussion.

DISCUSSION OF YESTERDAY'S NEW BOOK

Little Plane Big Dream
Infer the author's message.

Active participant in discussion. Refers to text to compose language.	Defines confident.	Provides a detailed description of the character's traits – sometimes inferring them from his actions.	Summarizes the author's message well.

REVISITING YESTERDAY'S NEW BOOK:
COMPREHENSION, VOCABULARY, OR FLUENCY

Analyze the author's craft–why authors of biography include information from the subject's childhood.

Refers to text to infer character's motivations.		Uses the photo and caption to infer the character's actions.	

Fountas & Pinnell *Leveled Literacy Intervention*. Copyright ©2013 by Irene C. Fountas and Gay Su Pinnell. This page may be photocopied.   LESSON RECORD 4-STUDENT

Odd-Numbered Lesson (cont.) (Top Right Form)

Lesson Record: 4-Student Version   Odd-Numbered Lesson (cont.)

PHONICS/WORD STUDY

Understand and use agent nouns.

understands and uses agent nouns.	Understands and uses agent nouns.	Needs support with beggar and cheaper.	Needs support with beggar.

READING A NEW BOOK

The History of Chewing Gum

Needs time to translate thoughts into English. Anticipates information by using headings. shares new information. References the text to support inference.	Unfamiliar vocabulary: modern times Defines: archeologist makes inaccurate inferences about new gum invention and reasons that gum is forbidden in school.	forbideded/forbidden T: Prompt to take that word apart in syllables Reads in a phrased and fluent manner. dropped/draped T: defined draped and wad.	Shares new information learned from the text.

ASSESSING READING AND WRITING BEHAVIORS:

Refers to the text to use new vocabulary. Good literal and inferential understanding.	Good literal understanding of the text. Needs support inferring the author's message.	Articulates understanding of information well. Needs support with new vocabulary.	Contributed to discussion unprompted. Infers and synthesizes information.

Fountas & Pinnell *Leveled Literacy Intervention*. Copyright ©2013 by Irene C. Fountas and Gay Su Pinnell. This page may be photocopied.   LESSON RECORD 4-STUDENT

Even-Numbered Lesson (Bottom Left Form)

Lesson Record: 4-Student Version   Even-Numbered Lesson

Date: _____ Teacher: **Mrs. Ha** Grade: **4** Lesson **150**

GOALS:

Sothearith	Louly	Cynthia	Angelia
Learn and use new vocabulary. Compose ideas in English.	Monitor accuracy + understanding. Synthesize information and write about it.	Infer author's message. Synthesize information and write about it.	Participate actively in discussions

REVISITING YESTERDAY'S NEW BOOK:
COMPREHENSION, VOCABULARY, OR FLUENCY

Analyze the author's organization of text.

Relates the order of the information in the text to the timeline.	Contributes to the conversation.	Contributes to the conversation.	Didn't participate in discussion.

REREADING AND ASSESSMENT

What do inventors and entrepreneurs have in common?

Inventors and entrepreneurs both try things out to make them better.			Reading record: 97%. fluent and phrased. Articulates how inventors and entrepreneurs are different, not the same.

WRITING ABOUT READING

Needs supportive conversation to help him compose his thoughts in English. "Inventors need to test things out"	"Inventors need to be confident and determined " "Entrepreneurs upgrade the product"		"Inventors invent interesting things. Entrepreneurs sell those things to make money."

Fountas & Pinnell *Leveled Literacy Intervention*. Copyright ©2013 by Irene C. Fountas and Gay Su Pinnell. This page may be photocopied.   LESSON RECORD 4-STUDENT

Even-Numbered Lesson (cont.) (Bottom Right Form)

Lesson Record: 4-Student Version   Even-Numbered Lesson (cont.)

PHONICS/WORD STUDY

Change verbs to nouns by adding -ion or -tion. Sometimes the base word changes.

Notices how the base word changes.	Understands and applies principle.	When working in pairs, actively discusses the principle with partner.	Notices that some words add -tion to the end.

READING A NEW BOOK

The Old Knife - historical fiction

Lots of new vocabulary and language to take in during book introduction. Alex/Alex's T: attention to the end-told. Twelth/twelfth T: Look at that word in parts.		Understands the banks collapsed. Predicts incorrectly.	Understands The Great Depression. Predicts incorrectly.

ASSESSING READING AND WRITING BEHAVIORS:

Shows good understanding but needs support articulating his thinking in English.	Articulates understanding well. Actively participates.	Needs encouragement to participate in whole group discussion.	Good literal understanding but inferring and synthesizing information is challenging.

Fountas & Pinnell *Leveled Literacy Intervention*. Copyright ©2013 by Irene C. Fountas and Gay Su Pinnell. This page may be photocopied.   LESSON RECORD 4-STUDENT

FIGURE 6.9 Completed Odd-Numbered and Even-Numbered Standard Lesson Record Forms

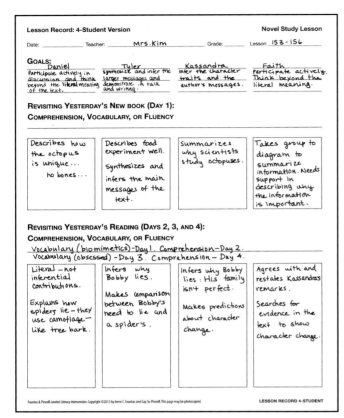

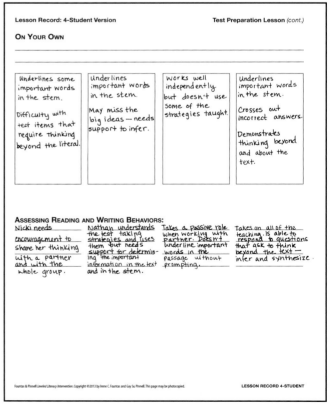

FIGURE 6.10 Completed Novel Study Lesson Record Form

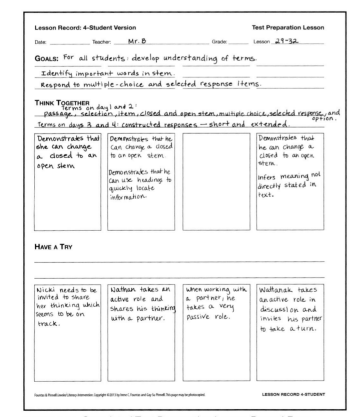

FIGURE 6.11 Completed Test Preparation Lesson Record Form

Student Achievement Log

This optional form can be used to document students' performance as they enter and exit *LLI*. Enter the Fountas & Pinnell Benchmark Assessment scores for each student in the group at the beginning and end of their series of *LLI* lessons. Include any other assessment information you wish to collect in the final column (see Figure 6.13).

FIGURE 6.12 Intervention Record

Intervention Record

Student Name: Corey Year: ___ Teacher: Mrs. Ha

Group: ___ System: _Orange _Green _Blue _Red ✗Gold _Purple_ Teal School: ___

Attendance Record						Weekly Reading Record						
Date	Week	M	T	W	Th	F	Lesson	Reading Record Book Title	Level	Acc. %	Comp.	SC	Fluency	#SGI
9/10	1	G-1	G-2	G-3	G-4	G-5	2	Revolting Recipes	O	96%	7/10	1	3	5
9/17	2	G-6	G-7	G-8	G-9	G-10	10	The Shiner	O	97%	7/10	O	3	5
9/24	3	G-11	G-12	G-13	G-14	G-15								5
10/8	4	SH	G-16	G-17	G-18	G-19	18	Trying Out	O	95%	7/10	2	3	4
10/15	5	G-20	G-21	CA	CA	G-24								3
10/22	6	G-25	G-26	G-27	G-28	G-29								4
10/29	7	G-30	G-31	G-32	G-33	G-34	34	Best Enemies	P	95%	8/10	2	3	5
11/5	8	G-35	G-36	G-37	G-38	G-39								5
11/12	9	SH	G-40	G-41	G-42	G-43	42	Shining Star of Science	P	98%	8/10	O	3	4
11/19	10	G-44	G-45	G-46	SH	SH								3
11/26	11	G-47	G-48	G-49	G-50	G-51	50	Keeping the Light	P	97%	8/10	1	3	5

NOTES:

Corey reads fluently with a degree of accuracy. His ability to think and talk beyond the literal understanding of the text, especially infer & synthesize information, has improved greatly. He will continue to need encouragement to participate actively in conversations about books read.

KEY:
Acc.% = Accuracy
Comp. = Comprehension Total Score
SC = Self-Correction
#SGI = Small Group Instruction (in addition to LLI)
TA = Teacher Absent
CA = Child Absent
TN = Teacher Not Available
CN = Child Not Available
SH = School Holiday

Fountas & Pinnell *Leveled Literacy Intervention*. Copyright ©2013 by Irene C. Fountas and Gay Su Pinnell. This page may be photocopied.

INTERVENTION RECORD

FIGURE 6.13 *LLI* Student Achievement Log

Leveled Literacy Intervention Student Achievement Log: 4-Student Version

School Year: ___ Teacher: Mrs. Ha Assessment Used: F & P Benchmark 2

School: ___ District/State: ___

GROUP ENTRY DATA

Student	Grade	Entry Date	Level	Accuracy %	Comp.	SC	Fluency	Notes
Sothearith	4	9/16	Q	95%	8	0	2	ELL Very new to this country.
Louly	4	9/16	Q	97%	8	2	3	
Cynthia	4	9/16	R	99%	7	1	3	
Angelia	4	9/16	R	98%	7	1	3	Very quiet – not a risk taker.

GROUP EXIT DATA

Student	Grade	Exit Date	Level	Accuracy %	Comp.	SC	Fluency	Notes
Sothearith	4	2/20	S	95%	8	2	2	Good thinking beyond and about texts. Continues to need support with new vocabulary and language structures.
Louly	4	2/20	S	97%	8	0	3	Good vocabulary. Needs support for conventional language structures in English.
Cynthia	4	2/20	S	95%	8	0	3	Good vocabulary. Needs support for conventional language structures in English.
Angelia	4	2/20	T	99%	8	0	3	Great improvement in thinking beyond and about texts. Continues to need invitation to talk about her thinking.

Fountas & Pinnell *Leveled Literacy Intervention*. Copyright ©2013 by Irene C. Fountas and Gay Su Pinnell. This page may be photocopied.

STUDENT ACTIVITY LOG: 4-STUDENT VERSION

Communication Sheet—Individual

This form can be used to communicate with the classroom teacher regarding an *individual's* weekly progress. You may want the classroom teacher to share the same kind of information with you. Close collaboration with the classroom teacher will contribute greatly to your students' progress in *LLI* lessons and in the classroom literacy program. You can write notes about the student's strengths in both reading and writing, as well as the present focus of your instruction (see Figure 6.14).

Communication Sheet—Group

This form can be used to communicate with the classroom teacher about a *group's* weekly progress. Write notes in each area that you feel will be helpful (see Figure 6.15).

Leveled Literacy Intervention Communication Sheet: Individual

Date: _____ Student: _Corey_ Classroom Teacher: _Mrs. Ha_

LLI Level: _____ System: __Orange __Green __Blue __Red X Gold __Purple __ Teal Reading Teacher: _____

Strengths:
Corey reads at a level O with a degree of accuracy. His reading is fluent and phrased, reflecting a literal understanding of the text.

Working toward proficiency with the following strategic actions:
Corey is being encouraged to infer character traits and the larger messages of fiction stories and nonfiction books.

Recent writing vocabulary:
because, people, their, they're, these, though

Other comments:
He is also working at expanding and clarifying his thinking in his writing about the reading.

FIGURE 6.14 Communication Sheet—Individual

Leveled Literacy Intervention Communication Sheet: Group

Date: _____ Teacher: _Mrs. Ha_ System: __Orange __Green __Blue __Red X Gold __Purple __Teal

Group Level: _S_ Students: _Sothearith, Angelia, Kassandra, Louly_

Strengths: This group works well together. All participate in book discussions, take turns, and listen to one another.
All read with high accuracy at level S.
Angelia, Kassandra, and Louly read integrating all dimensions of fluency.
Sothearith reads in a phrased manner. He continues to learn vocabulary and English language structures from the books he reads.

Working toward proficiency with the following strategic actions:
Inferring character traits, change and motivation in fiction.
Inferring and synthesizing authors' messages in fiction and nonfiction.
Using context (convinced, obsesses), morphology (previous, biomimetics) and reference tools to learn new vocabulary.
Notice the meaning of word roots (astro, photo, bio, micro, mega, therm)

Other comments:
All students would benefit from practicing the word games, if there is class time.
Sothearith would benefit from reading the take home books in class whenever time allows. Rereading will provide additional opportunities for controlling new vocabulary and language structures.

FIGURE 6.15 Communication Sheet—Group

Flip Record

An informal alternative form of record keeping is the Flip Record (see Figure 6.16), which you can quickly make using index cards and a sheet of paper or stiff card stock. Holding a sheet of 8.5" x 11" paper or card stock lengthwise, tape 5" x 8" index cards to the paper so that the cards overlap down the sheet. If you use a sheet of paper, you can place the Flip Record on a clipboard for stability. Have one card for each student, and write each student's name at the bottom of a card so the names will be visible when the cards overlap. You can then flip up the cards to write anecdotal notes about each student's progress; words, letters, or patterns that are challenging to the student; or any other notes you wish to make on the student's reading and writing behaviors. As each card is filled, peel it off the sheet and place it in the student's Student Folder.

Writing Sample in Literacy Notebook

The Literacy Notebook also serves as a record of progress. Students generally do their writing on right-hand pages (Figure 6.17). The opposite (left) page can be used to work on words (Figure 6.18). You can have students practice writing a word quickly or saying words in syllables while you provide (Elkonin) letter boxes. The notebook provides a record of the learning you are supporting in writing about reading. The samples in the book show the student's progress over time in learning about sounds, words, word parts, and the ability to compose and write sentences.

Reading Graphs and Reports

It will be helpful to keep a graph of progress for each reader. As suggested in the standard (even-numbered) lesson, take a reading record of one student's reading of the previous day's new book. Record the reading level on the Reading Graph (printable from the Online Resources site and found on the interior of each Student Folder). You can record the level by hand, using a circle with a dot in it for reading at the instructional level (95–97% with satisfactory comprehension for levels L–Z). Use an open circle for reading at the independent level (98–100% with

FIGURE 6.16 Flip Record

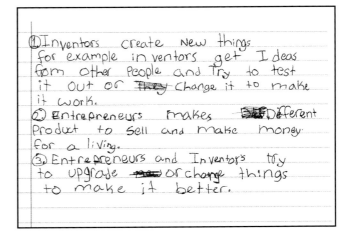

FIGURE 6.17 Writing About Reading Sample

FIGURE 6.18 Word Study Sample

satisfactory comprehension for levels L–Z). If the reading is below those levels, fill in the circle to make it black. If comprehension is unsatisfactory, make the circle black regardless of accuracy (see Figure 6.19). This tool allows you to enter the information from the student's reading record each week to document the student's progress on a graph. Be sure to share the information on the graph with the classroom teacher.

You can also enter the student's reading record information in the Online Data Management System (ODMS). The System will generate a graph using the data you entered (see Figure 6.20). Be sure to consult the material found at www. heinemann.com/ fountasandpinnell.com/student-progress-monitoring. aspx for a comprehensive tour and downloadable user manual for ODMS.

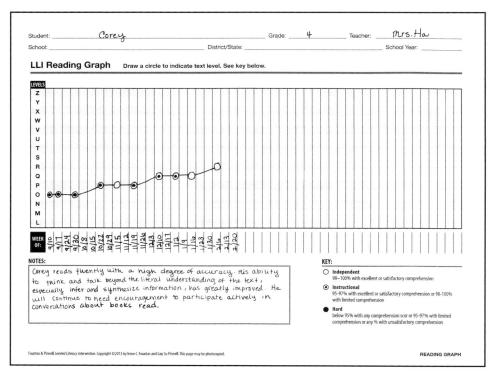

FIGURE 6.19 *LLI* Reading Graph

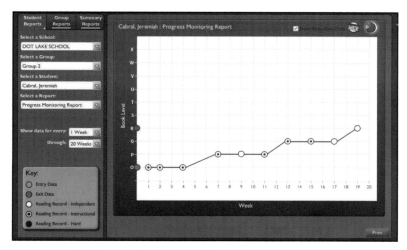

FIGURE 6.20 ODMS Report Showing One Student's Progress

section 7

Professional Development and **FAQs** for *LLI*

▶ Professional Development Options for *LLI*

❑ *System Guide*—This guide offers suggestions for implementing the intervention and also explains each of the *LLI* components in detail and many of the Recording Forms you will be using throughout *LLI* lessons. Appendices of useful resources and a bibliography of professional books are included for your reference.

❑ **Professional Development and Tutorial DVDs**— You can use the Professional Development and Tutorial DVDs from the Technology Package to support your work individually or with a study group of colleagues. There are three DVDs for *LLI Gold*. The two Professional Development DVDs provide an overview of the system and present demonstration lessons and details of the instructional procedures in *LLI*. The third DVD provides

a tutorial on coding, scoring, and analyzing reading records. It provides thoughtful guidance for your practice as well as information on how to use the data you have collected to inform your teaching.

❑ *When Readers Struggle, L–Z: Teaching That Works* (in press)—This professional book is a comprehensive tool for learning about a variety of difficulties readers have and how your teaching can move them forward.

❑ *Prompting Guide Part 1 for Oral Reading and Early Writing: K–8*—You can use this tool to support your students as they read or write. It contains precise language that can be used to teach for, prompt for, and reinforce effective strategic actions in reading and writing. The prompts call on the reader to take some quick action so as not to interrupt continuous processing of meaning.

❑ *Prompting Guide Part 2 For Comprehension: Thinking, Talking, and Writing, K–8*—This tool helps readers focus or expand their thinking. These prompts—during discussion, after the reading, and when revisiting the text—help to deepen understanding through talk.

❑ **Reflection Guide with a Videotaped Lesson**—Use the Reflection Guide (see Figure 7.1) to think about your own videotaped lesson, or you can audio- or videotape your lesson and discuss it with

LEVELED LITERACY INTERVENTION REFLECTION GUIDE — ODD-NUMBERED STANDARD LESSON GOLD SYSTEM

Name _____   Date _____

Discussing Yesterday's New Book
- How did I support the readers' thinking within, beyond or about the text?
- What new thinking was I able to help the readers attend to?
- How well did I help readers use evidence to support their thinking?
- How did I help the readers think about the genre and the big, important ideas?

Revisiting Yesterday's New Book for Comprehension, Vocabulary, or Fluency
- What was my rationale for selecting this lesson option?
- How clear and effective was my language?
- What is the evidence of student learning?

Phonics/Word Study
- How well did I engage the students in the inquiry process?
- How did I help the students construct the principle?
- How did I help the students understand how to apply the principle to other words?
- What was the evidence of new learning about words and how they work?

LEVELED LITERACY INTERVENTION REFLECTION GUIDE — ODD-NUMBERED STANDARD LESSON GOLD SYSTEM

Name _____   Date _____

Reading a New Book (Instructional Level)

Before Reading
- How did I help the students expand their knowledge of language structures and vocabulary?
- What new or important words did I help them notice in the text?
- What print features or text features did I help them notice?
- How did I help the students understand how the book works and understand critical aspects of the text meaning?

During Reading
- How did I teach for, prompt for, or reinforce effective processing strategies?
- What were the students able to do independently?

After Reading
- What was evidence of the students' understanding of the text?
- How did I support the readers' independent use of strategic actions through my teaching points?
- How did I help the readers think about the genre and the big, important ideas?
- What did the students learn how to do as readers?

LEVELED LITERACY INTERVENTION REFLECTION GUIDE — EVEN-NUMBERED STANDARD LESSON GOLD SYSTEM

Name _____   Date _____

Revisiting Yesterday's New Book for Comprehension, Vocabulary, or Fluency
- How did I support the readers' thinking within, beyond or about the text?
- What new thinking was I able to help the readers attend to?
- How well did I help readers use evidence to support their thinking?

Rereading and Assessment
- What strategic actions did the readers control independently?
- How did I teach for, prompt for, or reinforce processing strategies after coding the reading record?
- How did I teach for, prompt for, or reinforce the reader's control of strategic actions for comprehending?

Writing
- How did I engage the writers in composing sentences?
- What were the characteristics of the sentences students composed (language complexity, vocabulary, word difficulty, accuracy, etc.)?
- How did I help students use writing conventions?
- How did I draw the writers' attention to strategies for the construction of words?
- What links did I make to the students' previous knowledge?
- How did I use rereading to help students consider changes they needed to make?
- What did students learn how to do as writers?

LEVELED LITERACY INTERVENTION REFLECTION GUIDE — EVEN-NUMBERED STANDARD LESSON GOLD SYSTEM

Name _____   Date _____

Phonics/Word Work
- How well did I engage the students in the inquiry process?
- How did I help the students construct the principle?
- How did I help the students understand how to apply the principle to other words?
- What was the evidence of new learning about words and how they work?

New Book

Before Reading
- How did I help the children expand their knowledge of language structures and vocabulary?
- What print or text features did I help them notice?
- How did I help the children understand how the book works and understand critical aspects of the text meaning?

During Reading
- How did I teach for, prompt for, or reinforce effective processing strategies?
- What were the children able to do independently?

LEVELED LITERACY INTERVENTION REFLECTION GUIDE — EVEN-NUMBERED STANDARD LESSON GOLD SYSTEM

Name _____   Date _____

Rereading a New Book (Independent Level)

Before Reading
- How did I help the students expand their knowledge of language structures and vocabulary?
- What new or important words did I help them notice in the text?
- What print features or text features did I help them notice?
- How did I help the students understand how the book works and understand critical aspects of the text meaning?

During Reading
- How did I teach for, prompt for, or reinforce effective processing strategies?
- What were the students able to do independently?

FIGURE 7.1 *LLI* Reflection Guide

colleagues. You can download the Reflection Guide from the Online Resources site. You and your colleagues might take turns bringing a videotaped lesson or part of a lesson for a group discussion. At the end of the viewing and discussion using the Reflection Guide, share the new insights that will influence your own teaching.

❑ **Fountas and Pinnell website (fountasand pinnell.com)**—On this website (see Figure 7.2) you will find product updates, notices about new products and services, and a link to the Fountas and Pinnell blog and Facebook page to connect with teachers in the Fountas and Pinnell community.

❑ **Monthly Professional Development Calendar**— In Figure 7.3, we provide monthly suggestions for your continued growth as an *LLI* teacher. Work with your *LLI* colleagues in your school or district to set up meeting times once per month for approximately one and a half to two hours. You also have an array of suggested professional readings in the "Professional Development" section of each lesson that can be used for discussion. Bring your *System Guide* and *Lesson Guide* to each session. This calendar assumes beginning lessons in September, so if you begin in mid-year, you can adjust the calendar accordingly.

FIGURE 7.2 Fountasandpinnell.com Home Page

Monthly Professional Development Calendar

AUGUST	SEPTEMBER	OCTOBER
Knowing Your Readers	**Organizing and Making Transitions**	**Supporting Effective Reading**
You have collected important benchmark data on your students. Use the reading records from your assessment to talk with your colleagues about your groups and the starting levels. At the end of each level is your guide to what students need to be able to do—the behaviors and understandings to notice, teach for, and support from *The Continuum of Literacy Learning*. Use the guide to discuss the specific behaviors you observed in one group and the areas of *Prompting Guide, Part 1* and *Prompting Guide, Part 2* you will want to use as you start lessons. With a partner and the appropriate level book, role play how you demonstrate the reading behaviors you have identified.	You have had a few weeks to get to know the students in your groups and to help them get used to the predictability of the lessons. Select one of the lessons on your Professional Development DVDs to watch. Observe the teacher's organization and the transition from one part of the lesson to the next. Discuss what you notice about organization for teaching, for smooth transitions, and the pace of the lesson. Discuss how the teacher may have or could have facilitated active participation in the lesson activities and discussion.	Focus on the reading segment of your lesson. Think about how your introduction to the new text supports the students' effective processing. Prepare for your meeting by making careful notes of the problem-solving difficulties the students had as they read the new book during the last three lessons. Bring the book in these lessons, and share your observations with each other. Talk about what you might have done during the introduction to the text that would have prevented the processing difficulties. Look at the suggested language for the next instructional level book. Talk about how you will modify it to meet your students' needs.

NOVEMBER	DECEMBER	JANUARY
Using Ongoing Assessment to Inform Your Teaching	**Using *The Continuum* to Guide Teaching Decisions**	**Developing Phonics/Word Study Skills**
You have been taking a reading record on each student every eight days. Bring the last three reading records, including the key understandings, for one student from one of your groups. Work with a partner, using the goals from *The Continuum of Literacy Learning* and your data from the reading records. Talk about the reader's strengths and needs. Also talk about the change in the reader across the three reading records. Discuss what will be important to focus on next in your teaching.	Bring a set of Lesson Records, reading records, and Literacy Notebooks for one group of students. Work with a partner, and use the continuum for the level. Think about the three options you have for Revisiting Yesterday's New Book, and examine your students' present strengths and needs. Consider which of the three options for Revisiting Yesterday's New Book best meets the present needs of your students.	Bring the next odd- and even-numbered standard lesson, the instructional level book, the *Prompting Guide, Part 1*, and the *System Guide*. • Work with a partner to look at the Map for Phonics/Word Study in Appendix B. Use the Plan to think about the principles you have introduced with this group. • Next, look at the upcoming lessons, focusing on the new instructional book and the writing assignment. What opportunities are available for the students to use these phonics/word study principles while reading and writing about reading?

FIGURE 7.3 Monthly Professional Development Calendar

		JANUARY
		Developing Phonics/Word Study Skills
		• Now look for specific teacher language in *Prompting Guide, Part 1* to remind the students to use what they've learned about solving words in reading and in writing about reading.
FEBRUARY	**MARCH**	**APRIL**
Observing Change in Writing About Reading	**Supporting Writing About Reading Development**	**Supporting Fluent, Phrased Reading**
Bring *The Continuum of Literacy Learning*, Literacy Notebooks, and Lesson Records for one of your students. With your colleagues, discuss the changes you see in the writing. Look at the quality of ideas and composition in independent writing. Notice places where the student used correction tape and tried a word or received your support on the trial page. You can even look under the tape at the writer's first attempt. Discuss: • Writing high-frequency words • Using spelling patterns • Constructing multisyllable words • Using complex language structures • Increasing the amount of writing • Ability to hear sounds and record the letters that represent them • Ability to notice how words look • The content or kinds of thinking the student is sharing about text Identify your next teaching moves by referring to the Writing About Reading section in *The Continuum of Literacy Learning* at the grade level that matches the text reading level.	Bring the shared writing pieces you created with one group of students. Take turns presenting your pieces to the group. Talk about your teaching decisions in each. • What do you notice about the sentences you and the students composed? • What do you think the students learned to think about as writers? • What might you have done differently? Look at *Prompting Guide, Part 1* and *Prompting Guide, Part 2.* What prompts did you find useful in supporting the writers as they composed language around their ideas and constructed the text?	Bring one of each book at a level you are using with a group to your meeting. With a partner, look through the books for characteristics that provide opportunities to teach for fluent, phrased reading in each. Consider: • Phrases within sentences • Punctuation • Use of dialogue • Naturalness or complexity of language structures • Use of text features, such as bold letters or speech bubbles Share your insights with colleagues. As a group, talk about the implications for fluency as you introduce the texts and support the reading of the texts with your students.

FIGURE 7.3 Monthly Professional Development Calendar *(cont.)*

continues

section 7

Professional Development and FAQs

117

MAY	JUNE
Expanding Language Across the Lesson	**Supporting Comprehension Across the Lesson**
There are numerous opportunities to support students' use of language and expand their language across the lessons in both reading and writing. Think about one of your students who still has much to learn about the complex, and sometimes formal, English language structures found in written texts. With a partner, look at each element of two consecutive lessons. Talk about:	Bring two books you are using in *LLI* lessons. With a partner, look at the books and discuss how they work. Use the Analysis of New Book, and discuss the ten text characteristics in the corresponding lessons and the message statement. Refer to the New Book segment of the lesson as well as the Writing segment on the following day. Ask yourself:
• Opportunities for students to use language in each element	• How can I support students' attention to the meaning of the text in each element?
• Ways to increase the amount of student talk	• What aspects of the texts may be tricky for my readers?
• Opportunities to model and expand students' language	• How do I want to strengthen their thinking within, beyond, and about the text through the use of these books?
• Opportunities for students to use book language	Share your insights with the group as well as your reflections on a year of teaching.
• Opportunities to expand vocabulary	
• Opportunities and needs specific for ELL	
Share your insights with the group. Talk about changes you want to make in your teaching of the next lessons to provide stronger support for language development.	

FIGURE 7.3 Monthly Professional Development Calendar *(cont.)*

▶ Frequently Asked Questions About *LLI*

Implementing the *LLI Gold System*

What are the main differences between the* Red *and* Gold *systems and the* Orange, Green, *and* Blue *systems?

There are several differences as the *Red System* is the first in the series of *LLI* systems designed specifically for intermediate and middle-level students. You may want to read the research foundation paper at *fountasandpinnell.com./researchLLI.aspx*. The *Red* and *Gold* system lessons are built on a foundation of research related to preadolescent and adolescent literacy that is reflected in the design of the lessons. Each color in the system is designed to provide high-interest

books for the grade level. The books in the *Gold System* are designed to appeal to grade 4 students. Compared to the *Orange, Green*, and *Blue* systems, you will find a higher ratio of nonfiction texts (60 percent), and many are longer with additional nonfiction text features. The *Red* and *Gold System* lessons are designed for daily 45-minute instruction and include a variety of instructional procedures (related to comprehension, vocabulary, and fluency) that differ from the other systems. In addition, there is a four-lesson sequence with a novel at the end of every level and a four-lesson optional test preparation sequence. We believe you will find that the *Red* and *Gold* systems increase the intensity of the instruction to meet the needs of students who may have been struggling with reading for a longer time and at the same time are challenged by higher-level text demands.

Can LLI be used before or after school?

LLI is ideally suited for before or after school or for summer programs. Your important goal would be to group students using good data so that they are on appropriate levels for instruction.

Can LLI be used for tutoring?

The lessons can be used for tutoring with excellent results, although you will miss some of the social interactions of a group.

Does LLI replace guided reading?

LLI is intended to be supplementary instruction. That means that the power of the system is in the extra, intensive help students get in addition to good classroom teaching. Some classroom teachers have had successful results using *LLI* for a short time as a supplement with their lowest achieving readers. These students also had guided reading with their peers at least three times per week.

Is LLI the same as guided reading?

No, *LLI* is a much more intensive framework of components designed to support the accelerated progress of low-achieving students. It is highly systematic and sequential. The books are designed to build on one another. Although word work is provided in guided reading, *LLI* provides more intensive and longer work in phonics and word study. Most students do not need such an intensive approach.

Can a student continue in LLI if she has not made the progress we'd like in the 18–24 weeks?

You would want to do careful progress monitoring to be sure that it is being implemented as designed and the student is making progress throughout the intervention. In the case where there is no progress or extremely slow progress, you may want a thorough assessment of the student's learning needs by a psychologist. If the team then decides that *LLI* is the best intervention, you may decide the student should continue for a longer period of time.

Can I teach LLI lessons in the classroom?

The *LLI* lesson materials are portable enough that you can move from classroom to classroom to work with small groups. Work with the classroom teacher to find a small space that is far enough away from the guided reading table so that the two groups will not interfere with each other. Be sure you have a table and an easel. Working in the classroom is very efficient because students will have very little transition time.

Do I have to complete all of the lessons within each level?

No, but be cautious. Look at *The Continuum of Literacy Learning* for the specific level to be sure the children control most of the behaviors. If your readers are finding the books very easy and in your judgment they understand the phonics and word work principles, you can skip to the next level. (Sometimes teachers spend a lesson doing a "read in" just to experience all the good books on the level—or they send the books back to the classroom for students to read independently. If you choose this option, be sure that the books are within the independent range.)

Scheduling

How can I make the schedule work when there are so many conflicts?

A meeting of all the teachers at the grade level can be very helpful. Classroom teachers want students to have extra help but also have to consider all the demands on their time. Review the schedule and go over the different groups you are trying to convene.

Do all students need to finish the intervention at the same time?

No. If one student is clearly making accelerated progress, you or the classroom teacher can assess him and move him out of the group (or into a higher group) at any time. If a child needs more time in the intervention, have him join another group. It is all right for him to reread, talk about, and write about some of the books in the collection. You can also "borrow" books and lessons from a parallel strand to provide new texts at a level. Remember, there are no repetitions of books or lessons across the three systems.

Selecting Students for *LLI*

Can a student who is labeled a special education child for reading participate in LLI?

It depends on what services the district provides under the label of "special education." If the educational specifications parallel the specific teaching opportunities provided in *LLI*, then it is an option.

Should I use LLI with all my students?

LLI was designed to supplement the instruction that students receive in the classroom. Most students do not need such a structured approach, and teachers prefer more decision making in sequencing texts. Also, *LLI* does not provide enough lessons for daily small-group instruction across an entire year. However, you can decide to use the materials in any way you choose.

How do you decide to group students who are at the same reading level but have different needs?

All students will have slightly different needs. But you are working to place together four students for whom a particular reading level is appropriate. If that is true, then you can begin with lessons and books on a level. You can fine-tune your interactions with them during the lesson to account for their different needs. (For example, within a group reading at a level, one student may need more interactions around word solving and another around fluency.) Most of the time, however, students have multiple needs, and those will change from week to week. As with all teaching, observation is the key.

Attendance/Exiting the Intervention

What should I do when students are absent?

There will always be the problem of a student missing a lesson here and there. Meanwhile, others in the group will be moving on. You can send the missed book back to the classroom or home for the student to read and catch up. If attendance is spotty across the group, you can stop and have a "catch up" day to read and reread books they have missed and to review phonics principles. If a student has an extended absence, reassess and make a decision as to the level she should be reading. Be sure to use the Intervention Record included in the Online Data Management

System (ODMS) and also on the Online Resources site to track student attendance. These records will help you evaluate the success of the intervention.

How do you handle evidence of recurring attendance issues?

In this case, the student may fall behind the group not because he cannot make progress but simply because he is missing too many lessons. (The circumstance may require you to follow the same options listed under the question in this FAQ "What if one student consistently lags behind the others in reading?") But here, attendance is the real problem. Enlist the help of the classroom teacher or school administrator in investigating the problem. Talk with the family to be sure they know how important it is for the student to get to school. If there are health issues, work to understand them with the help of the school nurse and/or counselor, and try to work out a system for sending some materials home to the student.

What do I do if a student moves out of the school?

If possible, conduct a final assessment to get an ending level, and record it on the Recording Form. Look at reading records and reflect on your observation of the children remaining in the group. Working with the classroom teacher, select another child reading at the same instructional level to enter the group from the classroom or from another group if this is a better fit. The reader should be on the present level—not where the group originally started. It will not be necessary to "catch the child up" by reading all of the previous books. Just have this new group member begin where the others are.

Grouping

Do I have to limit the group size to four?

We strongly recommend four students for best results, though you might have to consider five or six. Where it is impossible to limit the groups to four, just try to keep the groups as small as possible. Occasionally, you will find that the levels do not always work out with an even number. At various times, you may find yourself teaching groups of three or even five or six. It is very important for readers to be working at an appropriate level. When working with odd numbers of students, have one student be your partner during word work or vocabulary instruction.

What if one student consistently lags behind the others in reading?

When you have students in a group, you cannot expect them all to perform in exactly the same way. Assess the student carefully using a reading record to be sure the text level is within reach with instructional support. It is a good idea to seat the student closest to you (making sure the student can see charts). You can give a little more individual support to this student to help the processing go a little faster, as fluent reading is important. Also, someone might be able to have the student reread the books in the classroom or at home. If the level is really too hard, try regrouping to place the student with another group at a lower level.

Should I regroup students as I notice differences?

Group members need to get to know each other and learn how to behave as a group. But if a student is clearly not placed at the right level, then you will need to move her right away. If you are working with several groups and you notice a student or two need a lower or higher level, adjust your groupings as best you can to meet the needs of the students. If there are small differences and no other grouping options, you may need to provide a bit more challenge or extra support to one of the group members.

What happens if one student in a group is accelerating faster than the others?

You can look for another group and move the student. It will not be necessary to have the student read all the books the students have read prior to entry. Just move the student into the group. If there is no group and the reader still needs intervention, keep her in the *LLI* group and provide some extra writing or word work. Select leveled books from the other collections to provide extra challenge. Most word work allows for students to go beyond the specific lesson.

What should I do if one student in the group is not moving along as quickly as the others?

This problem will almost always exist when you are working with a group—even a small one; you have three choices. (1) Give the student some extra help when possible. You can enlist the classroom teacher or any school helper or family member in doing some extra reading, word work, or writing with the student. (2) Slow the group down a bit by having a few "reading" or "writing" days to consolidate learning. (Be cautious with this option. It may not help and could slow the others down.) (3) Reassess the student, and move him to another group.

Lesson Time

Can I take longer to get through the lengthy books?

This should be very rare. Remember that students should be reading at a faster pace by the time they reach these levels. They will also be reading silently. Use your own sense of what is appropriate, but try not to "bog down." If you put in an extra day of reading, you can only briefly review the phonics principles and spend most of the time in extended reading, with discussion at the end.

What if my lessons are always too long and I find it hard to finish?

The 45-minute time frame is important as we have found that students start to lose attention after that. As you and the students get used to the routines, you will find it easier to keep the pace. Teach students to be aware of time and help you manage it. For example, they should put word magnets and other materials away quickly and make smooth transitions from one activity to another. You'll be taking a reading record during the even-numbered lesson, but the student will be reading only a short segment of the book. Keep the comprehension conversation brief, using only the prompts you need. Remember that you gained some evidence of the students' understanding during yesterday's discussion.

Organization will help. For example, keep the needed magnetic words together in a plastic bag or a small covered tub for a lesson. Keep all the student's materials in one accordion file or hanging file, and teach them to take them out and put them back quickly. Use a timer, as needed, to keep your lesson well-paced. Check students' reading fluency to make sure they are not simply reading too slowly. If that is the case, concentrate on fluency (see *Prompting Guide,*

Part 1). Finally, look at your lesson goals, and don't teach students things they already know how to do.

What happens if it takes more than 45 minutes to complete the lesson?

First, analyze—are you getting started on time? What is consuming time at the beginning? Try using a timer to determine where your lessons are running over. Where are you getting bogged down? Are the children reading too slowly? Is the discussion going in too many directions? Then tighten up the activities. It is important to get them all in; if you need to, you might use fewer examples to save some time.

Book Level

What if my group reaches the end of a level and I am not sure they are ready to move on to the next level?

Look carefully at the reading records, and then look at the first lesson on the next higher level. If you really think they need more time on the level, you can "borrow" books and lessons at the same level in one of the other systems. If you do not have the other systems, then find more books on the same level (from your guided reading books), and create your own lessons using the same lesson framework. You can review the phonics and word work from the level you are just finishing.

Is it all right to move to the next level without teaching all the lessons?

Yes, but be cautious. If readers are finding the reading material and the writing very easy, then you can skip the rest of the lessons at a level, or even an entire level. But, be sure to look at *The Continuum of Literacy Learning* for the level and think about evidence that the students have strong control of most of the behaviors and understandings required for the level.

What do you do about students whose reading might be at one level, but their writing is well below that level?

Go with the reading level for instruction in *LLI*. Be sure to give emphasis and attention to writing in the standard (even-numbered) lessons. Work closely with the classroom teacher to provide extra classroom writing opportunities.

Why are the novels one level below the instructional level being taught?

The students have completed the level of instruction and are ready to move to the next instructional level when they begin the novel study. We have selected novels one level below so students can enter the text with ease while at the same time learn how to sustain the reading of a longer text and also learn how to think deeply about issues in novels.

Teaching Decisions

How much can I vary the lesson (depart from specific instructions)?

We encourage you to adjust the lesson in any way justified by information from your ongoing assessment and observation of learners' strengths and needs. No lesson plan can be written to fit all students. It would not make sense to consistently eliminate lesson components or to drastically slow down instruction, but you will find yourself tailoring lessons to meet the precise needs of the students you teach.

If students are finding the new text too difficult, should I read it to them first?

No. If the text is so difficult that you need to read it to the students (or provide a very long introduction), then it is probably too hard. They need to experience proficient processing of new text that allows them to build their reading power. Move to an easier level.

If students are finding the new text very easy, should I cut back on the information in the introduction?

You can cut back a little bit, but remember that the introduction is designed to start readers *thinking*. It may be that students can move a little faster through the level or that your placement is too easy.

What do you do about students who have low vocabulary (including English language learners) when you get to books that have lots of concepts and new vocabulary?

You will need a richer introduction and perhaps a longer discussion after reading to be sure students are gaining the vocabulary they need. Also, they will be using these vocabulary words in the writing. After rereading, you can visit a few words just to use them and talk about their meaning. Talk with the classroom teacher to be sure that students are being exposed to new vocabulary daily through interactive read-aloud. Another way to help is to go to previous levels (for example, books that those students have not read) in any of the strands and give students some "extra" books to read that will be easy for them. They can do this in the classroom and will build vocabulary in the process. Finally, you could work into the lesson some word "collections," where you write words that are connected with each other in some way—names of pets, names of animals, words about weather, etc.

Can I carry the reading of the new book over more than one day?

It is best not to carry a book over unless you have no choice. The selections are short enough for one day's reading. You may need to have students finish a book at home, but this is not ideal. Check to be sure you have taught the students to read fluently.

What do you do when students have gaps in the phonics/word analysis area? Do you keep giving them extra practice? Do you stay longer on a level to make up for the gaps? Do you go back and teach previous concepts that they don't have?

These are complex issues and will depend a great deal on teacher decision making. If a student can read the texts at a level (meeting the criteria for instructional level), then usually they have phonics skills. But it would be a good idea to look at *The Continuum of Literacy Learning* and at the phonics and word study activities for that level and the previous level. It may be that you will need to spend a day or two just tidying up some phonics knowledge that will be essential as the children move into higher texts. Work closely with the classroom teacher to identify areas of support needed. You can also select enjoyable games and sorts from the Online Resources site.

How do you help children take on high-frequency words when there isn't enough time in the 45-minute lesson?

You are showing students how to look closely at the words, connect them with other words, and learn them—so their ability to take on new words should

speed up. Students will be doing a great deal of reading, and many new words will be acquired in this activity. Not all words have to be learned in isolation from word cards because the process of learning words is being established.

There are some ways to get extra word learning in. (1) Print out an extra copy of the high-frequency words, and show students how to cut them apart and take them home. Spend some lesson time "practicing" what they will do with their words at home. For example, they can lay them out and find connections. They can play Concentration. They can just turn them over and make piles of "easy words" and "words I'm still learning." (2) Have parents come to a conference, and show them a couple of easy games to play at home. (See the Online Resources site for game directions and word cards.)

How much flexibility do I have with regard to word work? Do I have to work with the suggested words?

The suggested words are there only for your convenience. You can select others that fit the principle you are teaching. If you feel a different principle is needed, make the decision to use the principle that fits your students' needs.

What should I do if the students are not learning words quickly enough?

Visit sections of this book for instructional procedures, and reflect on whether you are being explicit enough in your teaching. Also, look at the chapter in *When Readers Struggle, L–Z: Teaching That Works* (in press) on "Building and Using a Repertoire of Words." You may also select games or sorts from the Online Resources site.

Should all words in the Literacy Notebooks be spelled conventionally?

Most, because students have access to the books plus teacher support. Use white correction tape to help students use conventional spellings. Write some words for them. Also, they will be using letter boxes to help them write some multisyllabic words. There may be an occasional difficult word on which the student has made an excellent attempt and you do not want to take the time to make the spelling conventional. You may decide to ignore a few temporary spellings.

If the lesson specifies shared writing, could I use independent writing instead?

That is your decision. If you think students need a strong demonstration to focus their attention on one text, then use shared writing. If you think that each student needs to do the writing rather than observing some of the time, use independent writing. Sometimes you can write one shared sentence for students to copy (or you to write quickly for them) and then they can go on to write another sentence independently.

How do I support English language learners?

On the last page of every *LLI* lesson, you will find suggestions for fine-tuning the lesson to support English language learners. You will also find information in Section 1 of the *System Guide*. Also see *When Readers Struggle, L–Z: Teaching That Works* (in press).

Assessment

Why do I need to take reading records when I have the benchmark entry information?

The literacy levels of students change, and that is what you want to happen! You need up-to-date objective information to inform your decision making and your use of *Prompting Guide, Part 1*. Your weekly reading records will provide important information for teaching individuals in the group. Also, this information will help you in planning introductions to the text, phonics, and writing.

What if I started on a level that is proving to be too difficult for the group?

As a general practice, begin at a level that you are confident will allow the students to read very successfully. You can stop where you are and move down to a less difficult level if you find you started at the wrong place. As students go up levels, they may meet texts that they previously read and found hard. It will be a confidence booster to encounter these words again and find them within reach.

How often should I take a reading record?

If you take a record as recommended in the standard (even-numbered) lessons, then you will be taking a record every other day. Rotating around a group of four students, you will take one record on each student every eight days. Your daily observations and this procedure will provide enough specific information to guide your teaching.

Do I have to use the Recording Form to take reading records?

If you know how to take running records, you can use a blank form. (This may be more difficult at higher levels because there are so many words on a line and readers move along quickly.) For *LLI* books, you can also take a reading record electronically with the Fountas & Pinnell Reading Record App (in press).

Do you recommend administering a benchmark assessment before moving to the next reading level?

No. That would be too much assessment. If you are observing and taking reading records once every eight days on each student, then you will have a very good idea of how the student is performing at the present level. If they are reading at an instructional level on the first reading and at solid instructional level or independent level on the second reading, then they are probably ready to go on to the next level. Look at *The Continuum of Literacy Learning* for the present level to be sure that you are seeing evidence of the needed behaviors and understandings for thinking within, beyond, and about the text.

Parents

How can I support the student if she is not doing her homework?

LLI homework should take no more than about fifteen minutes. First, be sure that the student understands the homework task and that she can do it independently. If that is the case, the student may have a scheduling problem. Talk with her about the best time to do homework (right after school, right after dinner, etc.). Meet with the classroom teacher if it is very difficult for the student to find time or space at home. Maybe the homework assignment can be shortened somehow. There may be a short time during the school day when the student can do her homework. Another idea is to find a "homework buddy"—perhaps an older student who can support and encourage the *LLI* student.

How can I keep families involved?

Send home the parent letter introducing *LLI* to the family, and be ready to meet with families or talk by phone. (Note that Parent Letters are available in multiple languages—Spanish, French, Hmong, and Haitian Creole—from the Online Resources site.) Emphasize the value of this extra literacy support. Communicate how important it is for the student to participate in every lesson without missing any. Invite families to watch a lesson. Occasionally, attach an encouraging note to families to the student's portfolio to reinforce good thinking and effort. As time allows, make quick phone calls to families to share progress. Write a note to the student's family in the Literacy Notebook. Always encourage the students to show families the books they take home and teach them something they've learned. Encourage students to visit websites to learn more about topics.

Why are there no Take-Home (one-color) books with the Red, Gold, Purple, *and* Teal *systems?*

Students in grade 3 and beyond need to learn how to bring school materials home for work and return them to school the next day. They need to learn how to assume borrowing privileges such as those given in the public library. This is an opportunity to teach students responsibility. In addition, many of the *Red* and *Gold System* nonfiction books include scientific photographs, charts, maps, and diagrams that would not

be effective in black and white. Students can also enjoy the beautiful, colorful book in their original form in the classroom and at home. The sophisticated portfolio is a good tool for helping students become responsible and organized.

Should I send the LLI *books home with students?*

Yes! Students need to learn responsibility for caring for books—taking them home and bringing them back. They have a special portfolio for this purpose. Encourage them to keep the books in the portfolio so they will not forget them as they leave for school in the morning. They should take books home as needed. The new book in the standard (even-numbered) lesson will often be finished for homework.

Should I tell the parents the level I am working on?

We do not recommend the use of letter levels to show progress to parents. A level is a teacher's tool for selecting books. The level stands for a complex set of cognitive activities. You can explain the program to parents and other family members or caregivers as continuous progress. Show them the books their child was reading at the beginning of *LLI* and what he is reading now. Help them look at the books and understand progress. Explain that the level helps you monitor progress and teach the student. Try to avoid the "level" being something that parents and caregivers focus on too much.

appendix

System Book Chart

Book/Lesson Level O	1 Revolting Recipes (Level O)	2 Playing Tricks (Level M)	3 A Fresh Start (Level O)	4 The Broken Elevator (Level M)	5 The Truth About Bats (Level O)
	6 Animals and Their Tools (Level M)	7 Dinosaur Fleas (Level O)	8 Kangaroos in Trees (Level M)	9 The Shiner (Level O)	10 The Genius Club (Level M)
	11 Andromeda Clark Walks on the Moon (Level O)	12 Making Art for Fish (Level M)	13 The Pocket Watch (Level O)	14 Glow-in-the-Dark Animals (Level M)	15 Holding Up the Sky/Coyote's Dinner (Two-Way) (Level O)
	16 Fake Cake (Level M)	17 Trying Out (Level O)	18 The Turning Point (Level M)	19 The Story of Naismith's Game (Level O)	20 The Thorny Dragon (Level M)
	21 Double Double Trouble Trouble (Level O)	22 The Great Tug-of-War (Level M)	23 The Boy Who Saves Camels (Level O)	24 How to Train Your Human (Level M)	25–28* (Novel Study) Surviving Brick Johnson (Level N)
Book/Lesson Level P	33 The Paper Ball (Level P)	34 Best Enemies (Level N)	35 ER Vets to the Rescue (Level P)	36 The Great Back-yard Bird Count (Level N)	37 Animal Warnings (Level P)
	38 An Out-of-This-World Vacation (Level N)	39 Making Stories with Jeff Kinney (Level P)	40 The Absolute Worst Vacation Ever (Level N)	41 A Shining Star of Science: Cecelia Payne-Gaposchkin (Level P)	42 Kitty's Master Plan (Level N)
	43 A Young Hero with a Big Heart: The Story of Ana Dodson (Level P)	44 Ryan's Well (Level N)	45 The World Beneath Your Feet (Level P)	46 JT's Journal (Level N)	47 The Mystery of Anting (Level P)
	48 The Amazing Gecko (Level N)	49 Keeping the Light (Level P)	50 Message in a Bottle (Level N)	51 So You Speak African? (Level P)	52 Rashawn Steps Up (Level N)
	53 The Rock Garden (Level P)	54 The Summer I Met the City (Level N)	55 The Egg: Nature's Perfect Package (Level P)	56 The Mystery of the Missing Key (Level N)	57–60* (Novel Study) The PS Brothers (Level O)

*The four lessons following novel study are the optional test preparation lessons that do not have books associated with them.

System Book Chart

Book/Lesson Level Q	65 The Peculiar Platypus (Level Q)	66 Share the Seas with Manatees (Level O)	67 Yellow Feathers/ Cher Ami (Two-Way) (Level Q)	68 Wildlife in the City (Level O)	69 Octopus: Escape Artist of the Sea (Level Q)
	70 Bigfoot: What's the Evidence? (Level O)	71 Basketball: Changing the Game (Level Q)	72 Working Vacation (Level O)	73 The Great Debate (Level O)	74 A Real Family (Level O)
	75 Flying Fish: Take a Flying Leap/ Water Birds: From the Sky to the Sea (Two-Way) (Level Q)	76 Andromeda Clark, North Pole Explorer (Level O)	77 Alone in the Jungle (Level Q)	78 A Cliff Story (Level O)	79 Sapporo: A Snow Sculpture City (Level Q)
	80 People Powered: Pedaling on Land, Sea, and Air (Level O)	81 Countdown to Showtime (Level Q)	82 Circus Kid (Level O)	83 Why the Sea is Salty (A Tale from Iceland) (Level Q)	84 Rabbit and the Queasy Quivers (Level O)
	85 Knocked Out (Level Q)	86 Living in Space (Level O)	87 Born to Fly (Level Q)	88 Looking for Earth 2 (Level O)	89–92* (Novel Study) Switcharound (Level P)
Book/Lesson Level R	97 Rescuing Orangutans (Level R)	98 Mission: Dog Rescue (Level P)	99 The Yo-yo Caper (Level R)	100 Super Silk (Level P)	101 The Heroes of Pea Island (Level R)
	102 Surviving Cutts Island (Level P)	103 Shadow Magic: The Ancient Art of Shadow Puppetry (Level R)	104 Why Do I Have To . . . ? (Level P)	105 Seasick (Level R)	106 Jack at Sea (Level P)
	107 Odd Couples (Level R)	108 Look, Don't Touch! (Level P)	109 Flashy Flamingos (Level R)	110 Stranded! A Marine Mammal Mystery (Level P)	111 T. Rex: Scavenger or Predator? (Level R)
	112 Flying Money (Level P)	113 The Corpse Flower (Level R)	114 Chill Out! Science to Make You Shiver (Level P)	115 Andromeda Clark Makes Time Fly (Level R)	116 Andromeda Clark and the Mummy's Curse (Level P)

*The four lessons following novel study are the optional test preparation lessons that do not have books associated with them.

System Book Chart

Book/Lesson Level R (cont.)	117 *The Two Brothers: A Tale from Vietnam* (Level R)	118 *Amin and the Terrible Ogre: A Tale from Iran* (Level P)	119 *Geysers* *(Level R)*	120 *The Beast of Cross Mountain* (Level P)	121–124* (Novel Study) *Runt* (Level Q)
Book/Lesson Level S	129 *Tarantulas: Creepy, Crawly, and . . . Not So Scary* (Level S)	130 *Hidden Dangers of the Great Barrier Reef* (Level Q)	131 *Whitewater!* (Level S)	132 *Ice Climbing: The Frozen Challenge* (Level Q)	133 *Hero Rats* (Level S)
	134 *Upcycling: Turning Garbage into Gold* (Level Q)	135 *Spy Devices: Searching for Secrets* (Level S)	136 *Keeping a Secret: How to Create Codes* (Level Q)	137 *Buried Treasure* (Level S)	138 *Scarecrows and Girlfriends* (Level Q)
	139 *Crabs on the Run* (Level S)	140 *King of the Dogs* (Level Q)	141 *Sweet But Deadly: The Great Molasses Flood* (Level S)	142 *Partners In Crime* (Level Q)	143 *Escape to Freedom: The Story of Henry Box Brown* (Level S)
	144 *Snowmobiles: A Life-Saving Invention* (Level Q)	145 *The Science of Bread/Butter* (Two-Way) (Level S)	146 *What's For Breakfast?* (Level Q)	147 *The Robopoet 2000* (Level S)	148 *Little Plane, Huge Dream* (Level Q)
	149 *The History of Chewing Gum* (Level S)	150 *The Old Knife* (Level Q)	151 *The Mimic Octopus: A Master of Disguise* (Level S)	152 *The Octopus Project: How Nature is Shaping Robots* (Level Q)	153–156* (Novel Study) *Spider Boy* (Level R)

*The four lessons following novel study are the optional test preparation lessons that do not have books associated with them.

System Book Chart

Book/Lesson Level T	161 That's Gross (Level T)	162 Rowbear (Level R)	163 Rotten in Riverton (Level T)	164 Rescuing Entangled Whales (Level R)	165 Stopping Animal Invaders (Level T)
	166 Coconut: The Tree of Life (Level R)	167 Waiting for the Norah Ben (Level T)	168 Lornah Kiplagat: Long-Distance Hero* (Level R)	169 Jon Brooks: Art from Nature (Level T)	170 Amazing Brick Artists (Level R)
	171 The Good, The Bad, and the Piggy (Level T)	172 Project Lizard (Level R)	173 Rules of Survival (Level T)	174 Alien Stepmother (Level R)	175 Living Small: Life in a Tiny House (Level T)
	176 The Invitation (Level R)	177 Messages to the World: Art from Cape Dorset (Level T)	178 Joining Hands with a Village (Level R)	179 Splash! A Short History of Bathing (Level T)	180 Strange Rain (Level R)
	181 Scream Machines (Level T)	182 Accidental Inventions (Level R)	183 Jill Heinerth: Underwater Cave Explorer (Level T)	184 The Secret World of Caves (Level R)	185–189* (Novel Study) The Lemonade War (Level S)

*The four lessons following novel study are the optional test preparation lessons that do not have books associated with them.

Map for Phonics/Word Study				
SYLLABIC	**Level 0, Lesson 1**	**Level 0, Lesson 2**	**Level 0, Lesson 3**	**Level 0, Lesson 4**
Long and Short Vowel Patterns	Long and Short Vowel Patterns (*a, o*) Some words have a vowel pattern with a long or short sound (*a, o*). (*back, float, race, stop*)	Long and Short Vowel Patterns (*e, u*) Some words have a vowel pattern with a long or short sound (*e, u*). (*blue, chess, fruit, scrub, street, treat, tube*)	Long and Short Vowel Patterns (*i*) Some words have a vowel pattern with a long or short sound (*i*). (*hill, might, quick, twice, twist, why, write*)	Long and Short Vowel Patterns (*a, e, i, o, u*) Some words have a vowel pattern with a long or short sound (*a, e, i, o u*). (*brush, fight, class, float, frost, raise, knot, same, quick, throw, tell, treat, true, write*)
MORPHEMIC	**Level 0, Lesson 5**	**Level 0, Lesson 6**	**Level 0, Lesson 7**	**Level 0, Lesson 8**
Homophones **Multiple-Meaning Words** **Suffixes**	Homophones Some words sound the same but are spelled differently and have different meanings They are called homophones. (*board/bored, cents/scents, flew/flu, flower/flour, plane/plain*)	Multiple-Meaning Words Some words look the same but mean something different. They can be different parts of speech. (*play, nail, ruler, sink*)	Suffixes (*-ful, -ish, -y, -ly, -al*) Add a suffix to change a word from a noun to an adjective. Sometimes the spelling changes. (*breeze/breezy, child/childish, friend/friendly, nature/natural, noise/noisy, skill/skillful, storm/stormy, sun/sunny*)	Suffix (*-ly*) Add the suffix *-ly* to change a describing word (adjective) to a word that tells how (adverb). (*clear, clearly; lazy, lazily; quick, quickly; noisy, noisily; rough, roughly; smooth, smoothly*)
SYLLABIC	**Level 0, Lesson 9**	**Level 0, Lesson 10**	**Level 0, Lesson 11**	**Level 0, Lesson 12**
Long Vowel Patterns **Unique Vowel Sounds** ***r*-influenced Vowels**	Long Vowel Patterns in Two-Syllable Words Some two-syllable words have a long vowel pattern. The stress can be on either syllable. (*boastful, alone, frighten, approach, payment, complain, dislike, erase*)	Long Vowel Patterns in Two-Syllable Words Some two-syllable words have a long vowel pattern. The stress can be on either syllable. (*fewer, agree, freedom, complete, useful, defeat, weakness, include, outgrew*)	Unique Vowel Sounds in Two-Syllable Words (*oi, oy, ou, ow*) Some two-syllable words have two letters that make a unique vowel sound like the sound in *boy* or *cow*. (*loyal, around, moisture, powder, poison, thousand*)	*r*-Influenced Vowels in Two-Syllable Words (*er, ir, ur*) Some two-syllable words have a pattern that blends the vowel with *r*. (*person, circus, purple*)

Map for Phonics/Word Study

MORPHEMIC	Level O, Lesson 13	Level O, Lesson 14	Level O, Lesson 15	Level O, Lesson 16
Plurals **Irregular Past-Tense Verbs** **Inflectional Endings**	Plurals (*f* or *fe* to *v*) Change the spelling of some words to make them plural (*f* or *fe* to *v*). (*calf/calves, knife/knives, life/lives*)	Plurals of Words Ending in *-y* Add *-s* to nouns ending in a vowel and *-y* to make them plural. Change the *y* to *i* and add *-es* to nouns ending with a consonant and *y* to make them plural. (*bully, canary, donkey, valley, bullies, canaries, donkeys, valleys*)	Irregular Past-Tense Verbs Change the spelling of some action words to show they happened in the past. (*draw/drew, drive/drove, say/said, sleep/slept*)	Inflectional Endings (*-ed, -ing*) When you add *-ed* or *-ing* to a base word with two syllables, sometimes the spelling changes. (*escape, escaped, escaping, admit, admitted, admitting, visit, visited, visiting, carry, carried, carrying, destroy, destroyed, destroying*)

SYLLABIC	Level O, Lesson 17	Level O, Lesson 18	Level O, Lesson 19	Level O, Lesson 20
Vowel Patterns **Unique Vowel Patterns** **Closed and Open Syllables**	Vowel Patterns (*au, aw, o, ough*) Some words have a short vowel pattern, and it can be represented by different spellings. (*laundry, awful, softly, bought*)	Vowel Patterns (*augh, ough, al*) Some words have a vowel pattern that sounds like a short *o* and is represented by the letters *augh, ough,* or *al*. (*naughty, thoughtful, walkway*)	Unique Vowel Patterns (*ou, ow*) Some two-syllable words have a vowel pattern with a unique sound. It can be represented by the letters *ou* or *ow*. (*country, loudly, power, thousand, touchy, towel*)	Two-Syllable Words with Closed or Open Syllables Some two-syllable words have an open first syllable while others have a closed first syllable. (*bonus, insect, never, silent*)

MORPHEMIC	Level O, Lesson 21	Level O, Lesson 22	Level O, Lesson 23	Level O, Lesson 24
Prefixes **Comparative Endings**	Prefixes (*un-, re-*) Add a prefix to a word to change its meaning. Add *un-* to mean "not" and *re-* to mean "again." (*certain, uncertain, equal, unequal, kind, unkind, selfish, unselfish, steady, unsteady, cycle, recycle, model, remodel, tell, retell, view, review*)	Prefixes (*dis-, mis-*) Add a prefix to a word to change its meaning. Add *dis-* to mean "not" or "the opposite of" and add *mis-* to mean "doing something wrongly." (*place, displace, misplace*)	Prefixes (*non-, pre-*) Add a prefix to a word to change its meaning. Add *non-* to mean "not" and *pre-* to mean "before." (*nonfat, nonstick, prepay, prerecord*)	Comparative Endings (*-er, -est*) Add the suffix *-er* or *-est* to a word to show comparison. Sometimes the spelling of the base word changes. (*brave, braver, bravest, cool, cooler, coolest, happy, happier, happiest, hot, hotter, hottest*)

Map for Phonics/Word Study

Novel Study Week	**Level O, Lesson 25** n/a	**Level O, Lesson 26** n/a	**Level O, Lesson 27** n/a	**Level O, Lesson 28** n/a
Test Preparation Week	**Level O, Lesson 29** n/a	**Level O, Lesson 30** n/a	**Level O, Lesson 31** n/a	**Level O, Lesson 32** n/a
SYLLABIC	**Level P, Lesson 33**	**Level P, Lesson 33**	**Level P, Lesson 35**	**Level P, Lesson 36**
r-**Influenced Vowel Patterns**	Vowel Pattern *ar* in Multisyllable Words Some multisyllable words have a vowel pattern with *ar*. (*carpet, dollar, marble, sugar*)	*r*-Influenced Vowel Patterns in Multisyllable Words (*er, ir, ur*) Some multisyllable words have a vowel pattern with *er, ir,* or *ur*. (*hermit, circle, hurricane, jersey, firmly, purpose, permanent, virtue, turban, person, turtle*)	Vowel Pattern *or* in Multisyllable Words Some multisyllable words have a vowel pattern with *or*. (*border, corner, perform, report*)	Vowel Patterns *ur* and *ure* in Multisyllable Words Some multisyllable words have a vowel pattern with *ur* or *ure*. (*burning, mature, return, unsure*)
MORPHEMIC	**Level P, Lesson 37**	**Level P, Lesson 38**	**Level P, Lesson 39**	**Level P, Lesson 40**
Homophones **Homographs** **Compound Words** **High-Frequency Words**	Homophones Some multisyllable words sound the same but have different meanings and are usually spelled differently. (*ceiling/sealing, cellar/seller, morning/mourning, peddle/pedal*)	Homographs Some words look the same but mean different things. They may be pronounced differently. (*batter/batter, desert/desert, invalid/invalid, pupil/pupil*)	Compound Words Some words are made of two smaller words. (*lighthouse, daylight, sunlight, moonlight*)	High-Frequency Words Some words appear frequently in reading and writing. Notice the tricky parts to learn them. (*because, people, their, these, they're, though*)

Map for Phonics/Word Study				
SYLLABIC	**Level P, Lesson 41**	**Level P, Lesson 42**	**Level P, Lesson 43**	**Level P, Lesson 44**
Consonant Clusters **Silent _e_** **Silent Consonants**	Consonant Clusters in Multisyllable Words Some multisyllable words have consonant clusters or digraphs at the beginning that are blended together or make a unique sound. (_chocolate, gloomy, sprouting, squeamish, sweeter, thickness, triplets_)	Final Consonant Clusters Some words have consonant clusters at the end that are blended or make one sound. (_beneath, bridge, harvest, mustang, parent, publish, result, sandwich, sketch, telegraph_)	Syllables with Silent _e_ Some multisyllable words have a syllable that ends in a silent _e_. (_disgrace, donate, reptile, profile_)	Words with Silent Consonants Some words have consonants that are silent. (_design, honest, know, soften, write_)
MORPHEMIC	**Level P, Lesson 45**	**Level P, Lesson 46**	**Level P, Lesson 47**	**Level P, Lesson 48**
Adjectives to Adverbs **Nouns to Adjectives** **Suffixes**	Change Adjectives to Adverbs with _-ly_ Add _-ly_ to some describing words (adjectives) to make words that tell how something is done (adverbs). (_quickly, roughly, easily, lazily_)	Change Nouns to Adjectives with _-y_ Add the suffix _-y_ to change a noun to an adjective. (_breezy, cloudy, foggy_)	Change Nouns to Adjectives with _-ous_ Add the suffix _-ous_ to change a noun to an adjective. (_courageous, famous, mysterious, thunderous_)	Noun Suffixes (_-er, -or, -ist_) Add _-er, -or,_ or _-ist_ to a base word to name a person who does things. (_teacher, actor, pianist_)
SYLLABIC	**Level P, Lesson 49**	**Level P, Lesson 50**	**Level P, Lesson 51**	**Level P, Lesson 52**
Medial Consonants **Open and Closed Syllables** **_r_-influenced Vowels**	Multisyllable Words with Medial Consonants Some multisyllable words have single consonants in the middle. (_humor, moment, never, planet, seven, silent, wagon_)	Multisyllable Words with Open or Closed Syllables Some multisyllable words have an open or closed syllable. (_can/dy, hab/it, la/zy, mu/sic, se/cret, sto/len_)	Multisyllable Words with Two or Three Medial Consonants Some multisyllable words have two or three consonants in the middle. (_chapter, drummer, hollow, hundred, kingdom, method, mushroom, pattern, pumpkin, ticket_)	Multisyllable Words with _r_-Influenced Vowel Patterns Some multisyllable words have a syllable with a vowel pattern and _r_. Some have an _r_-influenced vowel pattern that sounds like long _e_. (_appear, cheerful, early, kernel. sincere_)

Map for Phonics/Word Study

MORPHEMIC	Level P, Lesson 53	Level P, Lesson 54	Level P, Lesson 55	Level P, Lesson 56
Prefixes **Suffixes** **Inflectional Endings**	Prefixes (*pre-, non-, mis-*) Add prefixes to words to change their meanings: *pre-* to mean "before," *non-* to mean "not," and *mis-* to mean "doing something wrongly." (*preheat, nondrip, misjudge, preplan, nonstop, mistreat*)	Prefixes (*re-, dis-, un-*) Add prefixes to words to change their meanings: *re-* to mean "again," *dis-* to mean "not" or "the opposite of," and *un-* to mean "not" or "the opposite of." (*rebuild, disappear, unfold, recycle, dishonest, unhappy, reuse, dislike, unsteady, rewrite, unusual*)	Suffixes (*-less, -ness, -ful*) Add suffixes to words to change their meanings: *-less* to mean "without," *-ness* to mean "state or quality of being," and *-ful* to mean "full of." (*color, colorless, colorful; bright, brightness; fear, fearless, fearful; fair, fairness; harm, harmless, harmful; ill, illness; pain, painless, painful; weak, weakness*)	Inflectional Endings on Multisyllable Words Ending with *y* When *-s, -es, -ed,* or *-ing* is added to a word ending in *y*, sometimes the spelling of the base word changes. (*buries, buried, copies, copied, enjoys, enjoyed, obeys, obeyed*)
Novel Study Week	**Level P, Lesson 57** n/a	**Level P, Lesson 58** n/a	**Level P, Lesson 59** n/a	**Level P, Lesson 60** n/a
Test Preparation Week	**Level P, Lesson 61** n/a	**Level P, Lesson 62** n/a	**Level P, Lesson 63** n/a	**Level P, Lesson 64** n/a
SYLLABIC	Level Q, Lesson 65	Level Q, Lesson 66	Level Q, Lesson 67	Level Q, Lesson 68
Hard and Soft *c* **Hard and Soft *g*** **Sound of *k*** **Consonant Digraphs**	Words with a Hard or Soft *c* Sound When *c* is followed by *a, o,* or *u,* it usually has a hard sound like *k.* When *c* is followed by an *e, i,* or *y,* it usually has a soft sound like *s.* (*cabin, central, cereal, cider, collect, cuddly, cyclist*)	Words with a Hard or Soft *g* Sound When *g* is followed by *a, o,* or *u,* it usually has a hard sound. When *g* is followed by an *e, i,* or *y,* it usually has a soft sound like *j.* (*garden, gentle, giraffe, gossip, gutter, gymnast*)	Words with the *k* Sound The sound of *k* can be represented by different letters (*k, c, ck, ch, qu*). (*token, attic, plastic, attack, buckle, stomach, conquer, plaque*)	Multisyllable Words with Consonant Digraphs Some words have two consonants that make one sound. They are called consonant digraphs. (*photograph, shampoo, chimney, thought, whistle, shelter, chocolate*)

MORPHEMIC	Level Q, Lesson 69	Level Q, Lesson 70	Level Q, Lesson 71	Level Q, Lesson 72
Plurals **Plural Possessives** **High-Frequency Words**	Plurals with Spelling Changes Change the spelling of some words to form plurals. (*child/children, life/lives, tooth/teeth, woman/women*)	Plural Possessives Add an apostrophe to a plural word ending in *s* to show it belongs to more than one person or thing. (*carpenter, carpenters, carpenters', girl, girls, girls', pilot, pilots, pilots'*)	High-Frequency Words Some words appear frequently in reading and writing. Notice the tricky parts to learn them. (*around, because, early, favorite, second*)	High-Frequency Words Some words appear frequently in reading and writing. Notice the tricky parts to learn them. (*against, already, although, definitely, somewhere, whether*)
SYLLABIC	Level Q, Lesson 73	Level Q, Lesson 74	Level Q, Lesson 75	Level Q, Lesson 76
Syllables	Words with Open Syllables Break words after the vowel when the vowel sound in the first syllable is long. (*broken, butter, chosen, helmet, pupil, number, solar, spider*)	Words with Closed Syllables Break words after the consonant when the vowel sound in the first syllable is short. (*absent, fever, blister, future, capture, rumor, pretzel, tablet*)	Words with Two Medial Consonants Break words between two medial consonants, but keep digraphs together. (*object, fashion, rugged, gather, rustic, machine, witness*)	Words with a Consonant + *-le* Syllable Break words, before a final consonant + *-le*. (*ankle, crumble, handle, middle, simple, table*)
MORPHEMIC	Level Q, Lesson 77	Level Q, Lesson 78	Level Q, Lesson 79	Level Q, Lesson 80
Synonyms **Antonyms** **Homophones** **Homographs**	Synonyms Some words have almost the same meaning. They are called synonyms. (*lucky/fortunate, voyage/journey, wonderful/marvelous*)	Antonyms Some words have opposite meanings. They are called antonyms. (*boring/exciting, forget/remember, guilty/innocent*)	Homophones Some words sound the same but are spelled differently and have different meanings. They are called homophones. (*aloud/allowed, cymbal/symbol, presence/presents*)	Homographs Some words are spelled the same but have different meanings and are sometimes pronounced differently. (*cricket/cricket, entrance/entrance, flounder/flounder, staple/staple*)

APPENDIX B

Map for Phonics/Word Study

SYLLABIC	Level Q, Lesson 81	Level Q, Lesson 82	Level Q, Lesson 83	Level Q, Lesson 84
Syllables	Words with Medial Consonants Break words with two medial consonants between the consonants, but keep digraphs together. When a multisyllable word has three medial consonants, break the word between consonants, keeping the digraph or consonant cluster together. (*chicken, fashion, harvest, napkin, support*)	Words with Long and Short Vowel Sounds Break two-syllable words after the first vowel when the vowel sound is long. Break two-syllable words after the consonant that follows the first vowel when the vowel sound is short. (*cradle, dragon, future, problem, humor, splendid, migrate, timid, private, wisdom*)	Words with Two Medial Vowel Sounds Break words between two vowels when you can hear the sound of each vowel. (*create, diet, duet, lion, poet, reuse*)	Words with a Consonant + -*le* Syllable Break words before the consonant + -*le*, but don't separate consonant digraphs. (*able, beetle, cycle, eagle, gentle, pickle*)
MORPHEMIC	Level Q, Lesson 85	Level Q, Lesson 86	Level Q, Lesson 87	Level Q, Lesson 88
Inflectional Endings	Inflectional Endings (-*ed*, -*ing*) When you add -*ed* or -*ing* to a base word that ends with a short vowel and a consonant, double the final letter; drop the *e* when the word ends with a silent *e*. (*dripped, dripping; hopped, hopping; liked, liking; raked, raking*)	Inflectional Endings (-*ed*, -*ing*) When adding -*ed* to a base word that ends with a consonant and *y*, change the *y* to *i* before adding the ending. No spelling change is needed when adding -*ed* to a base word that ends with a vowel and *y*. When adding -*ing* to a base word that ends with *y*, no spelling change is needed. (*played, playing, tried, trying*)	Inflectional Endings for Two-Syllable Words (-*ed*, -*ing*) When you add -*ed* or -*ing* to a two-syllable word with an accented second syllable, use the same principles that apply to one-syllable words. (*denied, denying; destroyed, destroying; refused, refusing; regretted, regretting*)	Inflectional Endings (-*ed*, -*ing*) Add a *k* to words ending in *c* before adding -*ed* or -*ing*. (*panic, panicked, panicking; picnic, picknicked, picknicking*)

Map for Phonics/Word Study

Novel Study Week	Level Q, Lesson 89	Level Q, Lesson 90	Level Q, Lesson 91	Level Q, Lesson 92
	n/a	n/a	n/a	n/a
Test Preparation Week	**Level Q, Lesson 93**	**Level Q, Lesson 94**	**Level Q, Lesson 95**	**Level Q, Lesson 96**
	n/a	n/a	n/a	n/a
SYLLABIC	**Level R, Lesson 97**	**Level R, Lesson 98**	**Level R, Lesson 99**	**Level R, Lesson 100**
Long Vowel Sounds **Unique Vowel Sounds** **r-Influenced Vowels**	Long Vowel Sounds in Multisyllable Words Some multisyllable words have an accented syllable with a long vowel sound. (*amuse, compose, contain, debate, delight, feeble, pollute, season, surprise*)	Unique Vowel Sounds in Multisyllable Words Some multisyllable words have a syllable with a unique vowel sound (*oi, oy, ou, ow*). (*around, avoid, drowsy, joyful, mountain, poison, vowel, voyage*)	r-Influenced Vowels in Multisyllable Words Some multisyllable words have an accented syllable with a vowel and the consonant *r*. Blend the sound of the vowel with *r*. (*circuit, concern, observe, stirring, urban, uncurl*)	Multisyllable Words with -*er* or -*ure* Some multisyllable words have a syllable with the *er* sound spelled -*er* or -*ure*. (*barber, creature, pleasure, butcher, mixture, treasure*)
MORPHEMIC	**Level R, Lesson 101**	**Level R, Lesson 102**	**Level R, Lesson 103**	**Level R, Lesson 104**
High-Frequency Words	High-Frequency Words Some words appear frequently in reading and writing. Notice the tricky parts to learn them. (*friend, once, should, thought*)	High-Frequency Words Some words appear frequently in reading and writing. Notice the tricky parts to learn them. (*beautiful, because, frequently, usually*)	High-Frequency Words Some words appear frequently in reading and writing. Notice the tricky parts to learn them. (*already, caught, happily, knowledge*)	High-Frequency Words Some words appear frequently in reading and writing. Notice the tricky parts to learn them. (*different, difficult, except, toward*)
SYLLABIC	**Level R, Lesson 105**	**Level R, Lesson 106**	**Level R, Lesson 107**	**Level R, Lesson 108**
Long e Vowel Patterns **Soft c** **Soft g** **Word Endings**	Vowel Patterns (*ie, ei*) Some words have an *ie* or *ei* pattern that sounds like the long *e* in *niece* and *receive*. (*briefly, cookie, prairie, relieve, deceive, receipt*)	Multisyllable Words with a Soft *c* Sound When the letter *c* is followed by *e, i*, or *y*, the sound of the *c* is usually soft. (*acid, advance, cyclone, distance, privacy*)	Multisyllable Words with a Soft *g* Sound When the letter *g* is followed by *e, i*, or *y*, the sound of the *g* is usually soft. (*edgy, fragile, legend, magic, village*)	Multisyllable Words Ending with -*el* or -*le* Some multisyllable words end with -*el* or -*le*. (*cancel, easel, fable, little, table*)

Map for Phonics/Word Study

MORPHEMIC	Level R, Lesson 109	Level R, Lesson 110	Level R, Lesson 111	Level R, Lesson 112
Inflectional Endings	Inflectional Endings for Two-Syllable Words (-ed, -ing) Add -ed or -ing to a two-syllable base word to change the tense or meaning. Sometimes the spelling of the base word changes. (*behave, commit, explore, figure*)	Inflectional Endings for Multisyllable Words (-ed, -ing) Add -ed or -ing to multisyllable base words to change the tense or meaning. Sometimes the spelling of the base word changes. (*decay, disobey, empty, reply, terrify*)	Inflectional Endings for Two-Syllable Words (-ed, -ing) Add -ed or -ing to two-syllable words accented on the first syllable to change the tense or meaning. (*edit, practice, vanish*)	Inflectional Endings for Two-Syllable Words (-ed, -ing) Add -ed or -ing to two-syllable words accented on the second syllable to change the tense or meaning. (*complain, decline, enlist, inflate, review*)

SYLLABIC	Level R, Lesson 113	Level R, Lesson 114	Level R, Lesson 115	Level R, Lesson 116
Words Ending with -ing **Long Vowel Patterns**	Words Ending with -ing When -ing is added to a base word, sometimes the spelling changes. (*admitting, complaining, completing, donating, inviting, maintaining, migrating, submitting*)	Long *a* Vowel Patterns in Accented Syllables Break words with a long *a* pattern in the accented syllable to read them. (*delay, erase, fable, famous, mason, payment, retain, safety, traitor*)	Long *i* Vowel Patterns in Accented Syllables Break words with a long *i* pattern in the accented syllable to read them. (*arrive, brighten, delight, final, lightning, ninety, silent, spider, unkind*)	Long *o* Vowel Patterns in Accented Syllables Break words with a long *o* pattern in the accented syllable to read them. (*frozen, abode, lonely, alone, lower, below, ocean, compose, slowly, enroll*)

MORPHEMIC	Level R, Lesson 117	Level R, Lesson 118	Level R, Lesson 119	Level R, Lesson 120
Prefixes **Suffixes**	Prefix (*in-*) Add a prefix to a word to change its meaning. Add *in-* to mean "not" or "in, into, or within." (*incomplete, inexpensive, invisible, indoors, infield, inset*)	Suffix (*-able*) Add a suffix to the end of a base word to change its meaning. Add the suffix *-able* to mean "capable of." (*admirable, affordable, changeable, enjoyable, identifiable, predictable, valuable, variable*)	Suffix (*-al*) Add a suffix to a word to change its meaning. Add *-al* to mean "having the characteristics of." (*accidental, ceremonial, political, tribal*)	Suffixes (*-ant, -ent*) Add a suffix to the end of a base word to change its meaning. The suffixes *-ant* and *-ent* mean "inclined to." (*defy/defiant, differ/different, observe/observant, repel/repellent*)

Map for Phonics/Word Study				
Novel Study Week	**Level R, Lesson 121** n/a	**Level R, Lesson 122** n/a	**Level R, Lesson 123** n/a	**Level R, Lesson 124** n/a
Test Preparation Week	**Level R, Lesson 125** n/a	**Level R, Lesson 126** n/a	**Level R, Lesson 127** n/a	**Level R, Lesson 128** n/a
SYLLABIC	**Level S, Lesson 129**	**Level S, Lesson 130**	**Level S, Lesson 131**	**Level S, Lesson 132**
Long Vowel Patterns **Unique Vowel Sounds**	Long *u* Patterns in Accented Syllables Break words with a long *u* pattern in the accented syllable to read them. (*amuse, conclude, human, include, pollute, rumor*)	Long *e* Patterns in Accented Syllables Break words with a long *e* pattern in the accented syllable to read them. (*defeat, needle, reason, succeed*)	Long Vowel Patterns in Accented Syllables Break words with a long vowel pattern in the accented syllable to read them. (*became, donor, indeed, lightning, rumor*)	Unique Vowel Sounds in Accented Syllables (*oi, oy, ou, ow*) Break words with a unique vowel sound in the accented syllable to read them. (*around, flower, coward, outrage, embroider, pointless, enjoy, voyage*)
MORPHEMIC	**Level S, Lesson 133**	**Level S, Lesson 134**	**Level S, Lesson 135**	**Level S, Lesson 136**
Prefixes	Prefixes (*uni-, bi-, tri-*) Some words have a prefix. A prefix can help you understand the meaning of a word. The prefix *uni-* means "single" or "one." The prefix *bi-* means "two." The prefix *tri-* means "three." (*unique, unicycle, bilingual, biweekly, triplets, triangle*)	Prefixes (*com-, sub-*) Some words have a prefix. A prefix can help you understand the meaning of a word. The prefix *com-* means "with" or "together." The prefix *sub-* means "under" or "lower." (*combination, common, compromise, subject, subway*)	Prefix (*ex-*) Some words have a prefix. A prefix can help you understand the meaning of a word. The prefix *ex-* can mean "out" or "without." (*exact, exclude, expand, expel*)	Prefix (*inter-*) Some words have a prefix. A prefix can help you understand the meaning of a word. The prefix *inter-* can mean "between," "among," or "together." (*interactive, intercom, intercontinental, intermediate, intertwine*)

Map for Phonics/Word Study

SYLLABIC	Level S, Lesson 137	Level S, Lesson 138	Level S, Lesson 139	Level S, Lesson 140
Vowel Patterns *r*-**Influenced Vowels**	Vowel Patterns in Accented Syllables (*au, aw, al*) Break words with the vowel patterns *au, aw, al* in the accented syllable to read them. (*author, awful, altar, because, drawing, faucet, laundry*)	*r*-Influenced *a* in Accented Syllables Break words with an *r*-influenced *a* in the accented syllable to read them. (*airless, aware, compare, market, remark, unfair*)	*r*-Influenced *o* in Accented Syllable Break words with an *r*-influenced *o* in the accented syllable to read them. (*afford, before, boredom, normal, shorten*)	*r*-Influenced Vowels in Accented Syllables (*er, ir, ur*) Break words with an *r*-influenced vowel in the accented syllable to read them. (*certify, circle, purpose*)
MORPHEMIC	Level S, Lesson 141	Level S, Lesson 142	Level S, Lesson 143	Level S, Lesson 144
Word Parts **Word Roots**	Word Part Terms (*base word, root, prefix, suffix, affix*) Some words name the parts that are put together to make a word. (*dependable, dishonest, misguide, nonsense, potatoes, preorder, quickly, submerge, successful, thermal*)	Word Roots (*astro, aud, photo*) Notice the meaning of the word root to learn the meaning of a new word. (*astronomer, astronomy; audible, audience; photocopier, photographer*)	Word Roots (*bio, sol, therm*) Notice the meaning of the word root to learn the meaning of a new word. (*biology, biography, solar, solarium, thermometer, thermos*)	Word Roots (*mega, micro*) Notice the meaning of the word root to learn the meaning of a new word. (*megavitamin, megaphone, microscope, microphone*)
SYLLABIC	Level S, Lesson 145	Level S, Lesson 146	Level S, Lesson 147	Level S, Lesson 148
Syllables **Long Vowel Patterns**	Words with *ar, er,* or *or* in the Unaccented Final Syllable Some words have *ar, er,* or *or* in the unaccented final syllable. (*hangar, splinter, doctor*)	Vowel Patterns *ur* and *ure* in Accented Syllables Break words with the *ur* or *ure* pattern in the accented syllable to read them. (*current, hurdle, mature, unsure*)	Words with *le, al, el, il, ile* in the Unaccented Final Syllable Some words have the *le, al, el, il,* or *ile* pattern in the unaccented final syllable. (*crystal, fossil, fragile, marble, model, nickel, oval, pupil*)	Vowel Patterns (*ie, ei, eigh*) Some words have an *ie* or *ei* pattern that sounds like the long *e* sound in *niece* and *receive.* Some words have an *ei* or *eigh* pattern that sounds like the long *a* sound in *vein* and *weigh.* (*belief, believe, freight, niece, receipt, receive, vein, weigh*)

Map for Phonics/Word Study

MORPHEMIC	Level S, Lesson 149	Level S, Lesson 150	Level S, Lesson 151	Level S, Lesson 152
Agent Nouns **Suffixes** **Commonly Misspelled Words** **Word Endings**	Agent Nouns Some words name people who do things (*farmer, driver, swimmer*). The *-er* ending is also used for comparison (*smaller*). (*actor, bigger, darker, farmer*)	Suffixes (*-ion, -tion*) Adding the suffix *-ion* or *-tion* to change a verb to a noun. Sometimes the spelling changes. (*create, creation, decorate, decoration, elect, election, introduce, introduction, protect, protection, reduce, reduction*)	Commonly Misspelled Words Some words require practice to learn how to read and write them correctly. Notice the tricky parts to learn them (*again, answer, although, definitely, eighth, familiar, separate*)	Word Endings (*-ure, -sure, -ture*) Some words end in *-ure, -sure,* or *-ture*. (*composure, injure, pleasure, structure*)
Novel Study Week	**Level S, Lesson 153** n/a	**Level S, Lesson 154** n/a	**Level S, Lesson 155** n/a	**Level S, Lesson 156** n/a
Test Preparation Week	**Level S, Lesson 157** n/a	**Level S, Lesson 158** n/a	**Level S, Lesson 159** n/a	**Level S, Lesson 160** n/a
SYLLABIC	**Level T, Lesson 161**	**Level T, Lesson 162**	**Level T, Lesson 163**	**Level T, Lesson 164**
Words with *qu* and *que* **Words with *ph* and *gh*** **Words with *g, gu,* and *gue*** **Words Ending with the *k* Sound**	Multisyllable Words with *qu* and *que* In some words, *qu* sounds like *kw* and in others it sounds like *k*. In some words, *que* sounds like *k*. (*conquer, question, unique*)	Words with *ph* or *gh* Some multisyllable words have *ph* or *gh* that sounds like *f*. Sometimes *gh* is silent. (*daughter, elephant, enough, laughter, paragraph, rephrase, roughly, telephone*)	Words with *g, gu,* or *gue* Some words have a hard *g* sound that is spelled *g, gu,* or *gue*. (*iceberg, guitar, prologue*)	Words Ending in the *k* Sound In multisyllable words, the sound of *k* at the end can be spelled in several ways (*c, ck, k, ch, que*). (*antique, attack, music, network, stomach*)

Map for Phonics/Word Study				
MORPHEMIC	**Level T, Lesson 165**	**Level T, Lesson 166**	**Level T, Lesson 167**	**Level T, Lesson 168**
Homophones **Suffix -ion** **Commonly Misspelled Words**	Homophones Some words sound the same but are spelled differently and have different meanings. They are called homophones. (*bolder/boulder, cellar/seller, desert/dessert, pedal/peddle*)	Suffix (*-ion*) Add the suffix *-ion* to some verbs ending with *ct* and *ss* to change the meaning. (*discuss, discussion, express, expression, predict, prediction, select, selection*)	Commonly Misspelled Words Some words require practice to learn how to read and write them correctly. Notice the tricky parts to learn them. (*address, different, library, often, receive, straight*)	Commonly Misspelled Words Some words require practice to learn how to read and write them correctly. Notice the tricky parts to learn them. (*advice, decision, except, lightning, ninety, surprise*)
SYLLABIC	**Level T, Lesson 169**	**Level T, Lesson 170**	**Level T, Lesson 171**	**Level T, Lesson 172**
Word Endings **Silent Letters** **Long *e* Vowel Patterns**	Words Ending with *et* or *it* Break words with *et* or *it* in the unaccented final syllable to read them. (*habit, planet, spirit, tablet, trumpet, visit*)	Words with Silent Letters Some words have silent letters. (*answer, castle, gnawing, honor, kneecap, rhino, wrinkle*)	Long *e* Vowel Patterns (*ie, ey*) Some words end with the long *e* vowel sound spelled *ie* or *ey*. (*hockey, movie, prairie*)	Multisyllable Words Ending with *ice, ace,* or *is* Some multisyllable words end with the pattern *ace, ice,* or *is*. (*palace, terrace, justice, notice*)
MORPHEMIC	**Level T, Lesson 173**	**Level T, Lesson 174**	**Level T, Lesson 175**	**Level T, Lesson 176**
Prefixes, Suffixes, and Inflectional Endings **Synonyms and Antonyms** **Multiple-Meaning Words**	Multisyllable Words with Prefixes, Suffixes, and Inflectional Endings Notice the base word and other meaningful parts to read new words. (*correctly, misfired, preheat, reconsidering, unequal, watches*)	Multisyllable Words with Prefixes, Suffixes, and Inflectional Endings Break words with prefixes, suffixes, and inflectional endings to read them. (*biweekly, disappearing, happier, homeless, quietly, strongest, unbeaten*)	Synonyms and Antonyms Some word pairs have almost the same meaning, while some word pairs have opposite meanings. (*defend/uphold, deny/reject, gentleness/ tenderness, increase/decrease, preserve/destroy, release/retain, request/reply*)	Multiple-Meaning Words Some words look the same but mean something different. They can be different parts of speech. (*nursery, patient, period*)

Map for Phonics/Word Study

SYLLABIC	Level T, Lesson 177	Level T, Lesson 178	Level T, Lesson 179	Level T, Lesson 180
Multisyllable Words	Multisyllable Words Some words have two, three, or four syllables. Every syllable has a vowel sound. (*dislike, elephant, coincidence, monster, gigantic, environment, steeple, invention, geography, tornado, unusual*)	Multisyllable Words Some words have two, three, or four syllables. Each syllable has a vowel sound. (*compare, actual, biography, describe, estimate, eliminate, problem, prediction, fortunately, identify*)	Multisyllable Words Some words have two, three, or four syllables. Each syllable has a vowel sound. (*climate, holiday, equivalent, culture, location, participate, freedom, terrible, justice*)	Multisyllable Words Some words have three, four, or five syllables. Each syllable has a vowel sound. (*instrument, anonymous, hippopotamus, numerous, biologist, organization, sensible, ridiculous, precipitation, summary*)
MORPHEMIC	**Level T, Lesson 181**	**Level T, Lesson 182**	**Level T, Lesson 183**	**Level T, Lesson 184**
Word Roots	Word Roots (*spec*) When you know the meaning of a word root (*spec*), it helps you figure out the meaning of a word. (*inspect, respect, spectacle*)	Word Roots (*therm*) When you know the meaning of a word root (*therm*), it helps you figure out the meaning of a word. (*geothermal, hyperthermic, thermal*)	Word Roots (*tele*) When you know the meaning of a word root (*tele*), it helps you figure out the meaning of a word. (*telecast, telegraph, telephoto*)	Word Roots (*photo*) When you know the meaning of a word root (*photo*), it helps you figure out the meaning of a word. (*photogenic, photograph, photon*)
Novel Study Week	**Level T, Lesson 185** n/a	**Level T, Lesson 186** n/a	**Level T, Lesson 187** n/a	**Level T, Lesson 188** n/a
Test Preparation Week	**Level T, Lesson 189** n/a	**Level T, Lesson 190** n/a	**Level T, Lesson 191** n/a	**Level T, Lesson 192** n/a

Map for Vocabulary					
Lesson 1	**Lesson 2**	**Lesson 3**	**Lesson 4**	**Lesson 5**	**Lesson 6**
Choose words from a previous reading.	fortunate **fortunately** **fortune** **unfortunately**	**interview** view	anxious jiggly nerve nerves **nervous** twitchy	**exercise** exert exertion	fertile **fertilizer**
Lesson 7	**Lesson 8**	**Lesson 9**	**Lesson 10**		**Lesson 11**
flexible	**adapt** **adaptation** **adapted**	sole **solitary** solitude	sympathetically sympathy **unsympathetically**		**genius**
Lesson 12	**Lesson 13**	**Lesson 14**	**Lesson 15**	**Lesson 16**	**Lesson 17**
propel **propeller**	**grave** gravely	sprawl **sprawled** **stretched**	bioluminescence **bioluminescent** illuminate **luminous**	**sauntered** **scampered** **slipped**	fertilize organ **organizing** sanitize
Lesson 18	**Lesson 19**	**Lesson 20**	**Lesson 21**	**Lesson 22**	**Lesson 23**
aggress **aggressive**	**stamina**	inspect prospect spectacles spectacular **spectators**	**camouflage** disguise	**capitulate** **commence**	belief believe disagree disappear **disbelief** gasped
Lesson 24	**Lesson 25**	**Lesson 26**	**Lesson 27**	**Lesson 28**	**Lesson 33**
assume assumed **assumes** assumption	fearful fearless **pitiful** pitiless pity	detain **detention** retain	thought thoughtful **thoughtfully**	**respect** respectful respectfully	Choose words from a previous reading.
Lesson 34	**Lesson 35**	**Lesson 36**	**Lesson 37**	**Lesson 38**	**Lesson 39**
collage	present **presentation**	**endoscope** microscope telescope	bicentennial bicycle bifocals **binoculars**	**vibrate** **vibrations**	inspect spectacle spectacles **spectacular**

Boldfaced words appear in *LLI Gold System* books.

Map for Vocabulary

Lesson 40	Lesson 41	Lesson 42	Lesson 43	Lesson 44	Lesson 45
distract **distracted** focus focused	**eternity**	**observation** **observatory** observe	**consequences** sequence	**donate** **donation** **donations** donee donor	persist **persistence**

Lesson 46	Lesson 47	Lesson 48	Lesson 49	Lesson 50	Lesson 51
submarine submerge **subway** subzero	**convince**	action **active** no action **passive**	adhere **adhesive**	**treacherous** treachery	impress **impressed** impression press pressure

Lesson 52	Lesson 53	Lesson 54	Lesson 55	Lesson 56	Lesson 57
irritable **irritate** **irritated**	impress impressed impression press **pressure**	inspect **inspector** spectacle spectacles	**chairlift** homesick **homesickness** **teacups**	incubate **incubates** **incubating**	**burglar** **burglarize** dramatize familiarize fertilize legalize modernize pressurize sanitize sterilize

Lesson 58	Lesson 59	Lesson 60	Lesson 65	Lesson 66	Lesson 67
pang	potent **potential**	autobiography **automatic** **automobile**	Choose words from a previous reading.	fake **genuine** **hoax** real true unreal	demolish **demolished** demolition

Lesson 68	Lesson 69	Lesson 70	Lesson 71	Lesson 72	Lesson 73
around round rounded **surrounded**	artist natural **naturalist** nature organist pianist	machine mechanic **mechanism**	**legend** **legendary**	**dribble** **dribbling** driblet dribs and drabs	**stifle** **stifling**

Boldfaced words appear in *LLI Gold System* books.

Map for Vocabulary

Lesson 74	Lesson 75	Lesson 76	Lesson 77	Lesson 78	Lesson 79
gyrate **gyrations**	collide **colliding** collision	**airborne** bear borne seaborne windborne	**bitter** embittered	cognition recognize **recognized** **recognition**	angle angler **angling**
Lesson 80	**Lesson 81**	**Lesson 82**	**Lesson 83**	**Lesson 84**	**Lesson 85**
intercontinental interdependent **international** Internet nation national	immerse immersible submerse submersible **submersibles**	redo **rehearsal** rehearse relight replay	**anticipation**	frustrate **frustrating** frustration	**queasy** **quivers**
Lesson 86	**Lesson 87**	**Lesson 88**	**Lesson 89**	**Lesson 90**	**Lesson 91**
ceremonial ceremony	dysfunctional **function** **functional**	immigrant immigrate immigration migrate **migration**	meter spectacle spectacles **spectrometer** spectrum thermometer	assert **assertive**	**miserably** misery
Lesson 92	**Lesson 97**	**Lesson 98**	**Lesson 99**	**Lesson 100**	**Lesson 101**
quiz quizzical **quizzically**	Choose words from a previous reading.	habilitate rehabilitate **rehabilitation**	evacuate **evacuated** evacuee vacant vacate	appropriate **appropriately** proper	coauthor co-op cooperate cooperation **cooperative**
Lesson 102	**Lesson 103**	**Lesson 104**	**Lesson 105**	**Lesson 106**	**Lesson 107**
anyone **graveyard** **lifeboat** **lifetimes** **nameplate** **sandbar** **shipwrecked**	**slogged** **staggered**	**audience** audio auditorium auditory	convince **convinced** persuade persuaded unconvinced	intoxicated **toxic** **toxin**	**horror-struck** **milk-white**
Lesson 108	**Lesson 109**	**Lesson 110**	**Lesson 111**	**Lesson 112**	**Lesson 113**
symbiosis **symbiotic** sympathy symphony	**conservation** conservator **conservators** conserve	**compatible**	autopsy necropolis **necropsy** optic optometrist	**depth perception** depth perception perceive	swivel **swiveled**

Boldfaced words appear in *LLI Gold System* books.

Map for Vocabulary

Lesson 114	Lesson 115	Lesson 116	Lesson 117	Lesson 118	Lesson 119
compose decompose **decomposes** decompress	conscious unconscious **unconsciousness**	**relative** **relativity**	**ancient**	marvel **marvelous**	**hospitality** host

Lesson 120	Lesson 121	Lesson 122	Lesson 123	Lesson 124	Lesson 129
constriction	trudge **trudged**	humiliated **humiliation** humility	echo reecho resonate resound reverberate **reverberated**	**contaminate**	Choose words from a previous reading.

Lesson 130	Lesson 131	Lesson 132	Lesson 133	Lesson 134	Lesson 135
append appendicitis **appendix**	**antidote** antifreeze antitoxin	real **realized** sanitary sanitize	**avalanche**	conquer **conquered** defeat overcome surrender win	bicycle cycle cyclic cyclist cyclone downcycle **downcycling** recycle **recycling** upcycle **upcycling**

Lesson 136	Lesson 137	Lesson 138	Lesson 139	Lesson 140	Lesson 141
microbe microchip **microdot** microfilm **microphone** microscope	symbiosis symbol symbolic symbolize **symbols**	**salvage** salvation save	misplace misquote misread misspell **mistook**	**scurried** scurry swarm **swarmed**	**crevasses**

Lesson 142	Lesson 143		Lesson 144	Lesson 145	Lesson 146
collapse **collapsed** collapses	backache backboard backbone backfire background backpack backstage **backup** backward backyard	checkup flashback horseback pickup uproot upset upstairs uptown upward	overalls overcoat overcome overdone overflowing **overjoyed** overlook **overpass**	mission **missionary**	glue **gluten** glutinous

Boldfaced words appear in *LLI Gold System* books.

Map for Vocabulary

Lesson 147	Lesson 148	Lesson 149	Lesson 150	Lesson 151	Lesson 152
tradition traditional **traditionally**	**reputation** repute reputed	preheat preschool preview **previous**	**convinced** invincible	plumb plumber plummet **plummeted** plump	**jet propulsion** propulsion propel propeller

Lesson 153	Lesson 154	Lesson 155	Lesson 156	Lesson 161	Lesson 162
biomimetics mimic mime mimicry mimetic	**disguise** **disguised**	obsess **obsessed** obsession	parasite **parasitic**	Choose words from a previous reading.	impersonal person personal **personality**

Lesson 163	Lesson 164	Lesson 165	Lesson 166	Lesson 167	Lesson 168
disgust **disgusted** distaste	collide **collision**	disentangle **disentangled** **entangle** **entangled** **entanglement** tangle	intoxicated poison poisonous toxic **toxin** venom **venomous**	**coir** fiber **fibers** fibrous **fronds**	ageless careless fearless hopeless joyless relent **relentless** thoughtless timeless

Lesson 169	Lesson 170	Lesson 171	Lesson 172	Lesson 173	Lesson 174
barriers bars blocks hindrances impediments **obstacle** **snags**	common extraordinary normal **ordinary** uncommon unusual usual	**inspiration** inspire spirit	menace **menaced** menacing	commerce **commercial**	apprehend **apprehensive**

Lesson 175	Lesson 176	Lesson 177	Lesson 178	Lesson 179	Lesson 180
alien alienate	dwell **dwellers** dwelling	apparel **garment** **garments**	nomad nomadic **nomads**	**epilogue**	aquamarine aquanaut aquarium aquatic **aqueduct**

Boldfaced words appear in *LLI Gold System* books.

Map for Vocabulary

Lesson 181	Lesson 182	Lesson 183	Lesson 184	Lesson 185
veracity **verified** **verify** **veritable**	flying-out-of-the-seat hard-kicking **heart-in-the-throat** stomach-dropping super-duper-fast-running sweet-to-taste **white-knuckle** yummy-licking	adhere **adhesive**	disintegrate **disintegrating** **integrate**	cave system **chamber** **chambers**

Lesson 186	Lesson 187	Lesson 188			
deflate **deflating** inflate	malice **malicious** **mischief**	conciliate reconcile **reconciliation**			

Boldfaced words appear in *LLI Gold System* books.

30-Minute Variation of Standard (Odd- and Even-Numbered) Lesson Framework

To accommodate a 30-minute variation, each pair of standard (odd- and even-numbered) lessons can be taught over the course of three days.

Day 1	Day 2	Day 3
Discussing Yesterday's New Book **or** **Revisiting Yesterday's New Book** Choose one: • Comprehension • Vocabulary • Fluency *5 minutes*	**Phonics/Word Study*** *10 minutes*	**Writing About Reading** *15 minutes*
Reading New Book (Instructional Level) • Introducing the Text • Reading the Text • Discussing and Revisiting the Text • Teaching Point *25 minutes*	**Revisiting Yesterday's New Book** Choose one: • Comprehension • Vocabulary • Fluency *10 minutes*	**Phonics/Word Study** *10 minutes*
	Rereading and Assessment *10 minutes*	**Reading a New Book (Independent Level)** • Introducing the Text • Reading the Text • Discussing and Revisiting the Text • Teaching Point *5 minutes*

* To accomodate this variation, you must return to the previous lesson for the Phonics/Word Study segment.

30 Minute Variation of Novel Study Lesson Framework

To accommodate a 30-minute variation for the novel study lesson sequence, the four lessons can be spread across six instructional days.

Day 1	Day 2	Day 3	Day 4	Day 5	Day 6
Discussing Yesterday's New Book *5 minutes*	**Revisiting Yesterday's Reading** Choose one: • Comprehension • Vocabulary • Fluency *5 minutes*	**Revisiting Yesterday's Reading** Choose one: • Comprehension • Vocabulary • Fluency *5 minutes*	**Revisiting Yesterday's Reading** Choose one: • Comprehension • Vocabulary • Fluency *5 minutes*	**Revisiting Yesterday's Reading** Choose one: • Comprehension • Vocabulary • Fluency *5 minutes*	**Concluding Discussion** • Reflections on the Book *10 minutes*
Revisiting Yesterday's New Book Choose one: • Comprehension • Vocabulary • Fluency *5 minutes*	**Reading a New Section** • Introducing the Text • Reading the Text • Discussing and Revisiting the Text • Introduction to and Assignment of Reading *25 minutes*	**Reading a New Section** • Introducing the Text • Reading the Text • Discussing and Revisiting the Text • Introduction to and Assignment of Reading *25 minutes*	**Reading a New Section** • Introducing the Text • Reading the Text • Discussing and Revisiting the Text • Introduction to and Assignment of Reading *25 minutes*	**Reading a New Section** • Introducing the Text • Reading the Text • Discussing and Revisiting the Text • Introduction to and Assignment of Reading *25 minutes*	**Writing About Reading** *20 minutes*
Reading a New Book • Introducing the Text • Reading the Text • Discussing and Revisiting the Text • Introduction to and Assignment of Reading *20 minutes*					

30-Minute Variation of Test Preparation Lesson Framework

To accommodate a 30-minute variation, two test preparation lessons can be taught over the course of four days.

Day 1 (familiar text)	Day 2 (unfamiliar text)	Day 3 (familiar text)	Day 4 (unfamiliar text)
Think Together • multiple-choice items *10 minutes*	**On Your Own** *30 minutes*	**Think Together** • constructed-response items *10 minutes*	**On Your Own** *30 minutes*
Have a Try *20 minutes*		**Have a Try** *20 minutes*	

LLI Gold System Series Books

Series books provide a strong scaffold for reading comprehension. Students have the experience of continuing meaningful reading over a longer period of time. They extend their ability to remember and use as prior knowledge important information and elements of texts.

A *series* is a set of texts that are connected in some way—characters, setting, or ideas. In the *LLI Gold System*, there are two kinds of series books—fiction and nonfiction.

- ❑ Fiction series books feature the same characters in the same settings (or couple of settings) by the same author. The characters are identifiable and remain pretty much themselves except that sometimes they learn by solving problems.

- ❑ Nonfiction series books are connected by a larger theme or idea. They have different content, but each elaborates on the overarching theme.

The series books in the *Gold System* may be read in any order, and it is not necessary to have read a previous book to understand a current one. (This feature is different from series books that are sequels and in which characters grow older, for example, Harry Potter.) Also, the series books in *LLI* are short (24 to 36 pages) so that they can be finished in a day; however, reading several or all of the books in a series will give readers a sustained experience in getting to know characters or thinking about a big idea. Some series are completed in the *Gold System*, but others cross over into the *Purple System*.

▶ Values of Series Books

FICTION

- ❑ Readers become interested in the characters and in following their adventures.

- ❑ Because they encounter a character across several texts, they can develop a richer understanding of the character.

- ❑ Readers become better able to talk about characters and infer their feelings and motivations.

- ❑ Students have the experience of reading connected text over time.

- ❑ They learn the process of making many connections between texts—typical situations, problems, settings, character traits, styles of writing and illustrations.

- ❑ Students encounter series books in different genres.

- ❑ It is highly motivating for students to meet the same characters again; they enter the text with *prior knowledge.*

NONFICTION

- ❑ Readers become interested in a larger idea or topic.

- ❑ Readers have the opportunity to encounter many examples that deepen their understanding of a theme or idea.

- ❑ Readers have the experience of connecting background information with new information.

- ❑ Readers sustain thinking about a big idea over a large amount of nonfiction reading.

- ❑ Readers have the opportunity to notice writers' treatment of a theme or idea.

- ❑ Readers acquire content that they can bring as *prior knowledge* to the reading of other texts.

In this appendix, we present the series books in the *LLI Gold System*. Since *LLI* is designed for flexible use, you may be starting your readers on any level appropriate to their current instructional reading level. That means that students may be reading a fiction series book without having read prior stories. This will not be a problem because every text stands alone; however, you may want to create chances for students to read and enjoy the easier books (on lower levels) in a series by adding them to the rereading segment or the choice library. They can use them for independent reading in the classroom or at home. Likewise, you can make available easier nonfiction series books so that students can explore a topic or idea independently. For example, having read one of the Intriguing Animals Series, they may want to read several more at independent level.

When students have read one or more of the books in a series, it will be easy for them to form expectations when they are introduced to a new book in the same series. The following are some suggestions for using series books.

❑ When introducing the first book in a series that students will be reading, be sure to identify the series and tell what the books will be like. Alert them that they will be reading more books with this idea or about these characters.

❑ When introducing another book in a series, make explicit connections between texts by holding up one or more previous books in the series and reminding students of what a character was like, what happened in a previous story, or what was important about the big idea. (As students gain experience, invite them to share their previous knowledge rather than telling them.)

❑ For nonfiction texts, remind students of the ways information has been presented in the earlier examples. Invite them to notice any similarities (nonfiction text features). In this way, you set expectations for how the information is organized.

❑ Substitute previous books in a series for the Revisiting Text portion of the lesson, choosing Comprehension, Vocabulary, or Fluency options. Using the series book for Revisiting will make it easier for students to make connections.

❑ Toward the end of a level (or several levels) set aside a lesson to reread and discuss all of the books in a series. Talk about what characters are like, the big idea, or the style of writing and illustrations.

❑ Add series books to the choice reading library or let students take them for independent reading.

❑ As students become more advanced, invite them to try writing their own stories about a character in a series. Or, based on their own lives or on further research and reading, they can write another book that would fit into a nonfiction series.

LLI Gold System NONFICTION Series Book List

Series Title	Description	Book Titles	Level
Wonders of Nature	Discover a few of the amazing secrets found in nature from silk made by spiders to glow-in-the-dark animals.	Super Silk	P
		The Egg: Nature's Perfect Package	P
		Glow-in-the-Dark Animals	M
		Geysers	R
		The Secret World of Caves	R
Against All Odds	In the face of the impossible, these real-life heroes succeeded despite their challenges.	Alone in the Jungle	Q
		The Heroes of Pea Island	R
Intriguing Animals	Texts present seven little-known and fascinating animals from around the world.	The Amazing Gecko	N
		Kangaroos in Trees	M
		The Peculiar Platypus	Q
		The Thorny Dragon	M
		Rescuing Orangutans	R
		Crabs on the Run	S
		Octopus: Escape Artist of the Sea	Q
		The Mimic Octopus: A Master of Disguise	S

Series Title	Description	Book Titles		Level
Art for All	Art can be found in surprising places, created for anyone and everyone to see.		*Messages to the World: Art from Cape Dorset*	T
			Jon Brooks: Art from Nature	T
			The Rock Garden	P
			Shadow Magic: The Ancient Art of Shadow Puppetry	R
			Sapporo: A Snow Sculpture City	Q
			Making Art for Fish	M
			Amazing Brick Artists	R
Remarkable Inventions	Some inventions make people's lives easier, some save lives, and some just make something good even better.		*Snowmobiles: A Life-Saving Invention*	Q
			People Powered: Pedaling on Land, Sea, and Air	O
			Accidental Inventions	R
Making a Difference	This series features true stories about people whose actions made the world a better place.		*Ryan's Well*	N
			Hero Rats	S
			Joining Hands with a Village	R
			A Young Hero with a Big Heart: The Story of Ana Dobson	P
			Mission: Dog Rescue	P

LLI Gold System NONFICTION Series Book List

Series Title	Description	Book Titles		Level
Unsolved Mysteries	Some people may think they know the answers to these mysteries, but no one knows for sure why these events occurred.		Strange Rain	R
			Stranded! A Marine Mammal Mystery	P
			Animal Warnings	P
			Looking for Earth 2	O
			Bigfoot: What's the Evidence?	O
			The Mystery of Anting	P
Sports for All	Sports weren't always the games we are used to playing today.		Ice Climbing: The Frozen Challenge	Q
			Basketball: Changing the Game	Q
			The Story of Naismith's Game	O

Series Title	Description	Book Titles		Level
Classic Tales	These traditional folktales include retellings of classic stories from Vietnam, Mexico, Iran, Iceland, and the United States		*The Two Brothers: A Tale from Vietnam*	R
			Holding Up the Sky and *Coyotes Dinner Two Trickster Tales from Mexico*	O
			Amin and the Terrible Ogre: A Tale from Iran	P
			Why the Sea Is Salty: A Tale from Iceland	Q
			Rabbit and the Queasy Quivers (A tale from the United States)	O
It's a Mystery	Get ready to follow the clues! From a smelly crime on a river to a set of "three-minute" mysteries, these stories will keep readers guessing as they try to determine "whodunit."		*The Yo-yo Caper*	R
			Partners in Crime	Q
			The Mystery of the Missing Key	N
			Rotten in Riverton	T
Andromeda Clark Series	Andromeda Clark isn't always the best student, but she makes up for it with an imagination that's in overdrive! In these fantasies, our heroine travels to important moments in history, where she joins the moon landing, finds King Tut's tomb, discovers the North Pole, and inspires Einstein's famous theory of relativity.		*Andromeda Clark Walks on the Moon*	O
			Andromeda Clark and the Mummy's Curse	P
			Andromeda Clark, North Pole Explorer	O
			Andromeda Clark Makes Time Fly	R

LLI Gold System FICTION Series Book List

Series Title	Description	Book Titles		Level
Alton School	Nick Everett just can't help himself. Whether he's challenging the reading assignments, facing down a bully, trying to outwit the teacher in poetry class, or debating the principal—Nick never looks before he leaps. But it's always fun watching him try to get out of trouble.		*Double Double Trouble Trouble*	O
			The Great Debate	Q
			The Robopoet 2000	S
			The Great Tug-of-War	M
Sports Action	The student athletes in these stories grapple with issues of competition, sportsmanship, teamwork, and friendship. Oh, and then of course there's Jack, who has to win a soccer game to save the world.		*Knocked Out*	Q
			Trying Out	O
			The Turning Point	M
			So You Speak African?	P

glossary

The following is a glossary of the terms, materials, and instructional procedures used in the *LLI System* and described briefly in this guide.

accuracy (as in oral reading) **or accuracy rate**
The percentage of words the student reads aloud correctly.

adjective
A word that describes or modifies a noun or pronoun. It usually tells what kind, how many, or which one (for example, a *huge* mountain).

adjust
To read in different ways as appropriate to the purpose for reading and type of text.

adverb
A word that describes or modifies a verb, adjective, or another adverb. It usually tells when, where, or how (for example, walked *quickly*).

affix
A part added to the beginning or ending of a base or word root to change its meaning or function (a prefix or a suffix).

agent noun
A noun that identifies someone or something as the performer of an action (for example, *actor, farmer*).

alphabet principle
The concept that there is a relationship between the spoken sounds in oral language and the graphic forms in written language.

analogy
The resemblance of a known word to an unknown word that helps solve the unknown word's meaning.

analyze (as a strategic action)
To examine the elements of text in order to know more about how it is constructed and to notice aspects of the writer's craft.

analyzing a reading record
Looking at errors, self-corrections, and sources of information and strategic actions to plan instruction.

animal fantasy
A make-believe story in which personified animals are the main characters.

antonym
A word that has the opposite or nearly the opposite meaning from another word (for example, *forget, remember*).

assessment
A means for gathering information or data that reveals what learners control, partially control, or do not yet control consistently.

assisted reading
An instructional procedure used to support students' fluent reading; the teacher models the text read fluently, then reads the same text along with the student.

autobiography
A book in which a person tells the story of her own life.

automaticity
Rapid, accurate, fluent word decoding without conscious effort or attention.

base word
A whole word to which affixes can be added to create new word forms (for example, *wash* plus *-ing* becomes *washing*).

behaviors
Actions that are observable as students read or write.

biography
A story that tells about all or part of a real person's life.

blend
To combine sounds or word parts.

bold (boldface)
Type that is heavier and darker than usual, often used for emphasis.

book and print features (as text characteristics)
The physical attributes of a text (for example, font, layout, and length).

break words
Actions readers take to solve words, breaking at the onset/rime, syllable, affixes, and inflectional endings.

callout
Text connected by a line or other simple graphic to a part of an illustration, diagram, or map to draw attention to that part.

capitalization
The use of capital letters, usually the first letter in a word, as a convention of written language (for example, for proper names and to begin sentences).

caption
Text that appears with an illustration or photograph and provides a title or short description of the artwork.

cause/effect
The writer why something happens and the resulting outcome.

choral reading
To read aloud in unison with a group.

chronological sequence
The writer presents information by describing events as they occurred in time.

closed syllable
A syllable that ends in one or more consonants (for example, *lem*/on, *in*/sect).

close reading
Returning to a previously read text to think more deeply about its meaning.

code (a reading record)
To record a child's oral reading errors, self-corrections, and other behaviors.

Coding and Scoring Errors at-a-Glance Chart
A chart containing a brief summary of how to code and score oral reading errors.

compare/contrast
The writer discusses two ideas, events, or phenomena, showing how they are similar or different.

compound word
A word made up of two or more words or morphemes (for example, *playground*); the meaning of a compound word can be a combination of the meanings of the words it contains or it can be unrelated to the meanings of the combined units.

comprehension (as in reading)
The process of anticipating the meaning before reading, constructing meaning while reading, and reflecting on the text after reading.

comprehension conversation
The conversation that takes place in the Rereading and Assessment section of the lesson, in which the student shares his understanding of the text.

concept words
Words that represent abstract ideas or names; categories of concept words include colors, numbers, months, days of the week, position words, and so on.

confirm thinking
An instructional procedure used to reinforce or validate student's thinking by restating.

connecting strategies
Ways of solving words by using connections or analogies with similar known words (for example, knowing *she* and *out* helps with *shout*).

consonant
A speech sound made by partial or complete closure of airflow that causes friction at one or more points in the breath channel; the consonant sounds are represented by the letters *b, c, d, f, g, h, j, k, l, m, n, p, q, r, s, t, v, w* (in most uses), *x, y* (in most uses), and *z*.

consonant blend
Two or more consonant letters that often appear together in words and represent sounds that are smoothly joined, although each of the sounds can be heard in the word (for example *tr* in *trim*).

consonant cluster
A sequence of two or three consonant letters that appear together in words (for example, *tr*im, *ch*air).

Consonant Clusters and Digraphs Chart
A chart of common consonant clusters and digraphs paired with pictures representing words beginning with each cluster (for example, *bl, block*).

consonant digraph
Two consonant letters that appear together and represent a single sound that is different from the sound of either letter (for example, *sh*ell).

content (as a text characteristic)
The subject matter of a text.

contraction
A shortening of a syllable, word, or word groups, usually by the omission of a sound or letters (for example, *didn't*).

conventions (in writing)
Formal usage that has become customary in written language. Grammar, capitalization, and punctuation are three categories of conventions in writing.

critique (as a strategic action)
To evaluate a text using one's personal, world, or text knowledge, and to think critically about the ideas in the text.

cumulative tale
A story with many details repeated until the climax.

decoding
Using letter-sound relationships to translate a word from a series of symbols to a unit of meaning.

dialect
A regional variety of language; in most languages, including English and Spanish, dialects are mutually intelligible—the differences are actually minor.

dialogue
Spoken words, usually set off with quotation marks, in texts.

distinctive letter features
Visual features that make every letter of the alphabet different from every other letter.

echo reading
An instructional procedure used to support fluent reading; the teacher reads a sentence or brief passage in a fluent manner, then the student echoes the sound of the reading that has been modeled.

Elkonin boxes
A tool for helping students think about the sounds and letters in words. The technique was developed by Russian psychologist, Daniil B. Elkonin, and includes placing visual frames around words to help in identifying sounds.

English language learners
People whose native language is not English and who are acquiring English as an additional language.

error
A reader's response that is not consistent with the text and that is *not* self-corrected.

expository text
A composition that explains a concept, using information and description.

F&P Calculator/Stopwatch
A device that will calculate the reading time, reading rate, accuracy rate, and self-correction rate for a reading.

F&P Text Level Gradient™
A twenty-six point (A–Z) text-rating scale of difficulty, in which each text level, from the easiest at level A to the most challenging at level Z, represents a small but significant increase in difficulty over the previous level; the gradient correlates these levels to grade levels.

factual text
(see **informational text**).

fantasy
An imaginative, fictional text containing elements that are highly unreal.

fiction
An invented story, usually narrative.

figurative language
Language that is filled with word imagery and metaphorical language to express more than a literal meaning.

fluency (as in oral reading)
The way an oral reading sounds, including phrasing, intonation, pausing, stress, rate, and integration of the first five factors.

fluency in reading
To read continuous text with good momentum, phrasing, appropriate pausing, intonation, and stress.

fluency in word solving
Speed, accuracy, and flexibility in solving words.

folktale
A traditional story, originally passed down orally over generations.

font
In printed text, the collection of type (letters) in a particular style.

form (as a text characteristic)
A kind of text that is characterized by particular elements; mystery, for example, is a form of writing within the narrative fiction genre.

genre
A category of written text that is characterized by a particular style, form, or content.

glossary
A collection of specialized terms and their meanings.

gradient of reading difficulty
(see **text gradient**)

grammar
Complex rules by which people can generate an unlimited number of phrases, sentences, and longer texts in a language; conventional grammar reflects the accepted conventions in a society.

grapheme
A letter or cluster of letters representing a single sound or phoneme (for example, *a*, *eigh*, *ay*).

graphic text
A text in which pictures tell much of the entire story or provide much of the information.

Guide for Observing and Noting Reading Behavior
Lists questions a teacher should ask himself about the ways a child is processing or problem solving texts.

hard reading level
The level at which the student reads aloud with less than 90% accuracy (levels A–K) or less than 95% accuracy (levels L–Z).

heading
Text placed at the beginning of a paragraph or part of a book that serves as a title and provides information about the text that follows.

high-frequency words
Words that occur often in the spoken and written language (for example, *the*).

high-utility words
(see **high-frequency words**)

historical fiction
An imagined story set in the realistically (and often factually) portrayed setting of a past era.

homograph
One of two or more words spelled alike but different in meaning, derivation, and sometimes pronunciation (for example, *desert* (dry region), *desert* (leave)).

homophone
One of two or more words pronounced alike but different in spelling and meaning (for example, *plane, plain*).

idiom
A phrase with meaning that cannot be derived from the conjoined meanings of its elements (for example, *raining cats and dogs*).

illustrations (as a text characteristic)
Graphic representations of important content (for example, art, photos, maps, graphs, and charts).

independent reading level
The level at which the student reads the text with 95% or higher accuracy and excellent or satisfactory comprehension (levels A–K) or 98% or higher accuracy with excellent or satisfactory comprehension (levels L–Z).

independent writing
Students compose and write a text independently with teacher support as needed.

individual instruction
The teacher working with one student.

infer (as a strategic action)
To go beyond the literal meaning of a text; to think about what is not stated but is implied by the writer.

inflectional ending
A suffix added to a base word to show tense, plurality, possession, or comparison (for example, *-er* in *darker*).

informational text
A category of texts in which the purpose is to inform or to give facts about a topic; nonfiction articles and essays are examples of informational text.

insertion (as an error in reading)
A word added during oral reading that is not in the text.

instructional reading level
At levels A–K, the level at which the student reads the text with 90–94% accuracy and excellent or satisfactory comprehension, or 95% or higher accuracy and limited comprehension; at levels L–Z, the level at which the student reads the text with 95–97% accuracy and excellent or satisfactory comprehension, or 98% or higher accuracy and limited comprehension.

integration
The way the reader consistently and evenly orchestrates pausing, phrasing, stress, intonation, and rate. When all dimensions of fluency are working together, the reader will be using expressions in a way that clearly demonstrates that he understands the text and is even thinking beyond the text.

intervention
Intensive additional instruction for students not progressing as rapidly as expected; usually one-on-one tutoring or small group (one-on-three or -four) teaching.

intonation
The rise and fall in pitch of the voice in speech to convey meaning.

italic (italics)
A type style that is characterized by slanted letters; often used for emphasis or as a part of references.

key understandings
Important ideas within (literal), beyond (implied), or about (determined through critical analysis) the text that are necessary to comprehension.

label (in writing)
Written word or phrase that names the content of an illustration.

language and literary features
(as text characteristics)
Qualities particular to written language that are qualitatively different from spoken language (for example, dialogue; figurative language; and literary elements such as character, setting, and plot in fiction or description and technical language in nonfiction).

language use (in writing)
The craft of using sentences, phrases, and expressions to describe events, actions, or information.

layout
The way print is arranged on a page.

letter and word games
(Lotto, Make It Match, and so on)
Games that require students to look carefully at words, letters, and parts of words.

letter-sound correspondence
Recognizing the corresponding sound of a specific letter when that letter is seen or heard.

letters
Graphic symbols representing the sounds in a language; each letter has particular distinctive features and may be identified by letter name or sound.

leveled books
Texts designed along a gradient from level A (easiest) to level Z (hardest).

lexicon
Words that make up a language; the vocabulary of a speaker of a language.

Literacy Notebooks
Special notebooks used by students to record newly learned words or vocabulary and their written responses to reading.

long vowel
The elongated vowel sound that is the same as the name of the vowel; the sound is sometimes represented by two or more letters (for example, c*a*ke, e*igh*t, m*ai*l).

M (meaning)
One of the sources of information that readers use (MSV: meaning, language structure, visual information); meaning, the semantic system of language, refers to meaning derived from words, meaning across a text or texts, and a meaning from personal experience or knowledge.

maintain fluency (as a strategic action)
To integrate sources of information in a smoothly operating process that results in expressive, phrased reading.

make connections (as a strategic action)
To search for and use connections to knowledge gained through personal experiences, learning about the world, and reading other texts.

memoir
An account of something important, usually part of a person's life; a memoir is a kind of biography, autobiography, or personal narrative.

metaphor
A figure of speech that makes a comparison of two unlike things without using the words *like* or *as*.

monitor and correct (as a strategic action)
To check whether the reading sounds right, looks right, and makes sense, and to solve problems when it doesn't.

morpheme
The smallest group of phonemes that carry meaning.

morphology
The study and description of word formation in language.

multigenre text
A writer uses more than one genre (for example, fiction and nonfiction) in a book.

multiple-meaning word
A word that means something different depending on the way it is used (for example, *ruler* (leader), *ruler* (instrument for measuring)).

narrative nonfiction
A book in which true information is presented in the form of a story.

narrative text
A category of texts in which the purpose is to tell a story; stories and biographies are kinds of narrative.

new word learning
A variety of ways students learn new words, including looking at the first letter and then running their finger left to right as they scan the word with their eyes.

nonfiction
A text whose primary purpose is to convey accurate information and facts.

notice parts
An instructional procedure in which students notice and underline word parts, or sort word cards with a common identifiable feature.

omission (as in error)
A word left out or skipped during oral reading.

Online Data Management System
The Online Data Management System (ODMS) is a web-based, password-protected tool that provides support for teachers and administrators to collect and analyze data on student achievement and to monito

Online Resources site
An online resources site that provides the specific materials for each lesson; it includes Recording Forms for taking reading records, word cards, games, Parent Letters, and other record-keeping and observation forms and resources used in *LLI*.

onset
In a syllable, the part (consonant, consonant cluster, or consonant digraph) that comes before the vowel (for example, *cr*eam).

onset-rime segmentation
The identification of onsets (first part) and rimes (last part, containing the vowel) in words (for example, *dr-ip*).

open syllable
A syllable that ends in a vowel sound (for example, *si*/lent, *mu*/sic).

oral games
Games teachers can play with students to help them learn how to listen for and identify words in sentences, syllables, onsets and rimes, and individual phonemes.

oral reading
In even-numbered lessons, the section called Rereading and Assessment—during which the student reads a text aloud and the teacher codes her reading behavior using the Recording Form, has a brief comprehension conversation, and makes a teaching point that will be helpful to the reader.

orthographic awareness
The knowledge of the visual features of written language, including distinctive features of letters, as well as spelling patterns in words.

orthography
The representation of the sounds of a language with the proper letters according to standard usage (spelling).

pausing
The way a reader's voice is guided by punctuation. A reader takes a short breath at a comma, a full stop with voice going down at a period and up at a question.

persuasive text
A text designed to convince the reader to agree with the point of view or opinion of the writer.

phoneme
The smallest unit of sound in spoken language; there are approximately forty-four units of speech sounds in English.

phoneme-grapheme correspondence
The relationship between the sounds (phonemes) and letters (graphemes) of a language.

phoneme substitution
The replacement of the beginning, middle, or ending sound of a word with a new sound.

phonemic (or phoneme) awareness
The ability to hear individual sounds in words and to identify individual sounds.

phonemic strategies
Ways of solving words that use how words sound and relationships between letters and letter clusters and phonemes in those words (for example, *cat, hat*).

phonetics
The scientific study of speech sounds—how the sounds are made vocally and the relation of speech sounds to the total language process.

phonics

The knowledge of letter-sound relationships and how they are used in reading and writing; teaching phonics refers to helping children acquire this body of knowledge about the oral and written language systems; additionally, teaching phonics helps children use phonics knowledge as part of a reading and writing process; phonics instruction uses a small portion of the body of knowledge that makes up phonetics.

phonogram

A phonetic element represented by graphic characters or symbols; in word recognition, a graphic sequence composed of a vowel grapheme and an ending consonant grapheme (such as *-an* or *-it*) is sometimes called a word family.

phonological awareness

The awareness of words, rhyming words, onsets and rimes, syllables, and individual sounds (phonemes).

phrasing

The way a reader puts words together in groups to represent meaningful units of language. Phrasing involves pausing at punctuation as well as at places in the text that do not have punctuation.

possessive

Grammatical construction used to show ownership (for example, *John's, his*).

predict (as a strategic action)

To use what is known to think about what will follow while reading continuous text.

prefix

A group of letters that can be placed in front of a base word to change its meaning (for example, *pre*heat, *un*do).

principle (in phonics)

A generalization or a sound-spelling relationship that is predictable.

problem/solution

The writer describes a problem and how it was or can be solved.

procedural text

A text designed to teach or show how to do something.

processing (as in reading)

The mental operations involved in constructing meaning from written language.

Professional Development and Tutorial DVDs

You can use the Professional Development and Tutorial DVDs to support your work individually or with a study group of professionals. The Professional Development DVDs provide an overview of the program and presents model lessons, while the Tutorial disc contains a tutorial on coding, scoring, and analyzing reading records as well as information on using the data to inform your teaching.

prompt

A question, direction, or statement designed to encourage the student to say more about a topic.

Prompting Guides, Part 1* and *Part 2

A tool you can use in each lesson as a quick reference for specific language to teach for, prompt for, or reinforce effective reading and writing behaviors; each guide is organized in categories and color-coded so that you can turn quickly to the area needed and refer to it as you teach.

punctuation

Marks used in written text to clarify meaning and separate structural units; the comma and the period are common punctuation marks.

***r*-influenced vowel sound**

The modified or *r*-influenced sound of a vowel when it is followed by *r* in a syllable (for example, p*er*son, c*ir*cus).

rate

The pace at which the reader moves through the text. An appropriate rate moves along rapidly with a few slowdowns or pauses and long pauses to solve words. The pace is also appropriate to the text and purpose of the reading—not too fast and not too slow.

readers' theater
A rewrite of an original text that is scripted into dialogue so the readers can take parts.

readers' tools
Features of the text that the reader can use to gather important information (for example, sidebars, maps, timelines).

reading graph
A graph that charts individual or group progress through leveled books.

reading rate (words per minute, or WPM)
The number of words a student reads per minute, either orally or silently.

reading record
The transcript of the text on which oral reading is coded.

realistic fiction
An invented story that could happen.

Recording Form
The form on which oral reading, the comprehension conversation, and the "Writing About Reading" assessment for a text are coded and scored; there is a Recording Form for each book in the *LLI System*—all are located on the Online Resources site.

repetition (in oral reading)
The reader saying a word, phrase, or section of the text more than once.

rhyme
The ending part (rime) of a word that sounds like the ending part (rime) of another word (for example, m-*ail*, t-*ale*).

rime
The ending part of a word containing the vowel; the letters that represent the vowel sound and the consonant letters following it in a syllable (for example, dr-*eam*).

root
A word part used to make other words. The same root can be found in many different words. A root is different from a base word because it is not a word; it is a word part (for example, *spec*tacle, *tele*graph).

rubric
A scoring tool that relies on descriptions of response categories for evaluation.

running words
The number of words read aloud and coded during the Rereading Books and Assessment part of even-numbered lessons.

S (structure)
One of the sources of information that readers use (MSV: meaning, language structure, visual information); language structure refers to the way words are put together in phrases and sentences (syntax or grammar).

say and sort
An activity in which the student has word cards to sort; the student says the word aloud and places it with other words with the same features.

science fiction
A form of fiction in which real or imagined scientific phenomena influence the plot.

scoring a reading record
Counting coded errors and self-corrections, which allows you to calculate the *accuracy rate* and the *self-correction ratio* on the Recording Form; the form also provides space for a *fluency score* (levels C–N) and *reading rate* (levels J–Z).

Scoring and Coding at-a-Glance
A summary of the steps for scoring the three parts of a running record: oral reading, comprehension conversation, and writing about reading.

search for and use information (as a strategic action)
To look for and to think about all kinds of content in order to make sense of text while reading.

searching
The reader looking for information in order to read accurately, self-correct, or understand a text.

segment (as a strategic action)
To divide into parts (for example, *c-at*).

self-correction rate
The proportion of errors the reader corrects herself.

semantic system
The system by which speakers of a language communicate meaning through language.

sentence complexity (as a text characteristic)
The complexity of the structure or syntax of a sentence; the addition of phrases and clauses to simple sentences increases complexity.

sentence strips
Strips of oak tag on which sentences have been written and then cut up and mixed up for students to put the sentences back together.

series book
One of a collection of fiction books about the same character or characters and the different events or situations they encounter; a collection of nonfiction books either on similar topics or that have similar themes.

shared writing
The teacher and students compose and construct a text on chart paper for everyone to see and reread.

short vowel
A brief-duration sound represented by a vowel letter (for example, c*a*t).

sidebar
A short piece of writing or graphic that accompanies and presents highlights of a major text.

silent *e*
The final *e* in a spelling pattern that usually signals a long vowel sound in the word and does not represent a sound itself (for example, mak*e*).

silent reading
The reader reading the text to himself.

small-group reading instruction
The teacher working with students brought together because they are similar enough in reading development to teach in a small group; guided reading.

solve words (as a strategic action)
To use a range of strategies to take words apart and understand their meaning.

sound boxes and letter boxes (Elkonin boxes)
(see **Elkonin boxes**)

sounding out
Pronouncing the sounds of the letters in a word as a step in reading the word.

sources of information
The various cues in a written text that combine to make meaning (for example, syntax, meaning, and the physical shape and arrangement of type).

spelling aloud
Naming the letters in a word rather than reading the word.

spelling patterns
Beginning letters (onsets) and common phonograms (rimes) form the basis for the English syllable; knowing these patterns, a student can build countless words.

split dialogue
Written dialogue in which a "said" phrase divides the speaker's words (for example, "Come on," said Mom, "let's go home.").

standardized
Remaining essentially the same across multiple instances.

strategic action
Any one of the many simultaneous, coordinated thinking activities that go on in a reader's head (also see **thinking within, beyond, and about the text**).

stress
The emphasis given to some syllables or words.

student folders
A set of folders to keep reading records and other data for each student; these folders can be passed on each year as part of students' records; the inside of the folder includes a graph for tracking a student's initial level, progress through *LLI*, and exit information.

subheading
Text placed after a heading dividing the section into smaller parts and providing information about the text that follows.

substitution (as in error in reading)
The reader reading aloud one (incorrect) word for another; a reader sometimes makes several substitutions.

suffix
An affix or group of letters added at the end of a base word or word root to change its function or meaning (for example, hand*ful*, hope*less*).

summarize (as a strategic action)
To put together and remember important information, while disregarding irrelevant information, during or after reading.

syllabic
Relating to the enunciation or separation of syllables.

syllabication
The division of words into syllables (for example, *pen-cil*).

symbolism
The use of an action, an object, or words to represent or suggest something else.

synonym
One of two or more words that have similar meanings (for example, *chair, seat*).

syntactic awareness
The knowledge of grammatical patterns or structures.

syntactic system
Rules that govern the ways in which morphemes and words work together in sentence patterns; not the same as proper grammar, which refers to the accepted grammatical conventions.

syntax
The study of how sentences are formed and of the grammatical rules that govern their formation.

synthesize (as a strategic action)
To combine new information or ideas from reading text with existing knowledge to create new understandings.

table charts
Charts the teacher constructs with the students, based on activities in the lessons, that are large enough for all the students in a group to see across a table.

temporal sequence
The writer presents ideas or events in the order in which they always happen (for example, life cycle and seasons).

text structure
The overall architecture or organization of a piece of writing; chronology (sequence) and description are two common text structures.

theme
The central idea or concept in a story; the message that the author is conveying.

think, pair, share
This instructional procedure is used to facilitate collaborative problem solving between peers; a question or problem is identified, and peers discuss and hypothesize and then share their thinking with the larger group.

thinking within, beyond, and about the text
Three ways of thinking about a text while reading: thinking *within* the text involves efficiently and effectively understanding what is on the page, the author's literal message; thinking *beyond* the text requires making inferences and putting text ideas together in different ways to construct the text's

meaning; thinking *about* the text, readers analyze and critique the author's craft and the quality or the authenticity of a text.

timeline
A graphic used to represent important events in chronological order.

told
The teacher telling the reader a word he cannot read. Usually follows a reader's appeal, "you try it" from the teacher, and an attempt.

topic
The subject of a piece of writing.

traditional literature
Literature that has been passed down over time.

understandings
Basic concepts that are crucial to comprehending a particular area.

V (visual information)
One of three sources of information (MSV: meaning, language structure, visual information); visual information refers to the letters that represent the sounds of language and the way they are combined (spelling patterns) to create words; visual information at the sentence level includes punctuation.

vocabulary (as a text characteristic)
Words and their meanings.

vowel
A speech sound or phoneme made without stoppage or friction in the airflow; the vowel sounds are represented by *a, e, i, o, u,* and sometimes *y* and *w*.

word
A unit of meaning in language.

word analysis
To break apart words into parts or individual sounds in order to read and understand them.

word bags
A collection of high-frequency word cards that are kept in a sealable, one-quart plastic bag.

word boundaries
The white space that defines a word; the white space before the first letter and after the last letter of a word; it is important for beginning readers to learn to recognize word boundaries.

word family
A term often used to designate words that are connected by phonograms or rimes (for example, *hot, not, pot, shot*); a word family can also be a series of words connected by meaning (affixes added to a base word—for example, *base, baseball, basement, baseman, basal, basis, baseless, baseline, baseboard, abase, abasement, off base, home base; precise, précis, precisely, precision*).

word magnets
Magnetic tiles used to write words or word parts that are then manipulated in phonics/word study lessons.

word-solving actions (see **solve words**)

words (as a text characteristic)
The decodability of words in a text; phonetic and structural features of words.

words in text
Students use their eyes to locate known and unknown words in text.

writing
Students engaging in the writing process and producing pieces of their own writing in many genres.

writing about reading
Students responding to reading a text by writing and sometimes drawing.

writing words fluently
Students learning to write words fast by writing a word several times.

"you try it"
A prompt given by the teacher that directs a student to make an attempt at reading a word during oral reading.

bibliography

Clay, Marie 1993. *Reading Recovery: A Guidebook for Teachers in Training.* Portsmouth, NH: Heinemann.

Elkonin, Daniil B. 1971. "Development of Speech." In Alexander V. Zaporozhets and Daniil B. Elkonin (Eds.). *The Psychology of Preschool Children.* Cambridge, MA: M.I.T. Press.

Fountas, Irene C., and Gay Su Pinnell. 2000. *Guiding Readers and Writers: Teaching Comprehension, Genre, and Content Literacy.* Portsmouth, NH: Heinemann.

Fountas, Irene C., and Gay Su Pinnell. 2006. *Teaching for Comprehending and Fluency: Thinking, Talking, and Writing About Reading, K-8.* Portsmouth, NH: Heinemann.

Fountas, Irene C., and Gay Su Pinnell. 2012a. *Genre Study: Teaching with Fiction and Nonfiction Books.* Portsmouth, NH: Heinemann.

Fountas, Irene C., and Gay Su Pinnell. 2012b. *Prompting Guide Part 1 for Oral Reading and Early Writing.* Portsmouth, NH: Heinemann.

Fountas, Irene C., and Gay Su Pinnell. 2012c. *Prompting Guide Part 2 for Comprehension: Thinking, Talking, and Writing.* Portsmouth, NH: Heinemann.

Lyman, Frank. 1981. "The Responsive Classroom Discussion." In *Mainstreaming Digest,* edited by A. S. Anderson, 109–13. College Park, MD: University of Maryland College of Education.

Pinnell, Gay Su, and Irene C. Fountas. 2008. *When Readers Struggle: Teaching That Works, A–N.* Portsmouth, NH: Heinemann.

Pinnell, Gay Su, and Irene C. Fountas. *When Readers Struggle: Teaching That Works, L–Z* (in press). Portsmouth, NH: Heinemann.

Shany, Michael, and Andrew Biemiller. 1995. "Assisted Reading Practice: Effects on Performance for Poor Readers in Grades 3 and 4." *Reading Research Quarterly* 50 (3): 382–95.